As the definitive social network for people doing business, entrepreneurs ignore LinkedIn at their own peril. Take the direct approach to reaching the movers and shakers by listening to what Ted has to say.
—JOEL COMM, NEW YORK TIMES BESTSELLING AUTHOR OF
TWITTER POWER 2.0: HOW TO DOMINATE YOUR MARKET ONE TWEET AT A TIME

Ted Prodromou wrote THE book on LinkedIn. I used to say the real secret to success is to get out there and work like hell but *The Ultimate Guide to LinkedIn for Business, Third Edition* is full of actionable strategies that will impact your bottom line immediately so you don't have to work as hard.
—FRANK KERN, ONE OF THE MOST SOUGHT AFTER DIRECT RESPONSE INTERNET MARKETING CONSULTANTS
AND COPYWRITERS ON THE PLANET. WWW.FRANKKERN.COM

Are you looking for a handbook to cover all that's possible with LinkedIn? Look no further than *The Ultimate Guide to LinkedIn for Business, Third Edition*. Filled with actionable insights you can use now, you'll want to grab a copy of this book today, and you'll hope your competitors don't get it first.
—PHIL GERBYSHAK, SALES TRAINER AND COACH

Everyone knows it's smart to connect with over 500 million business people on LinkedIn, but very few people know how to connect on LinkedIn profitably without wasting tons of time and money. If you want to know the behind-the-scenes, real-world strategies, you need to read this book filled with applicable tips and tricks to save you time and money, and to give you a roadmap to actually making money on LinkedIn.
—SCOTT KEFFER, BESTSELLING AUTHOR AND FOUNDER OF DOUBLE YOUR AFFLUENT CLIENTS

Ted keeps his finger on the pulse of LinkedIn. When a LinkedIn feature changes, he's one of the first to know about it. He teaches you how to connect in a way that's genuine and well received.
—CEDRIC CRUMBLEY, BESTSELLING AUTHOR OF *PROVEN SALES AND RECRUITING METHODS*

When it comes to marketing, there are loads of marketers that talk a good game, but Ted is truly knowledgeable and always up to date on any social media platform changes. His strategies and ideas have given me an increase in business and helped streamline my processes. I recommend anyone looking for a marketer to read this book.
—CHRISINE VERHULP, WWW.VBSVIRTUAL.COM

The LinkedIn techniques Ted teaches in this book are remarkably effective and super simple to implement. Follow Ted's lead, because I've seen firsthand how powerful it can be.
—ADAM FRANKLIN, BESTSELLING AUTHOR OF *WEB MARKETING THAT WORKS*

WOW—*The Ultimate Guide to LinkedIn for Business, Third Edition* is a must-read book that will guide you through how to become an influencer in your industry and how to connect effectively with other influencers. As usual, Ted Prodromou holds nothing back. His tips, strategies, and formulas for LinkedIn success are simple but powerful. The end results will help you attract the affluent clients you've been waiting for!
—RAVEN BLAIR GLOVER, PRESIDENT'S LIFETIME ACHIEVEMENT HONOREE

After targeting my LinkedIn profile using just some of the techniques Ted teaches in this book, I received a LinkedIn Mail from an HR Director from Sherwin Williams to speak for one of their training events. Is doing business with a Fortune 500 company worth investing your time in your LinkedIn profile? YES!
—ELIZABETH MCCORMICK, INTERNATIONAL MOTIVATIONAL SPEAKER AND FORMER U.S. ARMY BLACKHAWK PILOT AT PILOTSPEAKER.COM

After meeting Ted and becoming aware of his LinkedIn knowledge, experience, and talent, I had the privilege to put his work into action by following the skill sets described in his bestselling books. The best is yet to come as we are already increasing our connections by several people a day! Thanks, Ted, for making LinkedIn easy to implement and fun to follow!
—ANDREA ADAMS-MILLER, CEO AND FOUNDER OF THE RED CARPET CONNECTION

Ted's insights in this book and coaching have been instrumental to our efforts for building an effective LinkedIn presence with our high-profile clients. The breadth and depth of Ted's expertise as well as his ability to patiently guide us through the LinkedIn maze has significantly impacted our bottom line. He is one of our most valued resources.
—SUSAN GATTON, EXECUTIVE COACH

I knew quite a bit about LinkedIn (so I thought), but gained so much more useful knowledge from *The Ultimate Guide to LinkedIn for Business, Third Edition*. It was one of the best investments I have made in my social media education.
—MAGGIE HOLBIK, BUSINESS AND SOCIAL MEDIA COACH

Ted is simply the master at communicating the best formulas for LinkedIn success. Ted helped me see that LinkedIn is so much more than the sum of its parts. He guided me through creating a synergy on LinkedIn that yielded a greater understanding and fast, solid results.
—MICHAEL FLINT, CEO OF SWEET SUCCESS & HISPANIC MARKETING SUCCESS

Ted provides an incredibly simple solution to understanding and using LinkedIn. I am looking forward to adding the latest edition of his book to my library.
—ANDY PETERSON, DIRECTOR OF CLIENT VICTORY, KAHUNA BUSINESS GROUP

Entrepreneur
MAGAZINE'S

ULTIMATE

GUIDE TO

Linked in
FOR BUSINESS
Third Edition

■ Access more than 500 million business professionals in 10 minutes
■ Leverage the latest tools to **create a steady flow of business**
■ Supercharge your personal and business profiles

TED PRODROMOU

Entrepreneur Press®

Entrepreneur Press, Publisher
Cover Design: Andrew Welyczko
Production and Composition: Eliot House Productions

This publication is designed to provide accurate and authoritative information in regard to the
subject matter covered. It is sold with the understanding that the publisher is not engaged in
rendering legal, accounting, or other professional services. If legal advice or other expert assistance is
required, the services of a competent professional person should be sought.

Entrepreneur Press® is a registered trademark of Entrepreneur Media, Inc.

Library of Congress Cataloging-in-Publication Data has been applied for.
ISBN-13 978-1-59918-640-5
ISBN-10 1-59918-640-3

Printed in the United States of America

23 22 21 20 19   10 9 8 7 6 5 4 3 2 1

Contents

Acknowledgments

This book is dedicated to my brother-in-law and best friend of 40 years, Dieter Schien. While Dieter wasn't an avid LinkedIn user or entrepreneur, he was always supportive of my family and me. Dieter used to attend local marketing events and networking meetings with me. He liked tagging along to meet new people and to learn something new, even though he was disabled and couldn't work for the last 15 years of his life. Dieter was a lot like Norm on *Cheers*. Everyone knew and liked Dieter because he was friendly, kind, helpful, and a lot of fun. When he entered a room, everyone would yell, "Dieter!"

I'm going to miss you, Dieter, and I love you.

Foreword
by Melonie Dodaro
Founder and CEO of Top Dog Social Media and the bestselling author of *LinkedIn Unlocked* and *The LinkedIn Code*

There is no question that LinkedIn is a gold mine for those who take the time to understand how to leverage it. The problem is that most don't take that time. So many people are still collecting connections instead of building long-term relationships. Ted is one of those people who really understand how to build relationships, so when he asked me to write the foreword for his book, I accepted immediately.

When it comes to social tools, nothing can beat LinkedIn for business-to-business (B2B) lead generation. In fact, I tell my clients all the time that the highest ROI that I (or anyone else) can help them achieve with digital marketing is to train their team on how to use LinkedIn to generate leads and build relationships. In my company, 80 percent of the B2B leads generated from social media come from LinkedIn.

As the author of two LinkedIn books myself, I am attracted to the no-fluff style of LinkedIn as a business social network, as opposed to platforms such as Facebook and Instagram. I also enjoy Ted's straightforward approach to LinkedIn in this third edition of the *Ultimate Guide to LinkedIn for Business*.

With the declining reach of Facebook and the social media fatigue that is setting in, you cannot afford to ignore LinkedIn any longer. Now, more than ever, it's vital that you tap into the LinkedIn gold mine—with more than half a billion professional members and growing—to build your personal brand.

Your personal brand is also more important than it's ever been. You may not even realize that you already have one. If you are showing up in Google search results, you have a personal brand. The question is, are you proud of it? LinkedIn is the first place people will look to learn more about you professionally. Having a professional presence on LinkedIn is crucial to your personal brand.

Once you are proud of how your profile positions you and what you offer, the next step is to use LinkedIn's incredible and robust advanced search function to find and connect with your perfect potential clients. You can proactively generate leads on LinkedIn, consistently and predictably.

These are only two of the many things you will learn by reading this book, but if you walk away with just those two, you will have made back your investment a hundred times over—providing, of course, that you implement what you learn.

LinkedIn continues to be the world's largest business network, so if growing your business is important to you, don't just read this book—put it into practice.

Introduction

Welcome to the third edition of *Ultimate Guide to LinkedIn for Business*. When I wrote the first edition of this book in 2012, I never imagined I would write a second edition, let alone a third.

Our world has changed so much since I began writing the first edition in late 2011. The world was slowly recovering from the Great Recession caused by the devastating collapse of our real estate markets and financial system in late 2008. Businesses small and large were forced into bankruptcy. Millions of people lost their homes to foreclosure, their jobs, and their careers.

My story was no different. I lost most of my marketing agency clients in 2009, and I was really struggling. This was the second career reset for me in a decade, and I had lost all confidence in my ability to successfully provide for my family.

With one child in college and another about to enroll, I was fortunate to find a full-time job as an online marketing manager for a software company near my home. Jobs were few and far between, and they actually hired a 51-year-old to work alongside a team of twentysomething marketers.

I was back in the game!

This software company was in the right place at the right time. From 2009 through 2013, their profits quadrupled in the worst economic times since the Great Depression. Unfortunately for me, the company restructured after a venture capital investment, and most of the marketing department was let go in 2013.

But by then, I had written the first edition of the *Ultimate Guide to LinkedIn for Business* and was in the process of establishing myself as one of the country's top LinkedIn experts.

Today, I feel confident that my career resets are over because I'm so well-connected on LinkedIn. I can fill in any gaps that may appear between now and when I ride into retirement in the not-so-distant future.

LinkedIn has changed so much over the past few years and is in a constant state of flux. Many features and tools have been retired while many new features and tools have been added, making the previous editions of this book almost obsolete.

That's why, in this edition, I focus on networking techniques that are not technology-dependent or time-sensitive. Technology changes quickly, and social networks come and go every few years. Instead, I teach tried-and-true techniques that help you build human-to-human relationships. Sales happen after relationships are built, and technology and social networks help you reach more people than face-to-face networking can.

LINKEDIN'S EVOLUTION

When I wrote the first edition of *Ultimate Guide to LinkedIn for Business*, LinkedIn had approximately 150 million members and I had a whopping 689 connections. To be honest, I wasn't completely sold on LinkedIn's value at the time, but I was a regular contributor to the Groups and LinkedIn Answers sections of the site. I did get some business from LinkedIn at the time, but nowhere near what I get today.

At the time, LinkedIn was primarily a website where you could look for a job, find great employees to hire, or connect with recruiters who could help you with those tasks. Almost all LinkedIn's revenue came from recruiters' premium accounts, job postings, and the LinkedIn Job Seeker (now called Premium Career) premium membership.

One of the most popular LinkedIn tools back then was LinkedIn Answers. You could demonstrate your expertise by answering questions posted by other LinkedIn members. You could also post your own questions, and experts would give you free advice. You earned points by answering questions and could appear at the top of a live leader board if you answered enough questions every day. Getting on the leader board meant lots of exposure for your business.

LinkedIn had a variety of third-party apps, including SlideShare Presentations (which it acquired in 2012), Google Presentations (now called Google Slides), E-Bookshelf, My

Travel, Polls, and many more. These apps were very random and really didn't fit into the LinkedIn platform. In my opinion, these apps were LinkedIn's halfhearted attempt to increase user engagement and give people a reason to log in more than once a month.

LinkedIn's in-house apps were limited to LinkedIn Mobile and CardMunch. The LinkedIn Mobile app was very rudimentary at the time and had only a fraction of the functionality provided by the desktop platform.

Do you remember CardMunch? It let you take a picture of a business card, and a data entry person on the other side of the world would type the information into the LinkedIn platform manually. A few days later, the new connection would appear in your LinkedIn network. We've come a long, long way in a few years.

In 2013, Jeff Weiner, CEO of LinkedIn, declared he wanted LinkedIn to be the largest publishing platform on the internet after LinkedIn Today began to become more popular. LinkedIn Today lets you subscribe to content being posted on LinkedIn by people like Richard Branson, Bill Gates, and other business moguls. You could also subscribe to content from publishers like *The New York Times, The Washington Post*, and most other major news outlets. This was a great way to let LinkedIn members create a custom newsfeed that would bring them back to LinkedIn every day.

There are many newsfeed apps like Flipboard, Feedly, and the now-defunct Zite that let you create custom content feeds on your tablets and mobile devices. One of the most popular newsfeed apps at the time was Pulse, so LinkedIn acquired it for $90 million in 2013. This was a big step forward for LinkedIn in their pursuit of being the top content website.

So LinkedIn Today turned into LinkedIn Pulse, and almost overnight, LinkedIn built a powerful publishing platform. Content was being pulled into LinkedIn from most major publishers, and LinkedIn members could publish their own content on the Pulse platform as well.

Before long, thousands of new articles were being published every day by LinkedIn members and influencers. This gave LinkedIn members a place to share their expertise and gain exposure to the entire LinkedIn network, which at the time had more than 300 million members.

The second edition of *Ultimate Guide to LinkedIn for Business* was released in 2015, as LinkedIn was once again overhauling the desktop platform.

I chuckle when I look at the screenshots of the LinkedIn dashboard in the second edition. Today, LinkedIn looks nothing like it did just a few years ago, and it continues to evolve. In fact, today more than 60 percent of users access LinkedIn with their mobile devices, so in this edition I'll show you how to get the most from LinkedIn's new mobile apps.

The LinkedIn newsfeed is now the heart of the "new" LinkedIn, whether on desktop or mobile. As you subscribe to topics (now called hashtag communities), relevant content will appear in your newsfeed. There is even talk of showing posts from your LinkedIn Groups right in your newsfeed to encourage further engagement in Groups.

LinkedIn is also preparing to roll out intelligent bots in LinkedIn messages, which will automatically schedule appointments when you agree to meet someone you are chatting with. LinkedIn will be integrated with your calendars, so the bot will find a time you are both available and automatically create the appointment when you both agree. It will even go one step further and suggest an available conference room if you both work for the same company, a location if you are both in the same city, or an online meeting room like Zoom or Skype.

Partnerships are at the heart of LinkedIn's new content strategy. For example, its integration with Microsoft products has exceeded Weiner's expectations so far. Here are some of the ongoing LinkedIn/Microsoft integrations, with many more on the way:

- The LinkedIn identity and network is included in both Microsoft Outlook and the Office suite.
- LinkedIn notifications are now added within the Windows Action Center.
- Members who draft resumes in Word can update their profiles and discover and apply to jobs on LinkedIn.
- The reach of sponsored content across Microsoft properties is extended.
- Enterprise LinkedIn Lookup is now powered by Active Directory and Office 365.
- LinkedIn Learning is now available across the Office 365 and Windows ecosystem.
- Expect to see more about the addition of a business news desk across the content ecosystem and MSN.com.
- Social selling will eventually look different through the combination of Sales Navigator and Dynamics 365.

The future is bright for LinkedIn and Microsoft, and I can't wait to share more success stories in future editions of *Ultimate Guide to LinkedIn for Business*.

MY PERSONAL LINKEDIN STORY

When I first moved to San Francisco in 1979, it was easy to find a job. Silicon Valley was growing like crazy, and the high-tech industry was desperately looking for skilled workers. Companies were growing so fast that they posted job openings on billboards outside their sprawling tech campuses. I could drive around Silicon Valley, drop off my resume at security desks, and have multiple job offers by the end of the day. For more than 20 years, I had a secure career, knowing I could change jobs and get a significant raise whenever I wanted.

The high-tech boom of the 1980s and '90s was a very wild ride, primarily straight up. I built a strong network of contacts in the high-tech industry in my career as a network manager, working for leading-edge companies like IBM, Cellular One, and Digital Equipment Corporation. Life was fabulous, and I was a recognized leader in my field, featured in many trade magazines and even the annual report of a networking company, Xyplex.

But the internet boom of the late 1990s was like pouring gasoline on a fire, accelerating the growth of the high-tech industry exponentially—and far beyond the economy's capacity to handle it. It was the era of the dotcom bubble.

Then came Y2K and the turn of the century. Do you remember hearing about the fears that computers would crash at midnight on New Year's Eve because they couldn't handle the year 2000? Electricity would stop flowing. Water would stop flowing. Banks would fail. Air traffic control would be in chaos and planes would be stranded in the air.

None of the crazy fears materialized, but the bubble did burst that year, collapsing the entire tech industry. High-tech companies began laying off employees for the first time ever. Many companies closed their doors. Others sold themselves off for pennies on the dollar. Within one year, more than 500,000 high-tech workers lost their jobs in Silicon Valley alone. Most of the remaining jobs were outsourced overseas. Salaries plummeted for those lucky enough to keep a job, but most of us were unable to find work for the first time in our careers.

When my consulting practice went under in late 2001, I began reaching out to my network of colleagues for work. I didn't care if it was a consulting gig or a full-time job. I was sure someone would have a lead for me.

But a scary thing happened when I reached out. I couldn't reach most of my network. Emails bounced back. Telephones were disconnected. I heard, "The number you have reached is no longer in service" over and over. Many of my colleagues had moved out of the area because of the high cost of living and the lack of career opportunities.

I felt lost. I had no way to reach a network that had taken 20 years to build.

There were no networking websites like LinkedIn in 2001, so I joined a local business networking group. We met once a week for breakfast and traded leads. Most of them were worthless, but occasionally a lead would pan out. It also gave all of us an excuse to get out of the house, since we were all struggling, work-at-home consultants.

My business treaded water for the next few years as the economy recovered from the dotcom crash and 9/11. The only way to get new projects was from referrals, in-person networking, and cold calling because I couldn't afford to advertise.

In 2004, I received an email invitation from a friend who wanted to connect with me on LinkedIn. I didn't know what LinkedIn was, but I registered to check it out and officially became LinkedIn member 2,239,835.

I signed in and looked around a bit, but there wasn't much to see. I joined a couple of alumni groups, searched for some old co-workers, and then pretty much ignored it for the next year. I considered LinkedIn nothing more than a resume website.

Over time, though, LinkedIn added more features, making the site more useful. Adding the ability to interact with others was the turning point, and membership began to increase.

I discovered that if I answered questions in the Answers sections, people started reaching out to me with contract opportunities. I also posted provocative questions, which attracted a lot of attention and led to some interesting conversations.

LinkedIn became a useful tool in my consulting practice. My network expanded significantly as I connected with more people and joined Groups. After being a passive observer of LinkedIn for years, I realized that the more I participated, the more consulting work came my way.

Today I run my own company, Search Marketing Simplified LLC. I use LinkedIn to generate leads for my business by posting useful content such as articles and videos, engaging with my connections through messages, and sharing their content if I think my network could benefit from it. I also manage our paid ads on LinkedIn, which are extremely targeted and very effective. I'll share more details about LinkedIn advertising later in the book.

WHAT YOU'LL FIND IN THIS BOOK

Throughout this book, I'll share my perspective of LinkedIn from the eyes of a direct marketer since I am a direct marketer by trade. As far as I know, I'm the only LinkedIn expert who treats the site like a search engine and marketing platform using a direct-marketing approach. I'll also share tips to help you get maximum exposure for your personal profile and your company using search engine optimization (SEO) techniques.

Most LinkedIn books teach you the fundamentals of LinkedIn but don't go into much detail. You learn how to create a basic profile and how to use the LinkedIn tools, but you don't get into the nitty-gritty details that make you a LinkedIn expert.

We're going to go deep in this book—very deep. We'll start with the basics, and then I'll show you the advanced tips and tricks that will help you stand out from your competitors.

You will find as you navigate LinkedIn that it is constantly being updated. This is good news for you because it means you always have the most innovative and up-to-date networking tools available to you. You may notice that interfaces change from time to time and tools/features may move or be renamed. This is typical to the LinkedIn experience. As such, please note that some protocols and images you see detailed in this book are subject to change on the live site. Where possible, I've tried to add links that should take you to the most recent pages on LinkedIn where you can find current information. And, of course, you can always go to the Help section for answers.

Since my use of LinkedIn has evolved over the years, I'm going to share my unique approach to generating more business from LinkedIn. My approach is based on an old-school method (yes, I prefer to use proven methods that have worked for years and still work) called *AIDA*.

AIDA is short for Attention, Interest, Desire, and Action, which are the four steps in the buying process. Before someone will become your customer, they must be aware of your business and your products. This is the Attention stage. Once they know you exist, they have to be interested in your products and services. This is the Interest stage, where they discover how your products and services can solve their problems. The Desire stage is where they've evaluated all of the options in the marketplace and are convinced you are the best solution to their problem. Finally, the Action stage is where you close the sale.

This third edition of *Ultimate Guide to LinkedIn for Business* is inspired by and mirrors that concept of AIDA so you can see how I apply this approach to my daily LinkedIn strategy. Throughout the book, you will learn lots of great tips to help you get maximum exposure and find what you need to grow your business or advance your career.

First, I'll show you the ins and outs of LinkedIn by introducing you to the vast array of features and tools available to you. I'll explain each feature and tool in detail and show you some best practices for each. Some of the LinkedIn features you will learn about include:

- your homepage
- profiles
- jobs
- Groups
- articles
- video
- hashtag communities
- LinkedIn Pages
- tools
- mobile
- settings/personalization
- advertising
- Premium for business, sales, and recruiters
- Sales Navigator
- ProFinder

I'm going to show you how to leverage the power of LinkedIn to create a searchable LinkedIn profile that will rise to the top of the search results in both LinkedIn and Google.

After you master the basics, I'll show you how experts get the most out of LinkedIn. We'll review step-by-step case studies demonstrating how to use LinkedIn for various outcomes. If you are looking to grow your business, I'll show you how to find your perfect clients or customers. If you're looking to hire someone new, I'll show you how to find your dream employee.

Today, the business world is changing faster than ever. You need to be well-connected so your business will thrive through the peaks and valleys of the economy. You need to build a strong, stable professional network that can provide guidance and support during trying times. During your boom times, you can provide guidance and support to those in your network who are struggling. In Chapter 1, I'll explain the benefits of joining LinkedIn and show you how it can help you build your ideal professional network and grow your business. Let's get started.

Why LinkedIn?

The better question is, "Why *not* LinkedIn?" With hundreds of millions of business professionals from nearly every company in the world just one click away, why wouldn't you spend more time on LinkedIn if you were trying to grow a business?

You know when you're thinking about buying a new car and suddenly you see that model everywhere? You never noticed many on the road, but now that you're considering buying one, it seems like everyone is driving it. It's called the Baader-Meinhof phenomenon, and it's a well-known psychological effect.

I have the same problem when I see online ads and keywords. Sometimes I feel like Don Draper from the TV show *Mad Men*, analyzing every ad and keyword I see. Since I'm an SEO and online marketing expert by trade, I see the internet from the perspective of online ads, keywords, and search rankings. I'm always trying to figure out how a company gets top rankings or maximum exposure from their marketing campaigns.

I look for the same patterns on LinkedIn. Which companies appear consistently in LinkedIn? Which people get the most exposure? Which keywords get the most traction?

THE DEMOGRAPHIC GOLD MINE

With approximately 575 million members (at the time of this writing) and growing, LinkedIn is considered the most trusted social media platform among Washington Insiders by the National Journal. Unfortunately, most LinkedIn members don't see the site as a powerful business tool but as a place to post their online resume. They expect others to hunt them down without providing any value to the site in exchange.

According to LinkedIn, only 23 percent of their members are considered active users, logging in more than once a month. The remaining 77 percent are considered static users, and LinkedIn is trying hard to engage them.

Today, LinkedIn has become the largest business-oriented search engine. With its advanced search features, you can find great employees to hire, find the perfect company to work for, find highly targeted leads to sell to, and network with the thought leaders of your industry—not to mention establish yourself as a thought leader, too.

You can mine deeply into the LinkedIn database and find a treasure trove of information that will change the way you do business. You'll know so much about a prospect, their company, their competitors, their industry, and their products before you ever meet the person. LinkedIn is making it easier than ever to find targeted prospects for your business.

BUSINESS PROFESSIONAL SEARCH ENGINE

Not many people consider LinkedIn a search engine, but I invite you to consider the possibility. You know the power of appearing at the top of Google search results. You get free, high-quality, targeted traffic to your website, which generates more business for your company.

What if your profile or company appeared when someone did a people search on LinkedIn? What if your personal LinkedIn profile or company profile appeared when a prospect searched Google for keywords related to your product or service? What would that do for your career or company? What would your bottom line look like if you could identify highly targeted prospects just by searching on LinkedIn and Google?

If you still don't believe LinkedIn is a powerful search engine, then why do LinkedIn search results so often appear on Google? If Google understands the power of LinkedIn, you should, too.

Throughout this book, I'll be sharing my view of LinkedIn from the keyword and search engine ranking perspective. I'll also share tips to help you get maximum exposure for your personal profile and your company using your professional network.

HIGH-VALUE PROFESSIONAL NETWORK

So what can that professional network look like on LinkedIn? As you can see in Figure 1–1 below, according to online statistics portal Statista, 54 percent of household members in the United States who use LinkedIn are high-income and medium-income earners. There are approximately 150 million users in the United States or 26 percent of LinkedIn's total membership according to Statista.

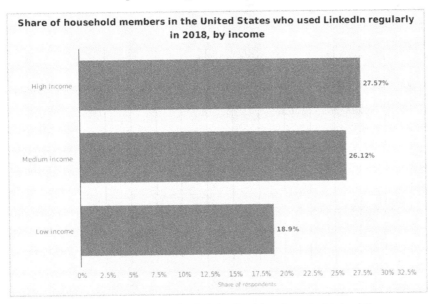

FIGURE 1–1. Income Level of LinkedIn Members in United States
Source: Surveys by Statista

LinkedIn's sweet spot by age is in the 25 to 44 age group, according to a 2018 study by Statista of internet users in the United States who use LinkedIn. Figure 1–2 on page 4 breaks down internet users in the United States who use LinkedIn by their age.

LinkedIn members are also well-educated. In a November 2016 Pew Research survey, 50 percent of internet users in the United States who have a college degree or advanced college degree use LinkedIn. See Figure 1–3 on page 4 to see the education level of LinkedIn users from the United States. These numbers are very similar to the education levels of European LinkedIn users.

If you are a consultant, executive coach, or professional service provider, you have an unlimited source of potential clients on LinkedIn who earn enough to hire you or have a corporate budget to hire you for their projects. This sure beats the old days of picking up the telephone book and cold calling people all day long.

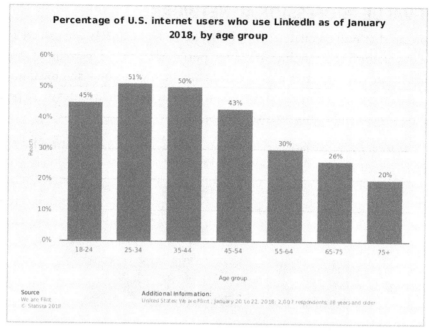

FIGURE 1–2. U.S. Internet Users Who Use LinkedIn by Age Group

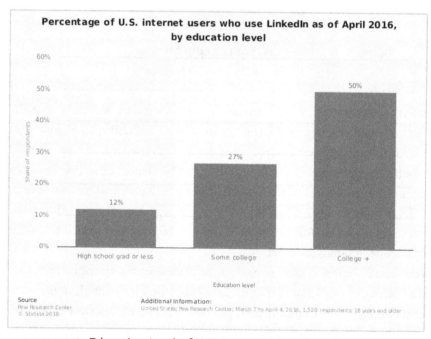

FIGURE 1–3. Education Level of U.S. Internet Users by Education Level

CONCLUSION

You now know that LinkedIn consists of well-educated, high-income members in the United States.

You can see the benefits of joining and participating in the networking Groups and demonstrating your expertise by helping others. In the next chapter, I'll show you how to get started on LinkedIn so you can begin growing your professional network and becoming a recognized thought leader in your industry.

For additional updates and how-to videos,
visit https://tedprodromou.com/UltimateGuideUpdates/.

Getting Started on LinkedIn

When did you sign up for LinkedIn, and what persuaded you to complete your registration? My guess is you registered years ago after a friend or colleague forwarded you an invitation to connect. If you're just starting your career, you were probably referred to LinkedIn by a friend, mentor, or even one of your professors from college or grad school.

Whatever your reason, you are now a member of the largest professional business networking community in the world. Today, LinkedIn is much more than just a networking website. It has become the largest job-related website with thousands of job postings. Recruiters and job seekers are finding LinkedIn to be the perfect place to connect. In fact, I recently heard an ad for LinkedIn on my local radio station that said a person is hired every ten seconds from a LinkedIn job posting. Not bad!

Many people ask me if LinkedIn is better than Facebook or other social media giants like Twitter and Instagram for connecting with people. A couple of years ago, I preferred to use LinkedIn to build my professional network and Facebook to connect with my personal network. Of course, I'm friends with some people on Facebook who are also connected with me on LinkedIn, which is fine. But I posted personal comments and pictures on Facebook and posted business-oriented information on LinkedIn.

I still don't like to see people's business-oriented status updates on Facebook unless they're also sharing posts about their personal life. When I was on Facebook, I wanted to turn off my business brain and have fun, and when I was on LinkedIn, I preferred to see only business-related information.

But Facebook is now trying hard to become both a personal and professional network, and it's succeeding in a big way. A few years ago, something interesting happened that changed my view of Facebook for business. My virtual assistant accidentally scheduled some automated posts in Hootsuite to post on my Facebook personal feed. I post excerpts from my *Ultimate Guide to LinkedIn for Business* and *Ultimate Guide to Twitter for Business* books on LinkedIn, Twitter, and other social media sites that link to landing pages where people can download free chapters of my books. I'm okay with posting these excerpts on my Facebook business page, which you can see at https://www.facebook.com/linkedincoach, but I felt embarrassed to share them on my personal Facebook page.

When I first saw the excerpts on my personal Facebook feed, I wasn't happy. But then I started seeing more downloads of my free chapters from Facebook than from Twitter and LinkedIn. After experimenting, I discovered Facebook is very effective at generating business leads. Now I use Facebook for personal *and* business while keeping my LinkedIn activity purely business. Posting content on Facebook, LinkedIn, Instagram, and Twitter generates most of the traffic to my website, where people can subscribe to my email list. Many eventually become clients.

Do you have a preference? I'd love to hear what you think. Send me an email at info@tedprodromou.com and let me know whether you keep your business and personal networks separate.

WHY CHOOSE LINKEDIN?

As the largest B2B lead-generation website where businesses can connect with their ideal customers and potential business partners, LinkedIn is the best place for you to reconnect with colleagues. LinkedIn has become so much more than a job-hunting website, which most people mistakenly think is its only function. Here is just a small sampling of its possibilities:

- Keeping up with news and trends in your industry
- Establishing your personal brand
- Demonstrating your particular expertise
- Finding great professional referrals
- Promoting your in-person and virtual events
- Introducing people to others in your network

LinkedIn has become the one-stop portal for you to connect with like-minded people. There is hardly anyone who doesn't benefit in some way from its network and tools. It's perfect for:

- An employee for a company
- Marketing and sales professionals
- Job seekers, HR personnel, and recruiters
- Entrepreneurs and business owners

You can do more than just advertise your resume. Through LinkedIn Groups, you can demonstrate your expertise to attract new clients and connect with other industry experts. You can share your knowledge, or you can keep up with the latest industry news by subscribing to specific industry-related content, which will appear right in your newsfeed. LinkedIn is expanding its tools and services to attract the best business professionals, so the quality of the community continues to improve and exceeds all other business networking communities.

Know Your "Why"

Unfortunately, many people become LinkedIn members and don't take advantage of the incredible opportunities and tools in the community. They create their account, partially fill out their profile, connect with a few close friends and only occasionally come back. They mistakenly think there is no reason for them to log in to LinkedIn because they haven't taken time to explore the "new" LinkedIn.

The real reason they are unimpressed with the site is because they don't have a reason to be an active member of the LinkedIn community. Like any community, you have to have a reason to join it if you want to take full advantage of all the opportunities it has to offer.

Think about why you joined other social networking platforms. For example, when people join Facebook, they expect to connect with past and current friends in a casual environment. Facebook is all about taking a break from our busy lives by viewing our friends' vacation pictures, chatting, and playing games. Your expectations are very clear when you join Facebook, and the level of engagement is incredibly high.

When people join LinkedIn today, they can expect to connect with hundreds if not thousands of like-minded business professionals. As LinkedIn provides more networking tools and ways to engage with others, the level of engagement increases proportionally. I spend much of my day logged in to LinkedIn, checking status updates from my connections, and learning about industry news. When I leave work (by walking from my home office to my living room!), I spend my personal time engaging with friends on Facebook. My expectations of both websites are very clear, so I have no problem engaging with people on both networks. In other words, I know my overall "why" (engaging with a professional community), which allows me to pinpoint my strategic objective.

DETERMINE YOUR LINKEDIN OBJECTIVE

What is your objective in joining LinkedIn? Most people don't have a specific reason to join unless they're looking to improve their career, which explains why many profiles are incomplete and show little or no activity. They signed up because they were invited to connect with a co-worker or colleague, but they weren't looking for a job or to network, so they think they have no reason to return.

I think most businesspeople don't understand the importance of building and nurturing a professional network. When you're working full time, you are usually overwhelmed with tasks and not thinking about networking. Most business professionals don't have a long-term career strategy and aren't preparing for "what's next."

If you lose your job (which happens frequently in today's work environment), you may not have a network to support you when you're looking for your next position. When you build and nurture your professional network with short, periodic updates, it will be much easier to reach out to them for help when the need arises because you are already on their radar. LinkedIn's networking tools (which I will show you in Chapter 14) make this very easy to do.

Even if you're gainfully employed and not looking for a job, it's still important to complete your LinkedIn profile. Your profile is a dynamic electronic billboard displaying your skills and expertise to millions of potential readers. By keeping your profile up-to-date, connecting with others, engaging in Groups, and demonstrating your expertise, you are showing the business world you are in touch with the latest trends and technologies. The more you participate on LinkedIn, the more your name will pop up in the LinkedIn sidebar and on search engines like Google, creating unexpected opportunities for potential customers, partners, and employers to find you.

You may not use LinkedIn on a regular basis, but other businesspeople do. It's become a common business practice to view LinkedIn profiles before meeting so you can learn something about each other. In fact, according to a study by Hubspot in their "State of Inbound" report, people will view your LinkedIn profile 83 percent of the time before they meet with you for the first time. Your LinkedIn profile is often their first impression of you, and as Will Rogers famously said, "You never get a second chance to make a good first impression."

With the uncertain job market and corporate instability, you never know when your company will be acquired or go out of business. It's also impossible to predict when you'll be restructured or downsized out of a job. Whether the economy is booming or declining, there is very little job security in today's marketplace.

My parents' generation got a job after they finished school, worked for the same company for 40 years, and retired. There was complete job security, and they never worried about being laid off or their company being bought. If a company was acquired, it usually kept all employees, whether they were needed or not. Layoffs were rare.

Unfortunately, those days are long gone; today we have to be prepared to change jobs, or even careers, in an instant. If your LinkedIn profile is active and current, there's a good chance you will land on your feet quickly if the worst happens. If you wait until you're unemployed to update your LinkedIn profile and build your connections, it will take much longer to find your next job. Take a few minutes every day and complete your profile, get the minimum ten recommendations, connect with some colleagues, and participate in Groups. Take it one step at a time, and soon you will be logging in to LinkedIn every day to participate in the vibrant community discussions or to catch up on the latest news in your industry.

How LinkedIn Can Help You

Once you are on LinkedIn and have completed your profile, you should determine how the site can best serve you. LinkedIn has four basic functions:

1. Establishing your professional profile
2. Staying in touch with colleagues and friends
3. Exploring opportunities
4. Finding experts and answers to your business-related questions

Your objective could be one, all, or any combination of these functions. But you should always work to establish your professional profile even if you aren't actively looking for work. Remember, LinkedIn is an electronic business card that can be seen by more than 500 million professionals, so you want a complete, up-to-date profile. You never know when a once-in-a-lifetime opportunity might arise because the right person spotted your profile in a search, watched one of the videos posted in your feed, read one of your articles, or noticed your comments in a group discussion.

It's also good practice to keep in touch with colleagues and friends, even just by commenting on one of their status updates. By "pinging" your network on a regular basis, you keep your name in front of them, and they'll be more likely to consider you for an opportunity when it arises. Many great career opportunities present themselves when you least expect it. Since I completed my profile and optimized it to appear when people search for popular search terms, I have received numerous opportunities even when I am not looking for them. LinkedIn is a powerful tool, and I will never have to worry about finding a new job if something unforeseen suddenly happens to my current role.

Using Interactive Content to Your Advantage

One way you can help achieve your objective is to use the power of LinkedIn's content platform. LinkedIn has been working hard to make its site more interactive so its users have a reason to log in every day. More than 50 percent of Facebook's 2 billion-plus members log in every day and spend at least one hour on the site. This is what LinkedIn is attempting to do.

Here's how: LinkedIn allows you to subscribe to content so it appears right in your newsfeed. You can subscribe to industry-related content, articles posted by Influencers, and content posted by members of your network. The platform is also experimenting with letting you see posts from your Groups in your feed.

LinkedIn has recently redesigned the desktop interface to make it easier to view content and interact with your network. The mobile app has been completely redesigned as well to encourage logging in more frequently. According to LinkedIn, engagement via LinkedIn Messaging increased 83 percent after the new app was released.

For example, LinkedIn now prompts you to wish connections a happy birthday or congratulate people when they have a work anniversary or start a new position in the Notifications link on the main menu. These new tools make it very easy to "ping" your connections to remain top of mind with them. One of my students recently reached out to wish an old colleague happy birthday, and it turned into a $3 million opportunity for him.

You can also use the content features of LinkedIn to research or look for expertise in an unfamiliar area. You will receive great advice from many experts in a matter of minutes by posting a question in one of LinkedIn's Groups. In the past, you would have to hire a consultant to help you navigate unfamiliar areas of expertise. Today, you have access to thousands of subject matter experts at your fingertips who will gladly answer your question for free in the Answers section. Many times, you will end up hiring the consultant who provides quality recommendations or advice—I know because I was hired many times after I answered questions—so it's a win-win for you and the expert. So think of how you can harness the power of this platform to help you achieve your goals, no matter what they are.

WHAT ABOUT OTHER NETWORKING WEBSITES?

There are other business communities online, but none is as vibrant and dynamic as LinkedIn. Many social media sites like Friendster and Myspace (talk about old school!) have come and gone and weren't focused on business networking.

One competitor to LinkedIn, Ryze, was launched a few years ago with a lot of fanfare, and it claims to have more than 500,000 members in 200 countries. Since then, it has lost momentum. Like the early days of LinkedIn, it seems people don't know what to do once they log in. The idea behind Ryze is that you "rise up" through quality networking. I see some current postings on the site, but it has disabled the ability to create new accounts, so it looks like Ryze's days are numbered.

Xing is the most popular business networking website in Germany and has a strong following in Europe. Xing is free to join and offers premium accounts for about $10 per month, which let you see who searched your profile, filter your searches for better targeting, and send messages to people you are not connected to. Xing has a lot of the same features and tools as LinkedIn, including groups, jobs, events, apps, and company pages. It's very user-friendly and a great business networking community for Europeans.

Occasionally, I receive invitations to join new business networking websites like Dock and Referral Key, but I don't bother signing up because I know I won't use them as often as I use LinkedIn. Some people prefer to network on these other sites for various reasons, but I think they're missing out by not focusing on LinkedIn. Maybe they have a niche network on another site that's working for them, but there is so much opportunity on LinkedIn that they're crazy not to build a network there, too. LinkedIn is exponentially larger than Xing (500 million users, compared to a bit more than 7 million, primarily in Germany, Austria, and Switzerland), so you can belong to both and expand your reach significantly. But at the end of the day, LinkedIn reigns supreme. Why be the salmon swimming upstream when you can easily ride the wave to success?

CONCLUSION

There are other business networking websites, but none come close to the power of LinkedIn for growing your professional network. At this point, you've established your reason for joining LinkedIn and your networking strategy is beginning to take shape. In the next chapter, we'll create your LinkedIn account, start creating your optimized profile, and begin expanding your professional network.

If you already have a LinkedIn account, you can skip the next chapter and jump to Chapter 4, where we will optimize your LinkedIn profile.

**For additional updates and how-to videos, visit
https://tedprodromou.com/UltimateGuideUpdates/.**

Creating Your LinkedIn Account

Whem you create your LinkedIn account, you will be prompted to answer some questions as you populate your profile. Filling out your profile completely will help you connect with others faster than if you leave out important details.

First, create your new account by entering your first and last names, your email address, and a password, as shown in Figure 3-1.

FIGURE 3-1. Creating Your LinkedIn Account

Next, select your Country/Region and enter your postal code. See Figure 3–2.

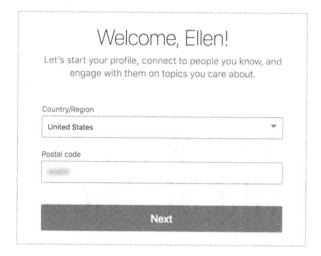

FIGURE 3–2. Selecting Your Country/Region

You will be asked to enter your Most Recent Job Title and Most Recent Company or to select Student. You will then be led through a custom wizard, as you see in Figure 3–3, which is tailored to your selection so you can easily build a profile optimized for your objective. After you enter your country, zip code, job title, and company, click Create My Profile and your profile will be created.

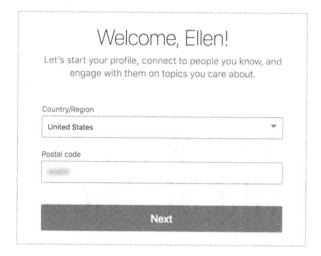

FIGURE 3–3. Enter Your Most Recent Job Title and Company/School

Next, confirm your email address to accept LinkedIn's privacy policy. LinkedIn will email you a code that you need to enter to verify your identity. See Figure 3–4 on page 17. You should also review the LinkedIn privacy policy so you understand their terms of service for using the website and who owns the content you publish on the website. As of this writing, LinkedIn says individuals still own any content they publish on the website, but it reserves the right to use the content any way it sees fit.

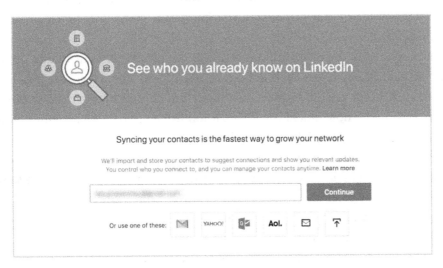

FIGURE 3-4. Confirm Your Email Address and Accept Privacy Policy

Next you will be asked if you want to import your contacts into LinkedIn. If you choose this option, LinkedIn will automatically import all your contacts from Outlook, Gmail, or whichever other email program you use. LinkedIn will tell you which of your contacts are already on LinkedIn so you can send them invitations to connect. If your contacts are not on LinkedIn, you can send them an email inviting them to connect with you. This is an easy way to quickly connect with your existing network on LinkedIn, as shown in Figure 3-5.

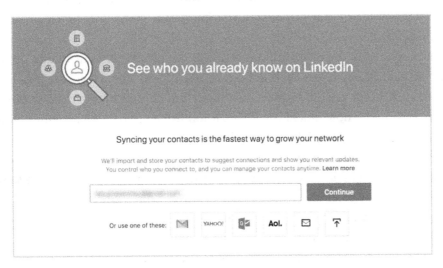

FIGURE 3-5. Importing Your Email Contacts

Personally, I do not like using automated connection tools. I feel it's impersonal almost like spamming your current network. LinkedIn sends a canned invitation to your contacts, and you can't customize the message for each person. I prefer to reach out to my existing network manually and choose whom I want to connect with on LinkedIn. That way, I can build my LinkedIn network with a small number of quality contacts instead of with everyone in my address book. I may have met someone at a networking event and exchanged contact information a few years ago, but that doesn't necessarily mean she's a good fit for my LinkedIn network today.

I do have clients who successfully used the automated connection tool to quickly build their network. They feel they're already connected to their contacts from previous business ventures, so it's fine to send the standard LinkedIn connection message. This approach allowed them to quickly grow their network, but only a small percentage of the automated emails resulted in LinkedIn connections. They had to reach out personally to connect with the rest of their email address book.

I'll leave it to you whether you want to use the automation tools, but most professionals prefer the "quality over quantity" method of building their network.

Next you will be prompted to share on Facebook and Twitter that you just joined LinkedIn. When people click on the link, you will be connected to them on LinkedIn. Again, I don't like this method of connecting with people because you are sending a blind invitation to all your Facebook friends and Twitter followers. I like to keep my Facebook personal life separate from my business life on LinkedIn. As I mentioned in Chapter 2, Facebook is becoming a great venue for business, but I still use it primarily for personal posts. With Twitter, I have no control over who follows me, and I may not want them to be part of my professional network on LinkedIn. Again, I'll leave it up to you if you want to share an open invitation on Facebook and Twitter, but I don't recommend it.

The next step in the registration wizard will ask you if you want to sign up for the premium, paid version or use the free, basic version of LinkedIn. I'll go into greater detail about the premium version later in this book, but I highly recommend staying with the free version for now unless you have an immediate need for LinkedIn's advanced features, such as InMail and Advanced Job Search.

The wizard will now prompt you to enter your current job information, including your hire date, details about the position, past job titles, responsibilities, and the dates you worked at that position.

As you enter your job information, the wizard will ask you, "What did you do as [your job title]?" Enter the details of your job responsibilities, and remember to include your skills when possible. Some people write a brief description of their responsibilities in the first person, while others create a bulleted list of responsibilities. An example of a first-person job description would be: "I was responsible for search engine optimization and online advertising for our regions around the world. I was also responsible for email marketing campaign development, brand development, and website traffic growth."

Other people write their summaries in the third person. An example of a third-person summary would be: "Ted is responsible for search engine optimization and online advertising for the company's regions around the world. He is also responsible for email marketing campaign development, brand development, and website traffic growth."

I prefer the first-person voice for my profile summary because it sounds more personal. To me, third-person narrative sounds like it was written by someone else, so it's not as friendly as a first-person summary. I know there is an ongoing debate about which style works better, so I suggest trying first person for a few months and then switching to third person to see which gets the best results.

Another way to phrase your summary would be the bulleted list:

A dynamic online marketing manager with more than ten years of experience, including search engine optimization (SEO), pay-per-click (PPC) advertising, and search engine marketing (SEM).

- *Thrives in chaotic environments, coolheaded in stressful situations, able to manage multiple projects concurrently and get things done*
- *Excellent communicator; often serves as the liaison between other departments, customers, and offshore teams*
- *Flexible and resourceful, applying exceptional organizational, time-management, and planning skills to deliver projects on time and on budget*
- *Drives adoption of new technologies and innovative solutions*

Here's another example of a bulleted-list job description:

Responsibilities included:

- *Search engine optimization (SEO)*
- *Online banner advertising for regions around the world*
- *Creating and managing pay-per-click (PPC) ad campaigns internationally*
- *Email marketing campaign development and management*
- *Brand development*
- *Website traffic growth*

Notice how the list contains keyword phrases and three-letter acronyms where appropriate. I added "(SEO)" after "search engine optimization" so the LinkedIn search algorithm can find these keywords and related acronyms in my profile. Now I'm easily found when someone searches for SEO *or* search engine optimization.

That's how I set my profile up, but there is no right or wrong way to create your profile summary. The main objective is to use your keyword phrases so you're easily found and people can get a quick overview of your skill sets as they scan your professional profile.

Once you've entered your current and past jobs, the LinkedIn wizard will prompt you to enter your education. Here, input the school you attended, the degree(s) you earned (if any), and the dates you attended the school. If you are a current student, you can use your expected graduation date. If you didn't graduate from that school, you can just note the dates you attended and the courses you studied. The wizard will continue to prompt you to enter more schools until you've entered all the ones you attended.

A lot of people who have college or advanced degrees ask me if they should also include their high school in their education profile. If you enter your high school, LinkedIn will show you people who also went to school there so you can add them to your network. If you think it would be valuable to have people from your high school in your professional network, then you should add your high school to your education profile.

After you complete the education portion of your profile, the wizard will move on to your skills. It's important to use keyword phrases in the skills section (as you did in your job description) so your profile is search-friendly. You can add up to 50 skills to your profile, which will dramatically increase the chances of people finding you when they search for that skill set. As you start typing, the system will suggest skills that are already being used on LinkedIn. Select as many variations of your keywords as possible to optimize your profile.

At this point, you should have a basic LinkedIn profile, and you will start seeing new items appear in your sidebar. LinkedIn is reading your profile and building a list of recommendations based on the keywords in your jobs, education, summary, and skills. The People You May Know feature will begin recommending new, targeted connections you may want to add to your network. As you add connections, your LinkedIn network will update automatically. It will tell you how many connections and how many new people are in your network. You will also see recommended jobs and Groups you may want to join based on your profile and network data. You will also see a list of companies you may want to start following so you can keep up with industry trends or see if you may want to work there someday.

Keep adding appropriate connections to your network, and this sidebar data will continue to update. LinkedIn is constantly learning and suggesting recommendations as your extended network grows. You receive targeted information automatically, which saves you a ton of time when you're looking for people to connect with or looking for companies to learn more about.

Your personal profile should complement your company profile, using the same terminology and keywords. People like to see congruency when they view your company profile and then visit your employee profile. This helps present a more professional image for you and your company, which gives potential clients a positive and lasting impression.

CONTACT INFORMATION

I teach my clients and students to make it easy for people on LinkedIn to reach out to you. Some of my clients are reluctant to share their telephone number and email address on their LinkedIn profiles because they fear they will receive spam messages and telemarketing calls.

My view is that we join LinkedIn so people can find us and do business with us. Hiding or not sharing your contact information is like trying to run a store without putting a sign on the building or listing your phone number. How are people going to know you are in business if you don't make it easy for them to find you?

So make it easy for potential clients to find you. You can add links to your website and blog right on your profile, which will generate lots of web traffic and help your search rankings. Links from popular sites like LinkedIn are very valuable, so make sure you take advantage of this feature.

Figure 3-6 on page 22 shows the available contact fields in your LinkedIn profile. One of the most common mistakes people make when adding their website or blog URLs to their profile is to choose one of the default options in the dropdown list, like Personal Website or Blog.

If you choose Company Website, for example, as shown in Figure 3-6, your listing will just say "Company Website" with no description. In Figure 3-7 on page 22, I chose the Other option, which allowed me to add some targeted keyword phrases. Now my website contact information displays "LinkedIn & Social Selling Tips," adding valuable links and keyword phrases to my LinkedIn profile that help improve my Google search rankings. Look at the difference between the two profiles.

When entering your website address into your contact information, type in the URL, choose Other, and enter your company name or keyword phrases in the box labeled Type (Other), shown in Figure 3-8 on page 23.

Now your website listing will look like Figure 3-9 on page 23, and your company name or keyword phrases are clickable links to your blog or website.

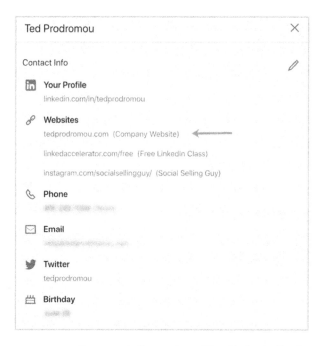

FIGURE 3–6. Contact Information—The Default Option

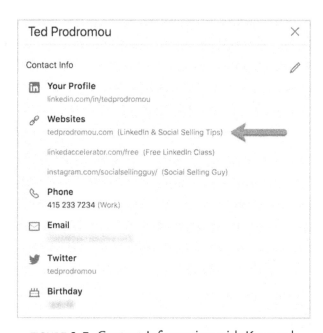

FIGURE 3–7. Contact Information with Keywords

FIGURE 3–8. Displaying Your Keywords Instead of the Words "Company Name"

FIGURE 3–9. Search-Optimized Links to Your Website

ADDING YOUR SOCIAL MEDIA ACCOUNTS

LinkedIn also lets you add social media feeds to your profile so your profile visitors can see what you're up to on the social media front. Let's explore some of your social media options.

Adding Your Twitter Account

Open your LinkedIn profile, click on Add Twitter Account, and enter your Twitter username. A popup box appears that authorizes your Twitter account (see Figure 3–10), then the checkbox appears. (As of this writing, LinkedIn uses a wizard tool to help you through the process.) I prefer to display my Twitter account on my profile by checking the *Display on your profile?* box. This allows me to tweet my LinkedIn status updates in one step.

FIGURE 3–10. Adding Twitter to Your LinkedIn Profile

Now my Twitter account is connected to my LinkedIn profile, and I can share my LinkedIn status updates on Twitter, as you can see in Figure 3–11.

FIGURE 3–11. Sharing Your LinkedIn Profile Updates with Twitter

You can easily see your full status activity by clicking on Me from the main menu, then Posts & Activity and Views of Your Posts, where you will see a full listing of your LinkedIn activity, as shown in Figure 3–12 on page 25.

FIGURE 3–12. See Your LinkedIn Activity

CONCLUSION

Your basic LinkedIn profile is now live, and you will start receiving invitations to connect with others. You can start reaching out to people yourself, but I recommend waiting until you are more familiar with LinkedIn and your profile is 100 percent complete. Think of this as a soft opening, so you can work out the bugs before the grand opening. In Chapter 4, I'll show you how to optimize your LinkedIn profile so you will appear near the top of LinkedIn and Google search results for your skills and target keyword phrases.

For additional updates and how-to videos, visit https://tedprodromou.com/UltimateGuideUpdates/.

Supercharging Your LinkedIn Profile

Your LinkedIn profile represents your professional image on the internet and can be found through searches on LinkedIn itself or search engines like Google, Bing, and Yahoo! When people search the internet for your name, your LinkedIn profile will likely be one of the top results, so you want to make a great first impression.

Think of LinkedIn as your online resume and your profile summary as the objective or professional statement. As people scan your profile, they should be able to understand exactly what you do or how you can help them.

Your LinkedIn profile provides people with a comprehensive summary of your education, work experience, and achievements. It also links people to other social media accounts and websites where you can showcase your expertise.

LinkedIn divides your profile into four high-level sections with corresponding subsections. These sections are:

- Background
  - Work Experience
  - Education
  - Licenses and Certifications
  - Volunteer Experience
- Skills

- ▨ Accomplishments
  - – Publications
  - – Certifications
  - – Patents
  - – Courses
  - – Projects
  - – Honors & Awards
  - – Test Scores
  - – Languages
  - – Organizations
- ▨ Additional Information
- ▨ Request a Recommendation
- ▨ Supported Languages

> **LINKEDIN PROFILE TIP**
>
> In this age of text messaging and autocorrect, our society has become very careless about spelling and grammar. Your LinkedIn profile is a reflection of your professional image, so be 100 percent sure it is correctly formatted and free of spelling and grammatical errors.

Your goal, of course, is to populate as many of these sections and subsections as possible to give the most comprehensive picture of who you are as a professional so you stand out among the crowd. In this chapter, I'll walk you through some of the best ways to do that, starting with what people see even before they click on your page: your profile headline and photo.

PROFILE HEADLINE

Your profile headline is the single most important part of your profile. Every day, your profile is automatically displayed to thousands of LinkedIn members in the right-hand column of their page under People Also Viewed and in search results when people search for skills and job titles.

When your name appears in the sidebar and search results, your headline must be compelling enough to make people want to click on your profile and learn more about you. You should never just include your name and company name in your headline. Bump up your discoverability with words that really show who you are.

In this section of your profile setup, you will also select your location and industry. LinkedIn has updated its dashboard so that you now see more information in the Intro section, as shown in Figure 4–1 on page 30. On my own profile, you can now see my background header, professional photo, name, headline, and location. In the right column, the gold "in" badge lets people know I'm a LinkedIn Premium member. Next you see my current company*, where I went to college, a link to my full contact information, and how many connections I have (they only show 500+ once you exceed 500 connections). On all profiles (not just mine), viewers can also see the first three lines of your summary and content you have shared in your profile.

* Note: My company name isn't really America's Leading LinkedIn Coach. I created a position in my Experience section and named the company America's Leading LinkedIn Coach so it is displayed prominently in my profile. It's a creative hack to get a tag line in front of your profile viewers.

GIVE UP THE GIMMICKS

Some people use tricks to get attention, but what it really does is show their inexperience. For example, some people like to add symbols to their headline. Some of the symbols I've seen include ™, ♦, #, *, ◊, and many other signs. I searched Google to see how people used the symbols, and they often just copied them from other people's profiles or used the Insert Symbols or Insert Shapes command in Microsoft Word.

Personally, I think it's unprofessional and diminishes your credibility. If you are really good at what you do, you shouldn't have to trick people into reading your profile. When I see symbols in someone's profile, I think of those restaurants with the neon signs advertising their cheap specials. You know the restaurant is a dive and the food is horrible, but they catch your attention with the flashing lights and low prices. This used to drive my father, a restaurant owner of more than 40 years, absolutely crazy. When he saw a flashing OPEN sign, he would always say, "If you serve good food and provide good service, people will know when you are open."

I feel the same way after seeing a LinkedIn profile that contains flashy symbols. Occasionally I will take a moment to read the profile. It's usually full of even more gimmicky symbols and buzzwords. The person typically overuses keywords (also known as "keyword stuffing" in SEO terms), overstates their experience, and uses other tricks to rank high in LinkedIn and Google searches. Eventually, LinkedIn and Google catch up with people like this and lower their rankings. They may get their 15 minutes of fame (and maybe even a few clients), but they rarely earn repeat customers or referrals.

Most people access LinkedIn through the mobile app, so Figure 4–2 on page 31 shows you what people see when they view my profile on a cell phone or tablet. Essentially they see the same information as they would on the desktop view but in a cleaner format.

FIGURE 4–1. Intro Section

When you sit down to write your profile headline, think of it as the title of an article or a book. The first two sentences of your summary are the teaser or subhead. They keep the reader interested enough to view the rest of your profile and learn more about you and your business.

Let's look at another example. Figure 4–3 on page 32 shows us the profile headline for Viveka von Rosen, a well-known LinkedIn expert. You know exactly what she does for a living within seconds of reading her profile headline. Notice that she incorporates strong keywords into her headline.

This strategy of using keyword phrases or skills in your headline is a popular one, and for good reason. Viveka's LinkedIn profile is the top organic search result in Google for "LinkedIn expert" out of 370 million search results (not bad!).

Also notice how she managed this powerful feat. Her public profile link, https://www.linkedin.com/in/linkedinexpert/, contains the phrase "LinkedIn expert," which Google sees as a keyword phrase, and it makes it very easy for prospective customers to find her on LinkedIn, as shown in Figure 4–4 on page 32.

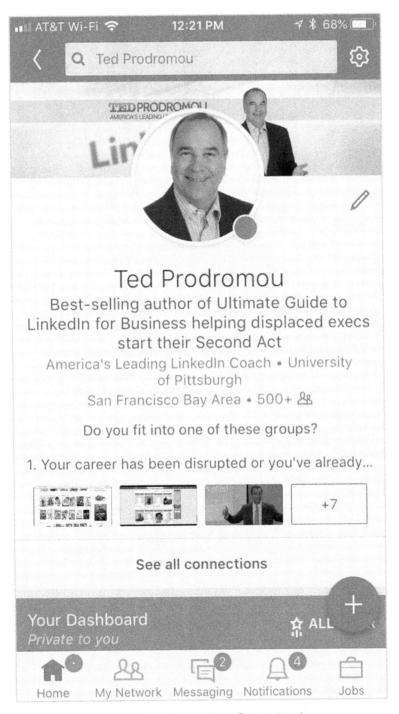

FIGURE 4–2. Mobile View of Intro Section

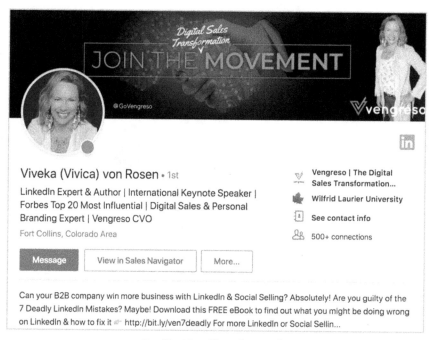

FIGURE 4–3. Profile Headline for Viveka von Rosen

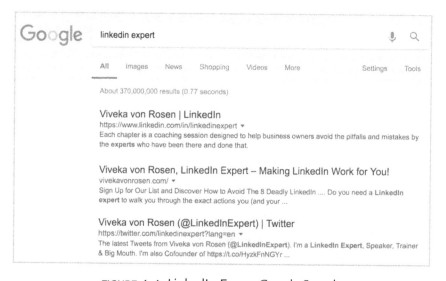

FIGURE 4–4. LinkedIn Expert Google Search

Take the time now to create a compelling profile headline using your target keyword phrases and claim your custom LinkedIn URL using a popular keyword phrase (if it's still available).

PROFILE PICTURE

Now that you have your headline wording optimized for discoverability, it's time to think about visuals. It's very important to use a professional picture in your LinkedIn profile. First impressions are everything, and people will judge you within two seconds of seeing your LinkedIn profile photo. Save the casual pictures for Facebook and Twitter.

The best LinkedIn profile pictures are engaging and inviting. I recommend a simple head shot focusing on your smiling face. You are establishing your professional brand on LinkedIn, and your profile photo is your personal logo. Your profile will be associated with your company, so you want to present a consistent, professional image. This is why I recommend using a professional head shot rather than an avatar, caricature, or another image that isn't congruent with the image you want for you and your business.

Never use your company logo as your personal profile picture. LinkedIn is a network where people connect with people. First, it's not engaging and doesn't give people a chance to get to know you. Second, it's a violation of the LinkedIn user agreement, which can be found at www.linkedin.com/legal/user-agreement. Your company logo will appear in your Experience section, and you can invite people to follow your company page where they will also see your logo.

Your profile photo must meet the following formatting guidelines:

- You can upload JPG, GIF, or PNG files
- Maximum file size is 8MB
- Pixel size: between 400 (w) x 400 (h) minimum and 7680 (w) x 4320 (h) maximum.

LinkedIn has added the ability to easily resize, crop, filter, and adjust your photo. See Figure 4–5 on page 34 to see how to edit your profile photo. As you upload your profile picture, you can choose who will be allowed to view it using the Visibility button. I recommend choosing "Public" so people can see your picture when they search on Google and when they are viewing your profile, even if you are not connected with them.

The choices under the Visibility menu are:

- *Your Connections.* Only people directly connected to you on LinkedIn will be able to see your photo.
- *Your Network.* Only people connected up to three degrees away from you.
- *All LinkedIn Members.* Everyone who is signed up to use LinkedIn.
- *Public.* People who do not belong to LinkedIn and find you through search engines (e.g., Google, Bing).

I feel strongly that you should have a complete profile on LinkedIn, including a professional picture. I feel a partial LinkedIn profile or a profile without a professional

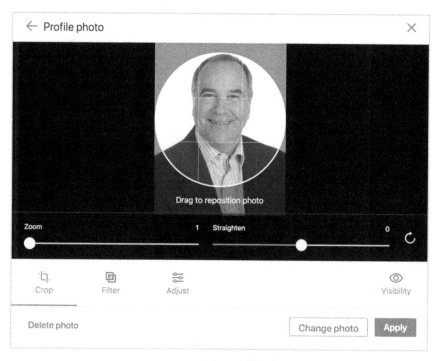

FIGURE 4–5. My Profile Photo

picture is a negative reflection on that person. If they don't take the time to complete their LinkedIn profiles, chances are they don't take the time to complete other work tasks as thoroughly as they should. I base this on the fact that some people I know don't have a complete LinkedIn profile and are not very detail-oriented. They finish 80 to 90 percent of a project but don't complete it. They are not the kind of people I want working for me, and I would not recommend them to others because it could reflect negatively on me. This is just my personal opinion, and while it may not hold true in all cases, I feel very strongly about finishing what you start.

STATUS UPDATE

Below your LinkedIn toolbar is your Status Update section. Your updates for "Share" will appear in the newsfeed, which is in the middle column of your LinkedIn homepage. LinkedIn now lets you share a variety of content or just a status update, which is similar to a tweet, as you can see in Figure 4-6 on page 35. Your updates can be Public, Public + Twitter, or just for your Connections. Your updates might include:

- *Write an article.* This is just like a blog post and can include text, embedded videos, links to your website, and hashtags.

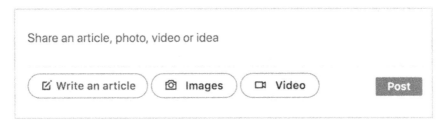

FIGURE **4-6**. Share an Article, Photo, Video, or Idea

- *Images.* Upload photos or illustrations with your marketing messages.
- *Video.* You can now upload native videos directly into the LinkedIn newsfeed.

You can share your status using this box, which is located at the top of your LinkedIn homepage. By selecting the Public + Twitter option you see in Figure 4-7, your status update will also be tweeted. You can prevent people from commenting on your status update if you choose.

I will go into publishing content on LinkedIn in Chapter 15. But for now, this is the basic way to do so—even if your profile setup is still in the early stages.

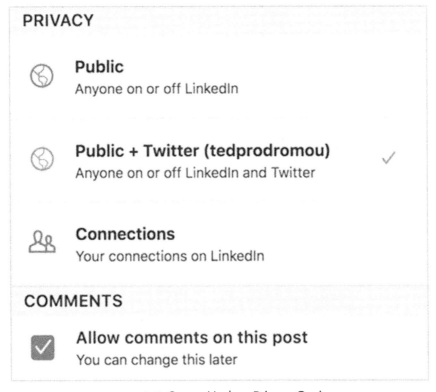

FIGURE **4-7**. Status Update Privacy Options

EXPERIENCE

Now we'll move into your Experience or Employment section. To add your current and previous positions, click on the **+** sign, as seen in Figure 4–8. Your current position and

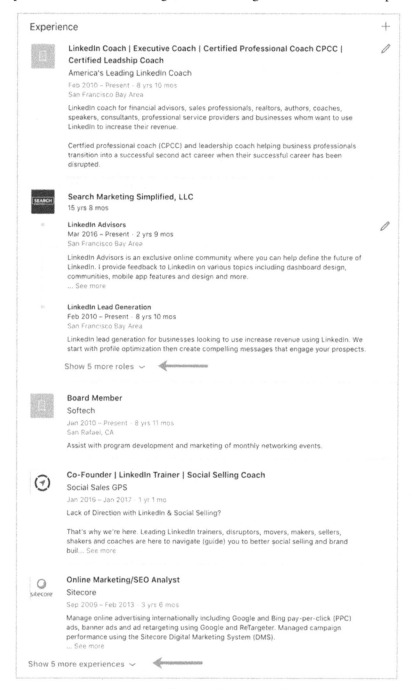

FIGURE 4–8. My Current Experience Summary

your most recent past four positions will be displayed in your profile. Five additional positions will be displayed if the viewer clicks on Show 5 more experiences. In my profile you can also click on View 5 more roles under my current company, Search Marketing Simplified, LLC.

Figure 4–9 shows you the Add Experience form. Simply fill out the form and click Save. Make sure you add a brief but clear description for each position. Use your target

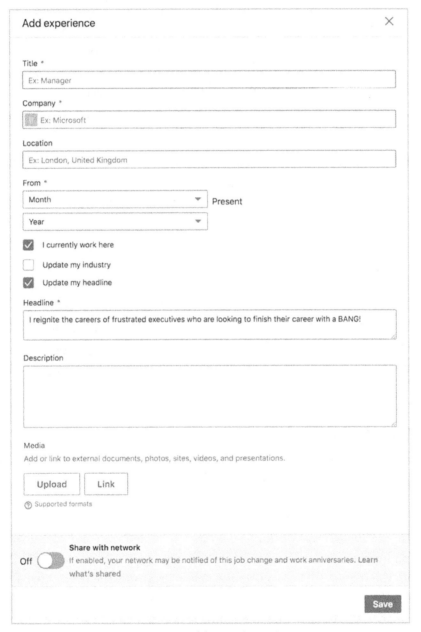

FIGURE 4–9. Add Experience Form

keywords in your job title and description, so you will be found when people search for your skill sets.

Notice you can create another profile headline in your Experience section, which lets you instantly replace your job title with a customized headline that appears only in this specific job. This headline grabs attention and tells people how you can help them when they view your profile. You can also upload media like a PDF, a relevant white paper you wrote, a video, or a podcast recording. This content is displayed within the job position and allows you to demonstrate your expertise.

EDUCATION

Once you've added your current and previous positions, you'll move on to your education. Simply click + Add Education to enter your school, degree, field of study, grade, activities and societies, years attended, and a description. Figure 4–10 on page 39 shows the Add Education form. Note: The only required field is the school name; all other fields are optional.

You can also add multimedia content and links to articles on websites, as shown at the bottom of the form.

> **LINKEDIN PROFILE TIP**
>
> Should you choose the Share With Network option when you update your profile? When I'm making a lot of changes, I leave the Share button turned off until I make the final update. If the Share button is on, your network will be notified every time you click Save, which can be annoying. I like to Share only when I'm finished updating, so my network is "pinged" with a notification that my profile has changed. The result is a lot of congratulatory messages from my network, which puts me back on their radar. I often reengage past clients with this strategy.

VOLUNTEER EXPERIENCE

Why does LinkedIn ask you to share your volunteer experience if the goal is professional development? Because it's a holistic view of who you are as a person. Adding volunteer experience shows people you contribute to your community by volunteering with organizations that are important to you. For example, when I was working as an IT director in the 1990s, I was working 80 hours a week and traveling a lot. I was an MIA father and husband, so I quit my job to spend more time with my young children and wife. This allowed me to drive on school field trips (I was the only father there most of the time). The best part of being my own boss was that I coached my son's baseball team with my sister, Connie. She was a tomboy growing up and the best baseball player in the neighborhood. We coached Little League against fathers who played college and

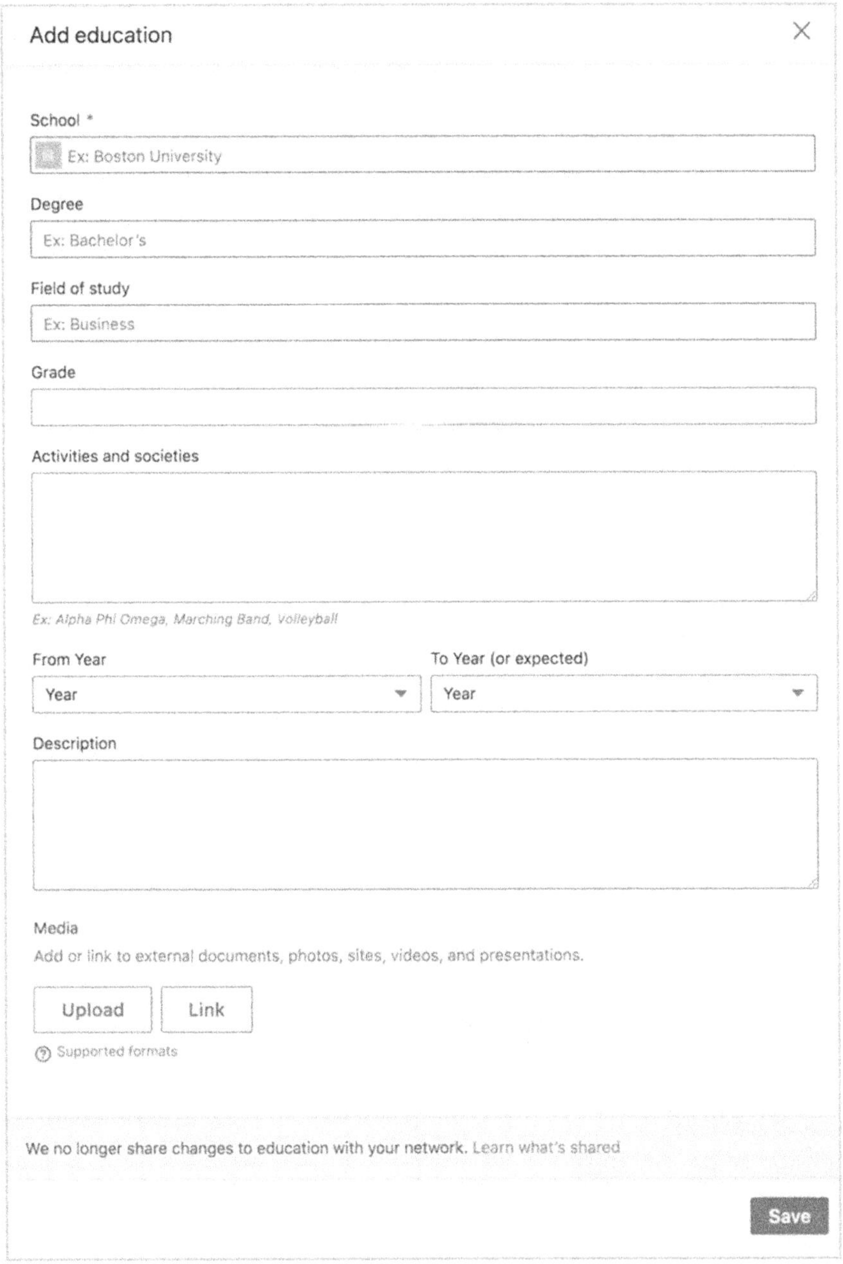

FIGURE 4–10. Add Education Form

minor league baseball, and we won the championship three out of four years because we focused on the basics of throwing, catching, swinging the bat level, and having fun. Sharing this story lets people know that family and community come first for me. To add your volunteer experience, fill out the form shown in Figure 4–11 on page 40.

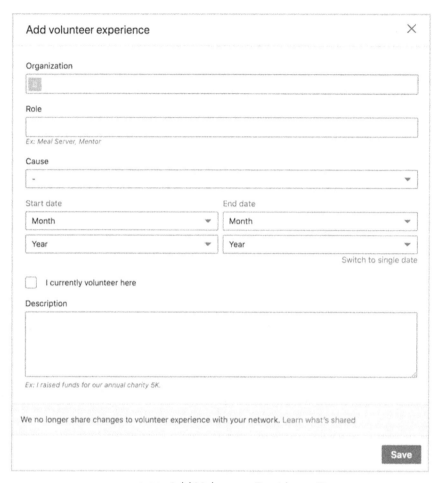

FIGURE 4–11. Add Volunteer Experience Form

SKILLS AND ENDORSEMENTS

Now that you've added your volunteer experience, you'll move to your skills. You can add up to 50 skills to your profile, and I recommend you use all 50 of them. Skills are used as keyword phrases in the LinkedIn search algorithm, so it's important to add as many skills as possible to increase your findability. Once you populate your profile with skills, people can endorse you for those skills. The more endorsements you have for each skill, the higher you will rank when people search LinkedIn for that skill. If you are an independent patent attorney, how great would it be to appear at the top of LinkedIn search results?

Let's add some skills to your LinkedIn profile. Click on Add a New Skill in the Skills & Endorsements section of your profile. As you see in Figure 4–12 on page 41, LinkedIn will suggest some skills based on your profile. Click on the appropriate skills, and they

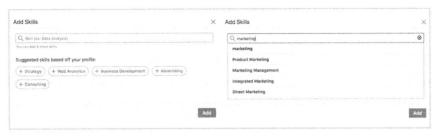

FIGURE 4–12. Add Skills to Your Profile

will be added to your profile automatically. You can also add more skills by typing the skill in the box next to the magnifying glass in the form. As you start typing, LinkedIn will autosuggest skills that already exist in their system. I recommend using these skills, since they are used in the search algorithm. Of course, if your skill is unique and not already in LinkedIn's database, you can certainly add it.

After you enter your skills, you can re-order them by dragging them up or down while in edit mode (see Figure 4–13 on page 42). You want to feature your top three skills so they appear prominently in your profile. This will result in more people endorsing you for those skills, which, in turn, moves you up the search rankings for those skills. The more endorsements you have for each skill, the higher you can rank. Your skills will be categorized as:

- Top Skills
- Industry Knowledge
- Tools & Technologies
- Interpersonal Skills
- Other Skills

RECOMMENDATIONS

I will cover giving and receiving recommendations in greater detail in Chapter 10. For now, I'll provide you with some important pointers to get started. Most important, it is critical to request recommendations personally. I know that I rarely recommend someone who sends me a mass request and doesn't take the time to write a personal request. This is a huge pet peeve of mine, and I will reiterate it numerous times throughout this book. *Do not use the tools in LinkedIn to send mass requests!* LinkedIn is about building strong personal connections, and using automated tools is not the way to build a strong connection with others. If you want a good recommendation from someone, take the time to write a personal message, and you will receive a much better recommendation than you would from a mass request.

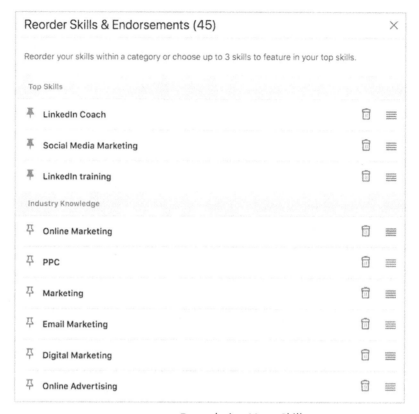

FIGURE 4–13. Re-ordering Your Skills

You can Request a Recommendation in this section by clicking on the link. Fill out the form shown in Figure 4–14 below, and a recommendation request will be sent to the contacts you choose.

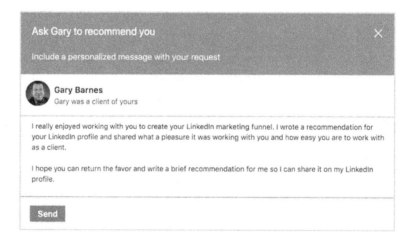

FIGURE 4–14. Recommendation Form

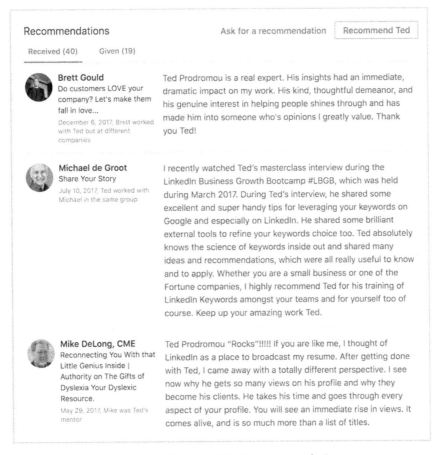

FIGURE 4–15. Some of My Recommendations

Make sure you include personal details about how you met, projects you've worked together on, and other details about your working relationship. Specify exactly what you want in the endorsement, such as focusing on a specific project you worked on or highlighting a certain skill set. Some people even prefer that you send them a brief endorsement you've written about yourself they can edit or modify to save them time.

Your recommendations are displayed next, as shown in Figure 4–15.

ACCOMPLISHMENTS

One of the big changes LinkedIn made in its overhaul of the dashboard was to create the Accomplishments section of your profile, reorganizing a lot of miscellaneous topics into one category, including:

- Publications
- Certifications

- Patents
- Courses
- Projects
- Honors & Awards
- Test Scores
- Languages
- Organizations

Figure 4–16 shows you the various topics in Accomplishments. Let's walk through them briefly.

FIGURE 4–16. Accomplishments Information

Publications

One of the powerful sections of your profile is Publications, where you can display your published books or articles. You used to need a valid ISBN number for your published book to use this section, but the rules have been relaxed. Your publication listing includes your book title, publisher, publication date, and a description of your book. You can also add a link to your website or any other retailer or site where people can purchase your book.

You can also add ebooks and self-published books in this section and link to your website or Amazon where people can purchase and download your books. I upload my digital magazine, *Social Selling Made Easy*, to Amazon and publish it as a free Kindle book, which I add as a Publication in my LinkedIn profile. It's a great way to get your content in front of millions of people for free. Another great feature of Publications is the ability to link to the LinkedIn profiles of your co-authors, as shown in Figure 4–17. I wrote one of my books with *New York Times* bestselling author Joel Comm, so both of our LinkedIn profiles are displayed in my profile, Joel's profile, and all the other book authors' profiles. This is a great way to associate yourself with famous authors, adding to your credibility.

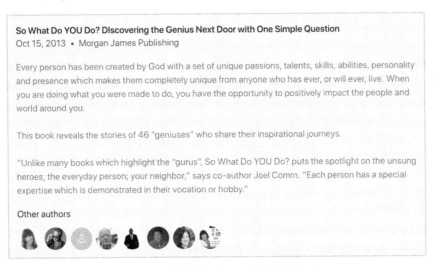

FIGURE 4–17. Publications with Co-Authors

Certifications

People often list multiple certification abbreviations in their name field. I recommend including only one or two of your top certifications, like CFA or CPA, at the end of your name and put the rest of your certifications under this section. When you add too many abbreviations at the end of your name, it can look cluttered, and it may be hard for people to search for you by your last name. If I add MBA and CPCC (my Certified Professional Co-Active Coach certification) to my last name, my name would be Ted Prodromou, MBA, CPCC. When people search for Ted Prodromou, the LinkedIn search algorithm might not easily find me because it thinks my last name is Prodromou, MBA, CPCC.

Patents

This is self-explanatory. Enter all your registered patents in this section. You can include single-owner patents, for which you are the sole patent holder, as well as patents for which you are one of many named on the project. This is a fairly common occurrence for engineers especially, so just make sure you denote that your name isn't the only one on the patent.

Courses

Have you created an online course or created a course for a school? You can enter all your courses in this section. I display my Linked Accelerator LinkedIn course here, which lets me link directly to the registration page. This is a great way to demonstrate your expertise and sell your courses. This is also one of the few places in your LinkedIn profile where you can add clickable links.

Projects

This is another section where you can add clickable links, so take advantage of it. I've created multiple projects, so I can share my *Social Selling Made Easy* magazine, a free LinkedIn training webinar, and my YouTube channel, Social Selling TV. Add any significant projects you have successfully completed or links to your promotional material.

Honors & Awards

This section is for any honors and awards you have received in your scholastic or professional career. When I was in the computer industry, I won many customer service awards, so I included them here.

Test Scores

When you are still in school, a recent graduate, or you receive a professional certification, you can share your test scores here. I've found that unless these are particularly pertinent to potential employers or possible business partners, they aren't terribly useful.

Languages

If you speak multiple languages, include each one in this section. Many companies are looking for multilingual employees, so recruiters and hiring managers will find you by searching LinkedIn for specific languages.

Organizations

Do you belong to professional organizations or are you a board member at a nonprofit organization? This is the section where you can share your membership in professional organizations like Rotary or your local Chamber of Commerce.

CONCLUSION

Your LinkedIn profile is now optimized for the search engines and ready to promote. To begin sharing your LinkedIn profile go to the main menu, select Me, View profile then select Edit your public profile at the top of the right column. At the bottom of the page, choose Create a Profile Badge to promote your LinkedIn profile or use your Public Profile link, which is at the top of the column. You can also add links to your LinkedIn profile from your website, blog, and email signature to generate traffic and improve your search rankings. LinkedIn frequently adds new sections to your profile, which lets you share more information about yourself. This helps people get to know, like, and trust you faster, accelerating the sales process dramatically. As you notice additional sections in your LinkedIn profile, fill them out to keep your profile as complete as possible.

In Chapter 5, I'll introduce you to the LinkedIn privacy settings so you can control when and where LinkedIn and its partner websites can use your profile information. I'll show you why it's important for you to configure your privacy settings properly to prevent your profile from appearing in inappropriate places, like in an ad near a competing company's profile.

**For additional updates and how-to videos, visit
https://tedprodromou.com/UltimateGuideUpdates/.**

Chapter 5

LinkedIn Privacy Settings

Now that your LinkedIn profile is complete, you can configure your privacy settings. LinkedIn lets you control how your data is displayed and who is allowed to see your activity on the site.

In today's world of cyber attacks, hacking, and data privacy issues, securing your LinkedIn profile is more important than ever. Internet privacy remains a controversial topic because people are rightfully concerned about how much personal information is being collected by websites and how they are using it. Your LinkedIn profile does not contain any personal information, like your home address or telephone numbers, unless you voluntarily add it to your profile. I do not recommend doing so. It *is* important to include your work or mobile number and office address so prospects and customers can easily reach you, though. Remember, more than 500 million people potentially have access to this information, which could be a blessing or a curse depending on who decides to use it. People will also be able to get your company phone number from your LinkedIn company page, so make sure you add a link to your company page in your profile. Make it easy for prospects and customers to contact you.

Speaking of choosing what to display, did you know you have two profiles on LinkedIn? Your *public profile* is what's displayed to people who aren't logged in to LinkedIn and is what shows up on Google searches.

Although you can customize it, it usually includes your photo, your name, your number of connections, your industry, and the general region where you're located. Your *primary profile* is what people see when they are logged in to LinkedIn: the details of your current and past jobs, your education, your recommendations, your websites, Twitter account information, and which LinkedIn Groups you have joined. In the center column of your profile, people will see all your LinkedIn activity, including your status updates, article posts, and when you share other people's updates.

People can also see all your LinkedIn connections, if you choose, which will help them get a sense of who you are. This helps users connect with like-minded people who may become clients or great referral partners. Many believe this is a great way to grow your professional network because you're being totally transparent with other LinkedIn members.

If you don't want to let people see your connections, you can change your privacy settings so you are the only one who can view them. Some people believe this gives them a competitive advantage.

For example, I used to work for a software company, and all the salespeople were connected with one another since they were on the same team. A few years later, many of the salespeople left the company and went to work for competitors. If these salespeople let everyone see their connections, their former co-workers could reach out to these connections and try to persuade them to switch to their business. If you don't share your contacts with other LinkedIn members, they won't have an opportunity to steal your customers away from your company. Be careful what you share!

When you recommend others on LinkedIn, your recommendation will appear in their LinkedIn profile if they choose to display them. This lets people see whom you do business with and helps them find great resources when they need assistance. People always prefer working with service providers that have been recommended.

The left column of your profile sidebar displays People Also Viewed. This section shows you the other profiles people viewed after they looked at yours. This lets you see people LinkedIn has associated with your profile because you work for the same company or in the same industry, have similar job skills, or have other similarities. This often leads you to people you should be connected with on LinkedIn.

Now let's dig deeper into the types of profiles you can set up.

PUBLIC PROFILE

Your public profile can be viewed by people who are not logged in to LinkedIn. This profile appears in Google searches if you choose to make it visible to the search engines. You can edit public profile settings and control which parts of your profile are displayed publicly. You can open your profile completely so all information is visible. You can also make your public profile completely private. The third option is to customize the display of different elements of your profile. For example, you can display your basic information, headline, and summary and block the rest of your profile from the search engines. Most people use the custom configuration to display only some information in their public profile.

To control which data fields people see in your public profile, go to the LinkedIn menu, select the dropdown menu under Me, and select Settings & Privacy. Figure 5–1 shows you the options you have to control your privacy.

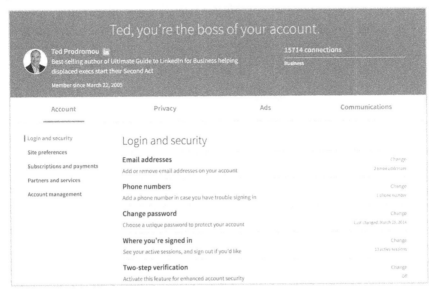

FIGURE 5–1. Settings and Privacy Dashboard

The dashboard is segmented into four sections:

1. Account
2. Privacy
3. Ads
4. Communications

Let's take a look at each one.

ACCOUNT

You can do a lot under the Account portion of your dashboard. You can edit, add, or remove email addresses associated with your account. You can also add or remove the telephone number displayed in your account and change your password. An interesting setting is Where You're Signed In, which tells you how many devices you are currently logged into. In Figure 5–1 above you can see I have 13 active sessions, so I need to look at this to see why I'm logged in so many times. I usually log in to LinkedIn from my desktop computer, laptop, iPad, or iPhone. You can log out of all your sessions to make sure there are no unauthorized users of your account. You can also turn on two-step verification as an added layer of security. With two-step verification, when you log into LinkedIn, you will receive a security code on your mobile device that you must enter to complete your login.

In Figure 5–2 below, you see Site Preferences. This is where you can select your preferred language, whether you want videos to autoplay, where your profile photos will appear (I highly recommend displaying them everywhere), your feed preferences, and your name, location, and industry preferences.

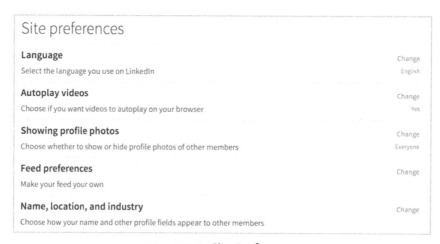

FIGURE 5–2. Site Preferences

Feed Preferences is where you customize the content for your newsfeed. When LinkedIn Pulse existed, we used to customize our newsfeed in Pulse settings. Now we select our content as you see in Figure 5–3 on page 53. Just click on + Follow to add content from a person, company, or hashtag topic. To unfollow, simply click on Unfollow.

You can also customize your newsfeed content by clicking on the ellipsis in an existing post and selecting Improve My Feed, as shown in Figure 5–4 on page 53.

If you have a LinkedIn Premium account, you can see the details of your plan and payment history in the Subscriptions and Payments section of your account. The Partners and Services section is important because you can see which outside

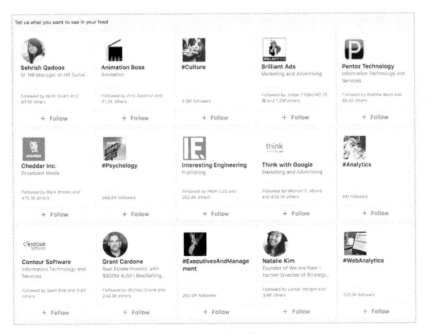

FIGURE 5–3. Feed Preferences

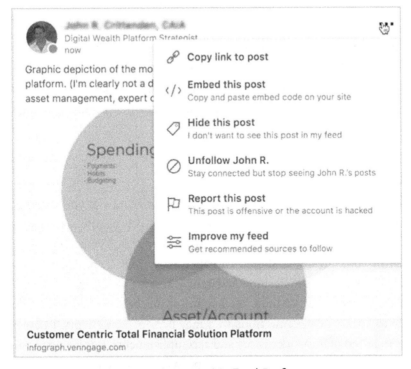

FIGURE 5–4. Improve My Feed Preferences

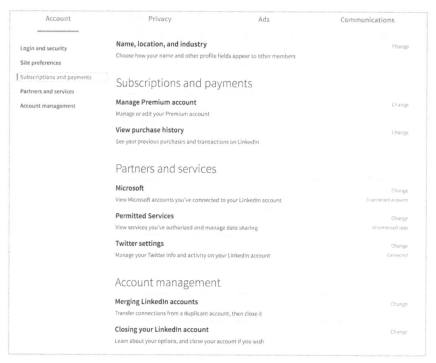

FIGURE 5–5. Permitted Services

services and websites you allow to access your LinkedIn data. As you can see in Figure 5–5 above, I don't allow any Microsoft services to access my account, but I have ten other services allowed. I like to review these services occasionally to make sure I'm not allowing apps I no longer use to access my LinkedIn account. I can also add my Twitter account in this section.

PRIVACY

The Privacy settings let you control who sees various portions of your profile, including your email address, your connections, who viewers of this profile also viewed, your last name, if your name will be mentioned when content about your employers is posted, how much of your profile is shared in your public profile, and whether your work experience will appear in the Resume Assistant (a feature in Microsoft Word).

In my case, I choose not to limit much in my profile because I want as much exposure as possible to attract new connections who may become new clients. I have nothing to hide, and I'm proud of my work history and accomplishments. But it's up to you what you share from your LinkedIn profile, and it all depends on your objective, which we discussed in Chapter 2. Figure 5–6 on page 55 shows you the available options on the Privacy tab.

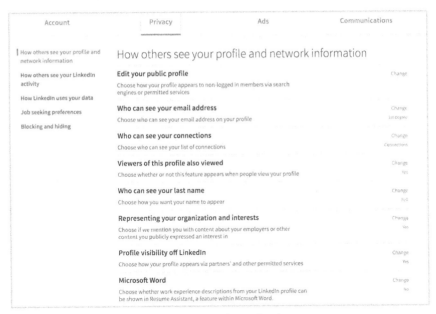

FIGURE 5–6. Privacy Settings

ADS

LinkedIn categorizes the Ads section into General Advertising Preferences, Data Collected on LinkedIn, and Third-Party Data. These settings may not make sense at first glance, but to a marketer, the distinctions are very important. To minimize the amount of data LinkedIn collects about you, I recommend turning off these settings. Figure 5–7 on page 56 shows the options for controlling your advertising preferences.

General Advertising Practices

This section covers three options you can use for advertising. Let's dig into them briefly; we'll talk more about LinkedIn advertising in Chapter 20.

1. *Websites you visited.* LinkedIn will ask to "use information about your visits to an advertiser's website to provide insights that help the advertiser understand which promoted jobs and ads may be relevant to you." If you say "yes," you are allowing LinkedIn to share data about you with a LinkedIn advertiser if you click on their ad. I recommend turning this setting off.

2. *Ads beyond LinkedIn.* LinkedIn will ask if you want to see their ads on other sites you visit on the web? I recommend turning this off as well.

3. *Profile data for ad personalization.* LinkedIn will ask if it can "use your profile photo and profile information (like name or company) to personalize the content of

promoted jobs and ads." You are the only one who can see ads with your photo, so I have no preference on this one.

FIGURE 5–7. Ads Settings

Data Collected on LinkedIn

In this section, you can control whether you see relevant ads based on your interest categories, connections, location, demographics, companies you follow, Groups, education, job information, and employer. I recommend turning all these settings on if you are looking for a job. For example, if you live in San Francisco, work for Twitter, belong to Groups related to social media, or attended Stanford, LinkedIn will only show you job ads related to these categories.

Third-Party Data

LinkedIn gives you two options to consider.

1. *Interactions with businesses.* LinkedIn will request to "use information about websites you've visited or information you've shared with businesses to show you relevant promoted jobs and ads." I recommend leaving this setting off. **This means LinkedIn is using cookies to track other websites you've visited so they can show you targeted job offers and advertising.**

2. *Ad-related actions.* LinkedIn asks if it can "use information about actions you took off LinkedIn (like applying to a job) in response to ads to understand which promoted jobs and ads are most relevant to you." LinkedIn only reports aggregate ad performance to advertisers and it won't tell them about specific actions you took. **I recommend turning this setting on if you want to see more jobs like the ones you already applied for.**

COMMUNICATIONS

If you want to control the amount of communication you receive from LinkedIn and your connections, it's easy to do so from the Communications tab.

To minimize the number of messages I receive from LinkedIn, I turn off almost all messages sent to the email address I have on file with LinkedIn. I interact with other LinkedIn members through the Messaging app and the Notifications tab. This also helps me avoid redundant messaging, as messages appear both in the LinkedIn Messaging app and my primary inbox if the feature is turned on.

I don't receive any update messages from my LinkedIn Groups because most of the posts in Groups are blog posts and self-promotions. I allow anyone to invite me to connect, and I am open to receiving messages from any of my 1st-degree or 2nd-degree connections who have a premium account with an open profile. I'll explain networking in more detail in Chapter 11, but for now, here's a quick summary of the LinkedIn network hierarchy:

- 1st-degree connections are your friends
- 2nd-degree connections are friends of your friends
- 3rd-degree connections are friends of your friends' friends

Here's how it works. If you connect with me on LinkedIn, we become 1st-degree connections. My network of 15,000+ connections and growing daily becomes part of your 2nd-degree network. For every 1st-degree connection you make, their network becomes part of your 2nd-degree network. This is why your LinkedIn network

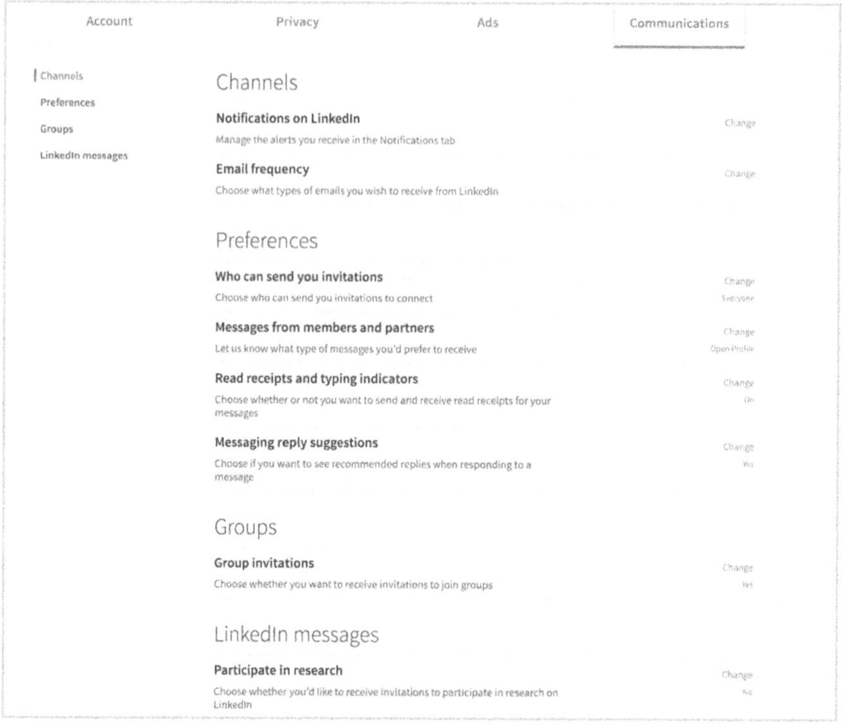

FIGURE 5–8. Communications Settings

powerful. You are one step away or one introduction away from millions of business professionals. So choose your Communications settings wisely. You can see what that menu looks like in Figure 5-8.

A new feature in LinkedIn messages is the Messaging Reply Suggestions, which I have turned on. When you are messaging with another person, LinkedIn will autosuggest a response to save time. It's convenient when you are on your mobile device and want to reply in a timely manner, but the suggested messages can be too simple or even cheesy at times, like "Sweet" or "Cool." See Figure 5-9 on page 59 for some examples of the reply suggestions.

CONCLUSION

If you are a consultant or business owner and want to get your name out there, I see no reason to block any of your content from the search engines. You are on LinkedIn so people can find you, and blocking your listing from search engines is self-defeating. It would be similar to having an unlisted phone number for your business. Opening up your profile completely will get your target keywords into the search engines, giving you maximum exposure.

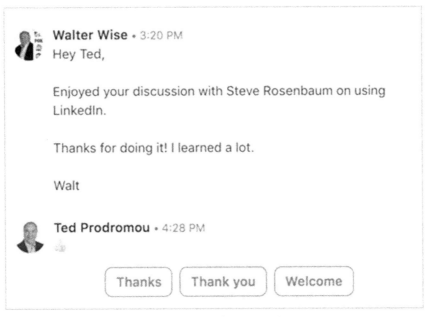

FIGURE 5–9. Reply Suggestions

In the next chapter, we'll take a tour of your LinkedIn homepage. I'll show you how to customize your homepage layout so you can easily see a snapshot of your important LinkedIn data.

**For additional updates and how-to videos, visit
https://tedprodromou.com/UltimateGuideUpdates/.**

A Tour of Your LinkedIn Homepage

N ow that you have a basic account set up, let's take a tour of your LinkedIn homepage. Every LinkedIn member has their own customizable homepage. When LinkedIn redesigned its platform in 2017, your newsfeed became the heart of your LinkedIn experience. You subscribe to content you want to appear in your newsfeed so you can easily see what's important to you in a single glance. Figure 6–1 on page 62 is a view of a typical LinkedIn homepage as seen on a desktop computer (the mobile view is obviously different). As you tour the homepage, note the following 11 features:

1. *LinkedIn Search*. This is where you search for people, companies, and Groups on LinkedIn. I'll show you how to do advanced searches on LinkedIn in Chapter 8.

2. *Toolbar*. This is your LinkedIn toolbar or menu and notifications section. When you have new LinkedIn mail or notifications (e.g., if someone comments on your status update or accepts your invitation to connect), the icon will show the number of new notifications. Currently, I have seven new notifications.

   Your LinkedIn toolbar or menu options include:

   - *Home*. Obviously, this takes you back to your LinkedIn homepage.

FIGURE 6–1. A Typical LinkedIn Homepage

- *My Network.* Add and manage your LinkedIn connections.
- *Jobs.* Post and manage job openings for your company, look for a job, and access premium services like Premium Career or Premium Career and Recruiter. I'll explain the premium solutions in Chapters 18 and 19.
- *Messaging.* Send and receive your LinkedIn messages.
- *Notifications.* Notifies you when your network is active or you receive activity on your LinkedIn posts.
- *Me.* View and edit your LinkedIn profile as well as manage your settings and privacy.
- *Work.* Access companies, Groups, and education.
- *Sales Navigator.* If you subscribe to Sales Navigator, this is where you access it. If you are not a premium member, it will say Try Premium Free for One Month.

3. *Self-Service Text Ads.* Near the top of Figure 6–1 above, you can see where your LinkedIn Text Ads will be displayed.

4. *Share an Update Box.* This is where you post your status updates, create articles, or post videos.

5. *Profile Snapshot.* This widget lets you see a snapshot of your LinkedIn profile photo and headline. This widget also provides quick access to Who's Viewed Your Profile, Views of Your Post, and all premium features if you subscribe to premium services.

6. *Your Communities.* These are hashtags or topics you can follow in your newsfeed. You can follow topics, thought leaders, or companies.

7. *Newsfeed.* This is where status updates and company news will appear. You can control the updates you see in this area by clicking on the three dots in the upper right corner of a post in your newsfeed then selecting Improve my feed.

8. *What People Are Talking About Now.* This is where LinkedIn shares breaking news from around the world that people are responding to.

9. *LinkedIn Learning.* This is for relevant courses from LinkedIn Learning, which is part of your premium subscription.

10. *Promoted Self-Service Ads.* When you place self-service ads with an image, they will appear here. See Figure 6–2 on page 64.

11. *People Also Viewed.* This widget shows you similar profiles that were recently viewed (see Figure 6–2). The LinkedIn algorithm creates a profile of you based on data in your profile and associates you with other professionals. Your LinkedIn profile will appear in front of thousands of people every day in this widget.

Figure 6–2 shows additional widgets displayed on your LinkedIn dashboard when you are viewing someone's profile. Next let's take a look at the mobile version of the homepage.

LINKEDIN MOBILE APP HOMEPAGE

The LinkedIn mobile app homepage layout obviously has less real estate than the desktop version, so you won't see all the features shown above. The mobile homepage contains:

1. LinkedIn search
2. Toolbar or menu
3. Share an update box
4. Profile snapshot

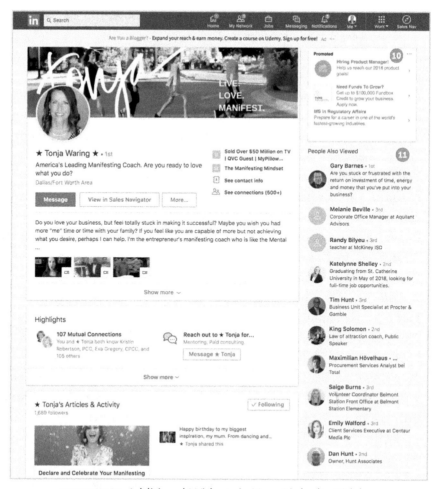

FIGURE 6–2. Additional Widgets in Your LinkedIn Sidebar

5. Your communities
6. Newsfeed

Figure 6–3 on page 65 shows you what the mobile app homepage looks like.

CONCLUSION

You are now familiar with your LinkedIn homepage and how you can configure it to display the newsfeed content that is most relevant to you. The goal of the homepage is to provide you with an efficient snapshot of your LinkedIn experience, including your newsfeed, network updates, new connection invitations, industry news, messaging, and more.

FIGURE 6–3. LinkedIn Mobile App Homepage

In the next chapter, I'll show you how to set up your LinkedIn company page and customize it to give your company maximum exposure.

For additional updates and how-to videos, visit
https://tedprodromou.com/UltimateGuideUpdates/.

LinkedIn for Companies

inkedIn Pages are like a LinkedIn personal profile for your company. Your company page is a mini-website for your company, but it's located on LinkedIn, so it's easy for members to find. You'll want to use some of the same SEO techniques that you used for your personal profile when you're setting up your company page, which I'll show you later in this chapter.

LinkedIn revamped company pages in 2018 to improve the user experience and increase brand awareness by making the pages more engaging. Now called LinkedIn Pages, you can add Showcase pages so it's easier for companies to feature their products and services. It's also easier to recruit new employees by featuring job openings and letting job seekers learn more about your company and your culture.

Your company page will always appear when a member types your company's name in LinkedIn's search box on his homepage or on the Companies link on the top toolbar under More. Your LinkedIn Page will also appear in Google search results. Because LinkedIn is a very popular and trusted website, LinkedIn Pages rank well in Google. This is very significant because people can view your LinkedIn Page even if they aren't logged into the site, giving your company significant exposure.

So make sure your company page is complete and updated frequently with your latest company news and product offerings.

Your LinkedIn Page will also appear when someone:

> **LINKEDIN PROFILE TIP**
>
> Your LinkedIn Pages url will be www.linkedin.com/company/YourCompany-Name.

- Views the LinkedIn profile of one of your employees
- Receives a notification when your products or services are recommended by one of your employees' connections
- Sees an open position in your company via a job search under Jobs You May Be Interested In
- Sees your company under Similar pages, which appears in the right sidebar on your homepage
- Follows your company and receives status updates

For LinkedIn members, company pages, now called LinkedIn Pages, are a great way to research companies. They are a treasure trove of detailed information, including company size, office locations, key executives, product offerings, and career opportunities. When you do a search from the LinkedIn top toolbar and switch the search type to Companies under the More tab, you will see search results from the company page (if there is one) and all companies that work closely or partner with that company.

For example, when you do a company search for Microsoft, you will see the Microsoft company page followed by a list of Microsoft Certified Partners. Click on the Microsoft company page, and you'll find a list of people in your network who are affiliated with Microsoft. You'll also be provided with a list of Microsoft employees who are your 1st-, 2nd-, or 3rd-degree connections.

You can follow companies on their company page so you can stay up-to-date with their new products or services, review their products or services, and see who they are hiring. You can also follow competitors and learn what they're up to.

LinkedIn Pages also let your customers and prospects get to know the people in your company. You can feature the employees behind your brand and show how customers use your products. Your company page is a great way to solidify your reputation and build trust with your clients and prospects.

COMPONENTS OF A COMPANY PROFILE

Before we dive more deeply into how to optimize your company's profile, let's look at the features of a typical company profile page. Figure 7-1 on page 69 shows a typical company profile.

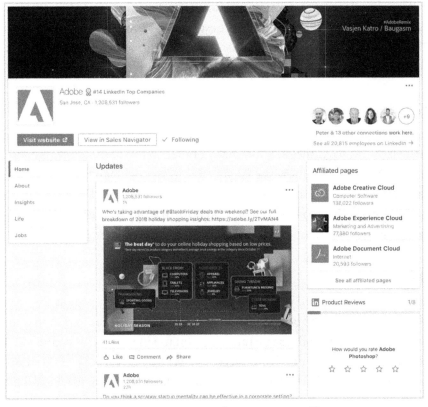

FIGURE 7–1. A Typical Company Profile

Overview of Your Company Homepage

The Home tab shows the viewer a snapshot of your company, including your recent updates, a brief description of your company, and all employees in the network, including 1st-, 2nd-, and 3rd-degree connections. You can also display your company's blog posts on the Home tab. It's a great way to give people a quick overview of your company and an opportunity for you to make a direct connection with them.

How You're Connected

This information is located on the right side of the header. It shows who you are directly connected to in this company and the total number of employees who are on LinkedIn.

Jobs

This is where any job openings you've posted on LinkedIn will appear. If you purchase a Premium Talent Solutions package, you can also add a brief description of your company culture so people can get a good idea of how fantastic it is to work there. The

Career Pages also let you feature top employees and create targeted messaging to help fill your open positions quickly with the best talent. To learn more about Career Pages and Talent Solutions visit https://business.linkedin.com/talent-solutions/company-career-pages.

Showcase Pages

You can feature your products and services on this sidebar widget. When a prospect or customer visits this page, they see how many of their network connections comment on, like, or share posts on the Showcase Page.

You can create a directory-style listing of your Showcase Pages in your sidebar. Each product or service can have its own page, including descriptions, features, images, display banners, videos, and special offers.

Feed Ads

LinkedIn advertising lets you promote posts from your company page as Feed Ads. When you sponsor an update, the post from your company page is featured in the timeline of a specified audience, using the same targeting you use in normal LinkedIn ads. This lets you get your message in front of your target audience so they'll see your Feed Ad in their personal timeline. You can read more about LinkedIn advertising in Chapter 20.

Analytics

This tab is visible only to an administrator of your company page. The Analytics tab shows you who your visitors are, what they do, and which other companies they follow. You can use this to gain valuable insight into what content they are most interested in, their job function, industry, company, and which products they are researching.

Updates

This data tells you exactly how many impressions your company updates reach, how many people click on the content, how many interactions (likes, shares, and comments) you are getting, how many new followers resulted from each post, and the engagement percentage.

Followers

This is where you see the demographics of who's following your company. You'll see how many people organically followed you and the number of people who followed you from promotions. You can sort your followers by seniority, industry, company size, function, and employee/nonemployee. This gives you valuable insight into the professionals who follow your company so you can structure Sponsored Content and other promotions targeted to your audience. You'll also see Follower Trends and How You Compare with similar companies.

Demographic Data

This data is similar to what you can get using Google Analytics but from LinkedIn's perspective. You'll see the number of visitors to your company page, so you'll know which content and products they're most interested in. You can also sort your visitor data by seniority, industry, company size, function, and employee/nonemployee. You will also see how many new Followers you have, where they are located, their job function, seniority, industry, and company size.

COMPANY STATUS UPDATES

Company status updates are posts made to share company news, product releases, promotions, or relevant industry news. Company status updates are a powerful communication tool, allowing you to send messages and links directly to your followers.

Company posts can be seen on the company's Overview tab by any LinkedIn member and in a member's network update stream. If you follow the company, you will see the company status updates directly on your homepage, so it's easy to know what's happening with that company, your competitors, or in your industry. All LinkedIn members can view company status updates, click on embedded links, or view posted videos. They can also comment on, like, or share a company status update, allowing your updates to spread virally to grow your following and engage your members.

CREATING YOUR COMPANY PAGE

When you are ready to create your company page, go to your main menu, Work, Create a company page.

Next choose Small Business, Medium to Large Business, Showcase Page or Educational Institution. You will enter a wizard (shown in Figure 7–2 on page 72) that will guide you through the setup of your new company page. Enter your company name, claim your LinkedIn public URL, your website URL, Industry, Company Size, Company Type, upload your logo and enter a short tagline or brief description of your company. Next check the box next to the verification message: "I verify that I am the official representative of this company and have the right to act on behalf of the company in the creation of this page." Click Create Page and your page will be created.

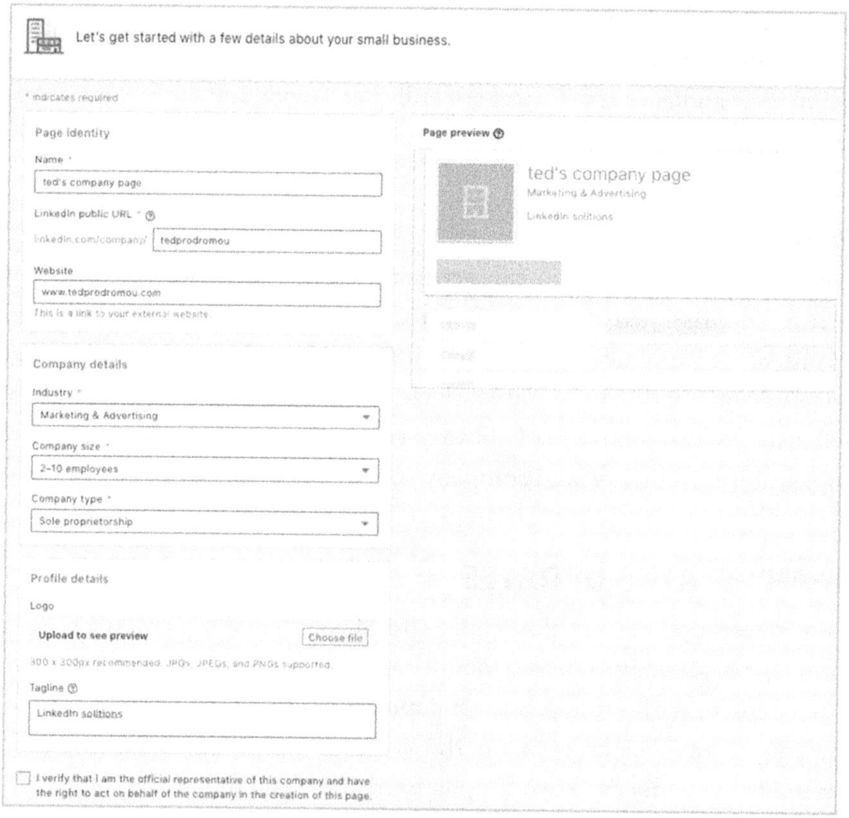

FIGURE 7-2. Company Page Setup Wizard

Designate at least two administrators for your company page. You may want to add more if you work for a large company and will have a lot of activity on your page. For example, if you will be posting a lot of job openings, you can designate a member of your human resources department as an administrator and allow them to post and remove job openings. It would be smart to have an administrator from each major department, such as HR, sales, public relations, and marketing, so they can each efficiently manage their areas of your company page. The marketing person could manage the Products & Services section, public relations could post your Share updates with current company news and product announcements, and sales could monitor the discussions in case any presales questions are posted.

It's imperative that you assign someone to constantly monitor your page for inappropriate content. Any offending content should be removed immediately.

That said, negative remarks don't necessarily have to be removed, if you address them in an appropriate way. Every company has at least a small number of dissatisfied customers who may post negative comments about their products. Instead of removing the comments, you can respond in a positive way by addressing the issue publicly. Sometimes it's a simple misunderstanding of how to use the product, which you can explain. On other occasions, there could be a legitimate problem with your product or service. If this is the case, then proper communication with the customer could resolve the conflict and even build your company's reputation. Admitting mistakes, offering speedy solutions, and promoting strong communication demonstrates that you care about your customers and provide excellent service.

CONCLUSION

Your LinkedIn company page is a mini-website where you can share company news, updates, and current job openings. It is easily found in LinkedIn searches and in Google search results, giving your company great exposure to millions of people.

In the next chapter, we'll explore LinkedIn Search, which is the most powerful tool on LinkedIn. Mastering the search function will give you access to the invaluable data in the rapidly growing LinkedIn database.

For additional updates and how-to videos, visit
https://tedprodromou.com/UltimateGuideUpdates/.

Chapter 8

LinkedIn Search

I t's hard to remember the days before online search engines. Today we search for everything, whether it's a good restaurant for dinner or a consultant with specific skills.

LinkedIn is a business-oriented search engine that works the same way as more general search engines, like Google, Bing, and Yahoo! LinkedIn has its own proprietary search algorithm, which isn't as sophisticated as Google's (no search algorithm is), but it's evolving rapidly. Once you master LinkedIn Search, you will have access to an unlimited number of prospects at your fingertips.

LinkedIn Search has two functions. First, it can be used to find other people, companies, and Groups on LinkedIn so you can build your professional network, follow companies, and join industry-related Groups. The second function of LinkedIn Search is for people to find you. Most people don't think of LinkedIn Search from that perspective, but I think you need to stop and consider the possibilities. What would it do for your business or career if you appeared when people searched for specific skills or industry terms? With more than 500 million of the best top business professionals looking for industry experts by searching LinkedIn, you career would skyrocket if you appeared on the first page of the search results. If you want to optimize your LinkedIn profile so you appear in search results, I invite you to visit Chapter 4.

WHY USE SEARCH

For now, let's start with using LinkedIn Search to find people, companies, and Groups. As you can see in Figure 8-1 below, the LinkedIn search box is located on the left side of the LinkedIn menu or toolbar. To see this expanded menu, click once in the search box then click on the magnifying glass icon.

FIGURE 8-1. The LinkedIn Search Menu or Toolbar

You have the ability to narrow your search results to People, Jobs, and Content. Clicking on More will expand your search to Companies, Schools and Groups. If you leave the search box on the default Search All and just click the magnifying glass, LinkedIn will display a list of all your 2nd-degree connections. You can also see a full list of your 1st-degree connections if you go to the My Network tab on the LinkedIn menu and click See All. If you want to find people outside your network, you need to enter specific keywords like a job title, company name, industry, school, or skill in the search box.

LinkedIn's people search is a very powerful tool that can help you find new customers, recruit new employees, and build your professional network. You can also use people search to:

- Find an industry expert to speak at an event your company is hosting
- Find an industry expert to hire as a consultant for a project
- Find people you want to meet with when you are traveling
- Find speaking engagements
- Find consulting engagements
- Connect with other industry experts to join you in a project or business venture
- Find people who want to join you for charity events
- Find people who want to start a local networking group

When you can search a database of more than 500 million business professionals, the benefits are endless.

KEYWORDS ARE STILL KING

Keywords, keywords, keywords! You are going to get tired of hearing me talk about keywords, but they are the foundation of LinkedIn Search so it's important you understand how to use them effectively. In Chapter 9, I'll teach you everything you ever wanted to know about keywords (and probably a little more!), but for now let's focus on the fundamentals of using the search function.

LinkedIn Search works a little differently from Google. If I search Google for *web marketing expert*, I will see results that contain the word "web" or "marketing" or "expert." This is called a *broad match search* because Google will return all results that contain any of the keywords I searched for.

I can also do a *phrase search* to narrow my results. If I search Google for "web marketing expert" with the quote marks, I will only see results that contain the entire phrase "web marketing expert." This gives me a more focused search result, saving me time.

When I do a phrase search for "web marketing expert" on LinkedIn, the search results will include every person who used the phrase "web marketing expert" in their profile, whether it is a job title, in their summary, or in one of their job descriptions. You can also sort by jobs, companies, content, and Groups when you select the appropriate sort option, as shown in Figure 8-1. As you are typing keywords in the search box, people, LinkedIn Pages, Showcase Pages, and Groups appear in a dropdown list, just like the Google Autocomplete dropdown you see when you do a Google search. By default, the initial search will show you 2nd-degree connections and jobs if you don't choose one of the sort options.

Once you have the basics down, you can use Search to your competitive advantage by reframing how you think about the feature.

Competitive Analysis

Let's get into more detail about doing a competitive analysis search, and I'll show you how to use the Search sort option to expand your search results and find exactly who or what you are looking for. A great example of a competitive search is looking to see what keywords your competitors are targeting. Let's say you're in the cloud computing business and want to see who's ranking well in LinkedIn search results. Figure 8-2 on page 78 shows your competitors once you enter your initial search term ("cloud computing").

The top search results begin to appear as you type your keyword phrase. In this example, we see the top search results for people and jobs. The top people result is a fake personal profile called Cloud Computing. This is proof the LinkedIn search algorithm isn't perfect and nowhere near as sophisticated as Google's.

One way to trick LinkedIn is to add your top skill as your last name. This will almost always rank you at or near the top of the search results for that skill. I don't recommend

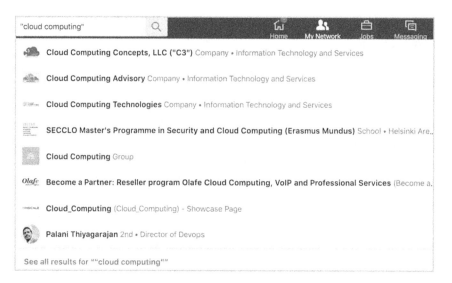

FIGURE 8–2. Keyword Instant Search Results

this tactic for a few reasons. First, it's against LinkedIn's terms of service, and it can suspend your account. Second, when you add extra words in your name field, it makes it difficult for people to find you when they search for your name.

Let's move on to the search results for companies. The top company for the phrase "cloud computing" is Cloud Computing Technologies. Let's reverse-engineer the search result and see how it achieved the top ranking and which other keywords it's targeting. Your goal is to outrank that company for the search term "cloud computing." Note that you will receive different search results if you search for *cloud computing*, which looks for LinkedIn profiles that contain the words "cloud" or "computing."

Reverse-Engineering

As I examined the Cloud Computing Technologies company page, I did a search to see how many times the phrase "cloud computing" appeared on the page, as you see in Figure 8–3 on page 79 (Ctrl-F on a PC or Cmd-F on a Mac).

Keywords

Using your target keywords in your company page title can help your search rankings significantly. It's also important to use the target keyword phrase a few times in the first two paragraphs of your summary. This strategy is almost identical to SEO best practices for ranking in search engines like Google. But be careful not to overuse your keyword

FIGURE 8-3. Checking Keyword Density

phrases. The summary should read naturally and provide a comprehensive overview of your company in the 2,000-character space you are provided. In this example, Cloud Computing Technologies uses the phrase "cloud computing" four times in the first two paragraphs of its company description.

Followers

To rank well in search results on LinkedIn, you must have a significant number of followers. I've seen companies with literally no summary or company information other than their company page title that have more than 800 followers, and they rank number one for their search terms. (I assume they hired offshore workers to follow their company just to receive the high ranking, and I obviously don't suggest you try the same thing.)

Take a look at the search results in Figure 8-4 on page 80 and click on each company to see how many followers they have. Cloud Computing Technologies has 771 followers, Cloud Computing Experts has 322 followers and Cloud Computing Intelligence Magazine has 390 followers. My assumption is Cloud Computing Experts has 25 employees and Cloud Computing Intelligence has only one, so it ranks lower. LinkedIn doesn't publicly share its search ranking factors, so we can only make educated assumptions.

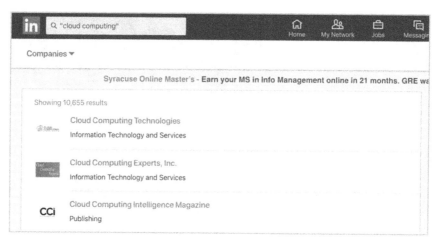

FIGURE 8–4. Company Search Results

LINKEDIN ADVANCED SEARCH

Now that you've had a taste of the basic LinkedIn Search it's time to dig into the main course: LinkedIn Advanced Search. This is the skill you need to master to become a top-tier LinkedIn user. Whether you are a salesperson hunting for prospects, a recruiter looking for top talent, or just a regular LinkedIn member, becoming an expert at searching on LinkedIn will take your career to the next level.

Advanced Search has changed dramatically with each LinkedIn redesign, and now you only have access to the additional search fields when you subscribe to Sales Navigator. In the old LinkedIn dashboard, you used to be able to sort the search results by relevance, relationship, relationship + recommendations, connections or keywords. This was confusing, and very few people knew what these categories meant. Today, it's much easier to sort your search results based on keywords, first name, last name, title, company, school, location, country, and postal code. When you subscribe to a LinkedIn Premium account, you will have access to even more data fields, like Groups, years of experience, function, seniority level, interested in, company size, Fortune 500 level, and when joined LinkedIn. The higher your subscription level, the more data you will see.

Figure 8–5 on page 81 compares the available search fields on LinkedIn and Sales Navigator. On the left you see the All People Filter search options when you are using LinkedIn's free or premium version. In the past, you received additional search fields when you subscribed to LinkedIn Premium, but today you need to upgrade to Sales Navigator to access Advanced Search.

On the right side of Figure 8–5, you see the Advanced Lead Search fields from Sales Navigator. This is what you need to dig deep to find your ideal clients and to be able to save your searches. You can read more about Sales Navigator in Chapter 19.

FIGURE 8–5. All People Filters vs. Sales Navigator Advanced Lead Search

Obviously, you don't need to connect with everyone on LinkedIn, but you can build a strong professional network of 150 colleagues that you can carry with you for the rest of your career. No longer will you have to worry about recessions and high unemployment. When you surround yourself with a strong international professional network, you can lessen the impact of an economic downturn on your career.

While the economy and unemployment were seesawing over the past 20 years, the number of millionaires and billionaires around the world increased significantly. According to *The Wall Street Journal,* there were 306 billionaires in the world in 2000. In 2017, there were *2,208 billionaires—*a 622 percent increase.

How did so many people become billionaires during the worst economic conditions in our lifetime? They built a strong personal network so they could withstand the recession and even make a significant amount of money.

This information is *directly* related to LinkedIn Search because you have the opportunity to build a powerful personal network from the LinkedIn database. Everyone you need to know professionally is on LinkedIn. If for some reason you need to connect with someone who is not on LinkedIn, a LinkedIn connection can lead you to that person. Remember, success in business is about *who* you know, not *what* you know.

The better you get at LinkedIn Search, the closer you come to putting your personal dream network together. Mining through the LinkedIn database and looking for the nuggets of gold will eventually put you in a position where you will always be able to earn money. When you need a new project, one of your connections will know someone who needs your expertise. Looking for some new sales prospects? A few of your 2nd- and 3rd-degree connections are sure to need your product. It's all about leveraging the power of LinkedIn's rapidly growing network.

USING LINKEDIN'S ADVANCED SEARCH FOR SALES

Advanced Search can be useful for all sorts of tasks. It is especially adept at helping you find sales leads. Say you are a sales rep who sells customer relationship management (CRM) software to enterprise-level clients. Your key decision-maker is usually at the CXO level, and your target companies are in the Fortune 500. Your software has a six- to 12-month buying cycle, and there are many departments involved in the decision-making process, including sales, information technology, and sometimes marketing. Project managers from these departments are also involved in the purchase decision.

Your initial contact is usually with a manager in the IT or sales department who does the initial evaluation of your product. After that, an IT or sales director gets involved. Use LinkedIn Advanced Search to find managers who are doing the initial evaluation or directors who are involved in the second phase of the project.

In the past, an easy way to find managers or directors shopping for CRM systems was to search LinkedIn Answers for phrases like:

- What is the best CRM software?
- I am looking for insight . . .
- Looking for advice . . .
- I want a GREAT CRM system. What is the best?
- What is your current CRM?

Now that LinkedIn Answers has been discontinued, we have to take another approach. One way is to join Groups related to CRMs. Most of these Groups are managed by vendors who are probably your competitors, so if they let you, joining will give you access to people who are evaluating your competitors' CRM products and to their current customers, who may be having problems with their CRM. Figure 8–6 on page 83 shows you how to start a focused search to find Groups related to the CRM business. Look at the first result. There are more than 242,000 members of the Sales/Marketing Executives Group, so this is a perfect place to start.

This is where you'll find the Groups of CRM consultants and providers, including your competitors. Consider joining Groups where decision-makers would hang out, like

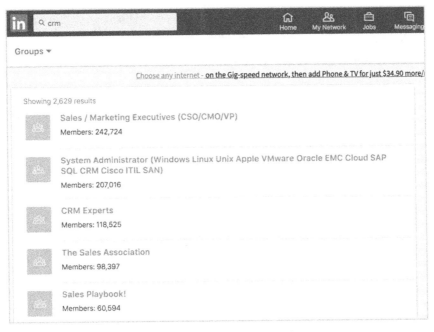

FIGURE 8–6. Finding CRM-Related Groups

CMO Network, Inbound Marketers, Marketing Profs Pro, and other popular sales and marketing–related Groups.

I use my competitors' Groups and Groups related to our products to find out what people are saying about them, good and bad. It's a great way to gain competitive intelligence about your competitors' products. People will be discussing what they love about your competitors' products—and, more important, what they don't. When you're making a sales presentation to a prospect, you will know your competitors' weaknesses and can show them how your product excels.

To find this competitive intelligence, you have to search each Group individually. Unfortunately, there isn't a way to search for keywords in all Groups at once, so you have to go one by one. In Figure 8–7 on page 84, you can see how to search for keyword phrases in Groups.

Next you should view the person's profile (see Figure 8–8 on page 85) to see if they are a potential prospect. Are they a decision-maker who can purchase your product or service? Are they connected to anyone in your network who can give you feedback about this person or can introduce you to this person? (See Figure 8–9 on page 86.)

If you think this person is a good prospect, you can send them a message if you are already connected and let them know why you're reaching out. For example, I know Ervin Grinberg, so it's easy to check in with him and say hello. One ice-breaking phrase

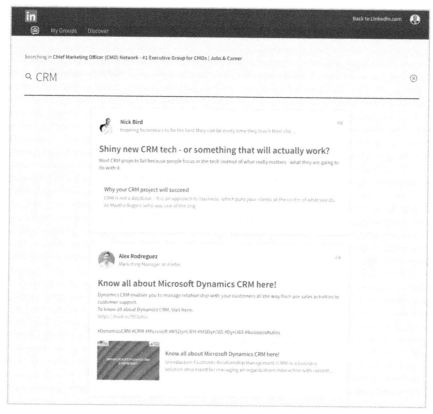

FIGURE 8–7. Keyword Searches in Groups

I like to use is, "Are you still looking to use LinkedIn to grow your business?" If they are successfully using LinkedIn, they will let me know. If not, this often leads to a phone call to explore ways we can work together.

You can customize the message to fit your needs. Start with something like, "Are you still looking to [fill in the blank with the solution you can provide]?"

Let's say I come across the profile of Mike Samboy, and I think he's a good prospect, but I'm not connected with him. In Sales Navigator, I can view our mutual connections and ask for an introduction. Figure 8–10 on page 87 shows you how to view our mutual connections and Ask for Intro with a single click.

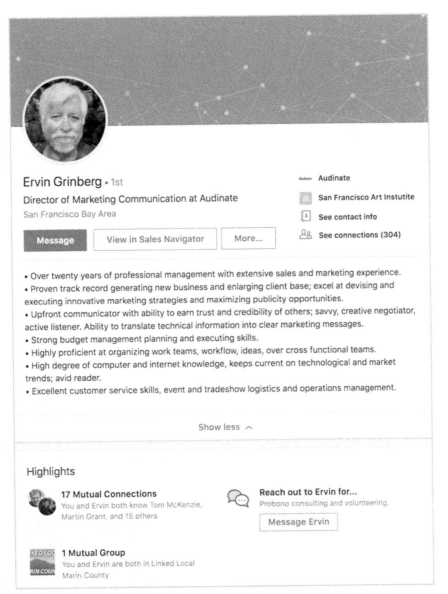

Ervin Grinberg • 1st

Director of Marketing Communication at Audinate

San Francisco Bay Area

Audinate

San Francisco Art Instutite

See contact info

See connections (304)

Message | View in Sales Navigator | More...

• Over twenty years of professional management with extensive sales and marketing experience.
• Proven track record generating new business and enlarging client base; excel at devising and executing innovative marketing strategies and maximizing publicity opportunities.
• Upfront communicator with ability to earn trust and credibility of others; savvy, creative negotiator, active listener. Ability to translate technical information into clear marketing messages.
• Strong budget management planning and executing skills.
• Highly proficient at organizing work teams, workflow, ideas, over cross functional teams.
• High degree of computer and internet knowledge, keeps current on technological and market trends; avid reader.
• Excellent customer service skills, event and tradeshow logistics and operations management.

Show less ∧

Highlights

17 Mutual Connections
You and Ervin both know Tom McKenzie, Martin Grant, and 15 others

Reach out to Ervin for...
Probono consulting and volunteering.

Message Ervin

1 Mutual Group
You and Ervin are both in Linked Local Marin County

FIGURE 8–8. View Their Full Profile

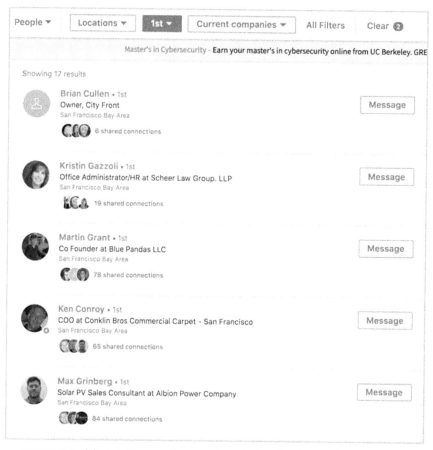

FIGURE 8–9. My 1st-Degree Connections Who Are Mutually Connected

A More Direct Route to Hot Prospects

While it is relatively simple to look for prospects in Groups, you can see the obvious drawback: There is no easy way to prequalify the potential leads you find there. You have to take that extra step of reviewing a member's profile to find out if she works for a company that meets your demographic target. Unfortunately, there isn't an Advanced Search capability for Groups that lets you filter by anything other than keywords. It would be nice to be able to filter group discussions by the same fields as people search, but LinkedIn doesn't offer that option as of this writing.

In my experience, it's rare to see high-level executives asking questions about products in Groups, since they enter the buying process toward the end, after much due diligence by managers and directors. You can target managers and directors in Groups, but you have to use a different approach to connect with the C-level executives who are the final decision-makers.

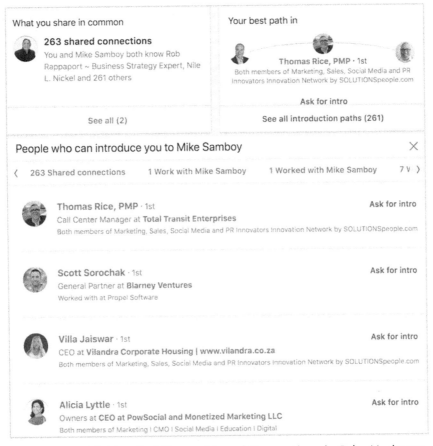

FIGURE 8–10. Viewing 2nd-Degree Mutual Connections in Sales Navigator

I prefer to use the Advanced Search for Leads when I'm looking for very specific information about a person or company. In this example in Figure 8–11 on page 88, you could do an Advanced Search to find C-level executives, managers, and directors in companies that have between 501 and 1,000 employees located within 25 miles of downtown San Francisco. If you notice a manager or director from a company with "CRM" in their profile, it's a good idea to connect with them and start a dialogue. To see the search results for this specific search, see Figure 8–12 on page 89.

You can see your relationship to them and ask for introductions from your 1st-degree connections when the time is right. You can also modify your search to focus on specific companies once you know which companies are researching new CRM systems.

There are also hundreds of ways to slice and dice your searches using the Advanced People Search. We don't have enough room in this book to get into every combination

FIGURE 8–11. Selecting CXO-Level People Within 25 Miles of Downtown San Francisco

of searches you can do, but here are the high-level categories offered in the Advanced People Search:

- Keywords
- First name
- Last name
- Title
- Current company
- Past company
- School
- Geography
- Industries
- Seniority level
- Groups

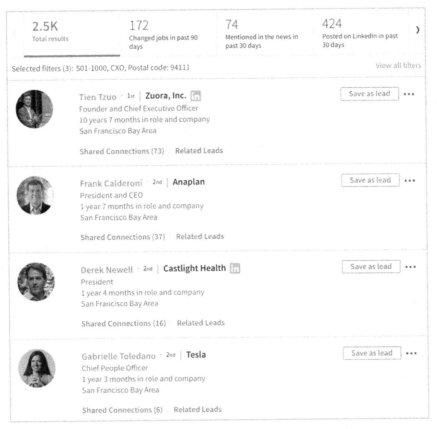

FIGURE 8–12. Viewing the Results of Your Search Specifications

- Relationship
- Interested in
- Language
- Company size
- When joined

Within each of these high-level categories, you can select many subcategories, making your filtering options almost limitless. You have access to the world's largest—and highest-quality—business intelligence database. Use it!

Saved Searches

Over time, you will create custom Advanced Lead Searches that return great results. With a free or LinkedIn Premium account, you can no longer save searches. You need to upgrade to Sales Navigator to be able to save your best searches. Once you save a search, it runs 24/7, finding new prospects literally while you sleep. This is very handy because it can take a lot of time to refine your searches to achieve your desired results. New leads are delivered to your inbox automatically when you use Saved Searches.

ADVANCED JOB SEARCH

Advanced Search is also useful for finding jobs. You can search for jobs using job title, keywords, or company name in the basic Jobs Search box. LinkedIn also provides advanced search capabilities in Jobs. The filters work the same way as the Advanced People Search filters, but they are tailored to help you narrow down your search results when looking for a new job. A great trick is to use the Advanced Job Search when you are looking to hire new employees. Search for jobs similar to the one you want to fill and see how other companies describe it, what skills and keywords they are using, and how they position the job. You can learn a lot by "spying" on your competitors.

You can filter your job search by the following categories:

- Keywords (located in the main search bar at the top of the page)
- Date Posted
- Salary
- LinkedIn Features
- Job Type
- Location
- Company
- Industry
- Job Function
- Experience Level
- Title

Each of these categories has numerous subcategories to help you zero in on jobs compatible for you that will pay the salary you want. The Advanced Job Search is a great tool, considering LinkedIn is becoming the top place for companies to post jobs and for people to find new jobs.

LinkedIn Jobs also lets you save your favorite searches in the Create Search Alert tab. When you find jobs you are interested in, you can save them in the Saved Jobs tab.

CONCLUSION

You now know more about LinkedIn Search and Advanced Search than 90 percent of all LinkedIn members, even though we've just scratched the surface of what you can do with these advanced search capabilities and a database of more than 500 million business professionals. Play around with LinkedIn Search and see what you can uncover in the treasure trove of business intelligence.

I'll show you some more advanced tricks later in the book when I teach you how different users approach LinkedIn, such as students, sales reps, recruiters, and job seekers. For now, take a short break and practice your LinkedIn searching while it's still fresh in your mind. Then move on to the next chapter, where I will show you how to get found on LinkedIn.

For additional updates and how-to videos, visit
https://tedprodromou.com/UltimateGuideUpdates/.

Chapter 9

Getting Found on LinkedIn

What do you do when you want to learn more about a product or service? I bet the first thing you do is go to Google and search the internet. With so much data available to us today, search engines are an integral part of our life. When you use Google, you can find information about literally anything in seconds. The word "Google" is so ingrained in our culture that it's now used as a verb.

Search has evolved beyond the desktop computer with many of our inquiries being voice driven, through our smartphones and at-home devices. It's only a matter of time before we pull up our LinkedIn app and request, "LinkedIn, find me a business coach in San Francisco."

The problem with broad searches, however, is that you get a broad result. If you search for "web marketing consultant," Google doesn't know if you want to hire a web marketing consultant or if you're trying to find out how to become a web marketing consultant. Google can't read our minds yet—but it's getting pretty close!

When you search LinkedIn for "web marketing consultant," chances are your search result will show you a list of web marketing consultants and jobs for "web marketing consultants." By narrowing your search, say, by searching for "web marketing consultant New York," you can generate a more targeted list that may give you the result you need.

LinkedIn is a *vertical search engine*. A vertical search engine shows you very focused results based on the keywords you search for. This is why it's so important to use your target keywords when creating your own LinkedIn personal and company profiles. You want to be found.

"What are target keywords," you ask. Target keywords are the phrases or specific skills you enter into a search engine to find targeted results. The more specific your keyword phrases are, the better your search results will be. This is why it's essential to use all 50 skills in your LinkedIn profile because they are the keyword phrases people use to find you. If someone did a Google search to find you or your business, what keywords would she have to enter?

Optimizing your LinkedIn profile by using these keywords is similar to the process used to optimize your website or blog so you can rank highly in Google. Optimizing your LinkedIn profile doesn't just help people find your profile through the search function; it also helps LinkedIn recommend people to connect with, companies you may be interested in, or your perfect job. LinkedIn scans your profile and uses your keyword phrases to make targeted recommendations for you. The more targeted your profile is, the more targeted LinkedIn's suggestions will be. Once your profile is fine-tuned, you will see targeted recommendations in your sidebar every time you log in.

The LinkedIn algorithm is a very powerful artificial intelligence tool. Let's explore how to use it to your advantage, starting with how to make these keywords do the heavy lifting for you.

KEYWORD SELECTION

The most important component of search engine optimization is keyword selection. Search engines use keywords and phrases to find and rank websites by following an algorithm, or set of rules.

The algorithms for the various search engines are not exactly the same, which is why searching the same keyword brings different results. However, they follow very similar processes. Most of the search engines rank websites based on where and how often a particular keyword is used on the website. They will rank a website higher if, for example, the keyword is used in the title, if it is placed near the top of the page, and if it is used often.

LINKEDIN SEO TIP

To increase your chances of having your LinkedIn profile rank highly, use your keywords in these sections of your profile:

- Profile headline
- Current work experience
- Past work experience
- Summary
- Skills

Think about these questions while creating your list of keyword phrases:

1. What are your skills? _____

   _____

2. What is your expertise? _____

   _____

3. What job titles best describe you or the job you are looking for? _____

   _____

4. What makes you different from your competitors? _____

   _____

5. What makes you better than your competitors? _____

   _____

FIGURE 9–1. Keyword Worksheet

Use the worksheet in Figure 9–1 to create a list of at least ten keyword phrases that best describe you and your expertise. The more focused your keyword phrases are, the more your profile will stand out.

If you are like most people, you have a hard time describing your skills and areas of expertise, so you're probably struggling to come up with your keyword list. If you're finding it difficult to come up with a list of what you're really good at, ask your friends or colleagues. They'll be glad to tell you what you're good at (and what you're not so good at, if you're brave enough to ask!).

COMPETITIVE ANALYSIS

One of my favorite ways to compile keyword lists is to look at my competitors' and colleagues' profiles to see what keywords they use to make their profiles stand out.

Let's say you're a certified public accountant in San Francisco and you want to see which keywords are being used in the profiles of the top search results. Start by doing a search on LinkedIn using "CPA" as your keyword and your city in the Location field. Leave the rest of the search boxes empty and click on Search as shown in Figure 9–2 on page 96.

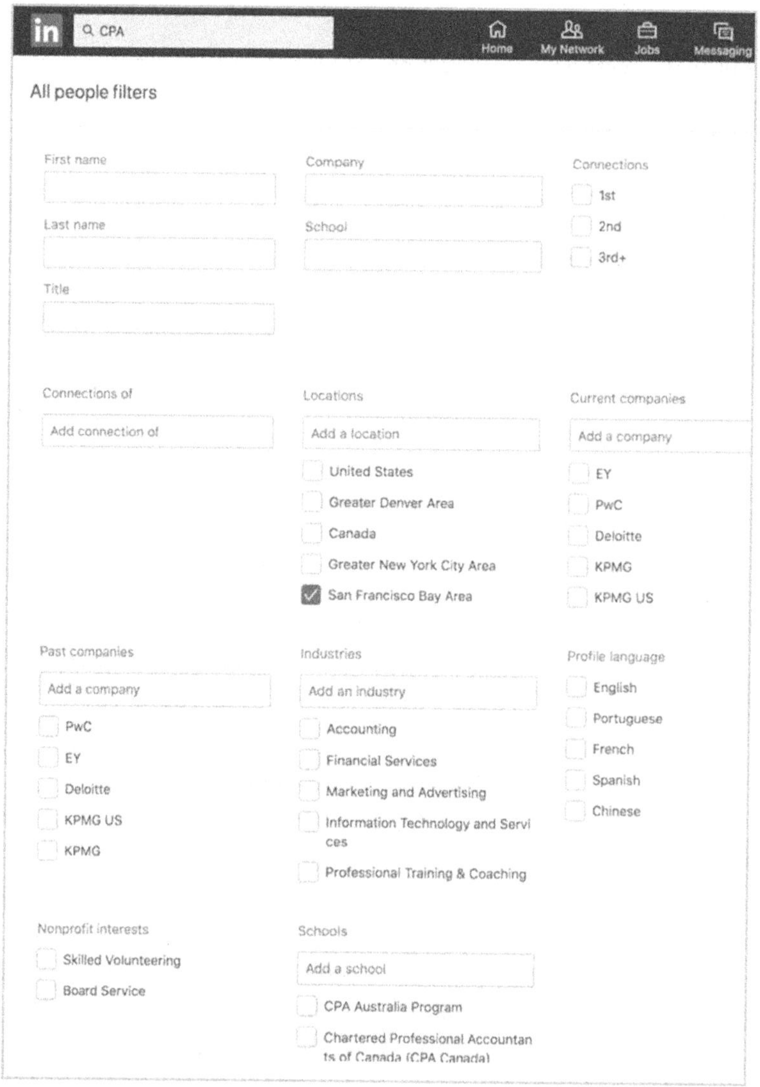

FIGURE 9–2. Advanced People Search for a CPA Located in the San Francisco Bay Area

Your search results will show the top rankings for LinkedIn members who have the letters "CPA" in their profile. In the past, you used to be able to sort by relevance, keywords, and other options, but LinkedIn discontinued the sort feature because it was rarely used. LinkedIn will rank the search results based on your search criteria, as shown in Figure 9–3 on page 97.

As you can see, the top search results have a few things in common. All the top results contain "CPA" at or near the beginning of their profile headline or in the last name field. In this search result, LinkedIn is only showing me CPAs in my 3rd degree, so the only way for me to reach them is to send them an InMail to see if they are

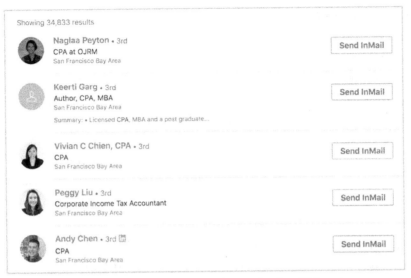

FIGURE 9–3. Your Search Results for CPA

interested in connecting or or if they want to get together do discuss referring business to each other.

You can modify your original search so you can see 1st-, 2nd-, and 3rd-degree connections, to see how they are ranking on the first page. In the Connections tab, select 1st, 2nd, 3rd+ as shown in Figure 9–4 below, and you can see the difference.

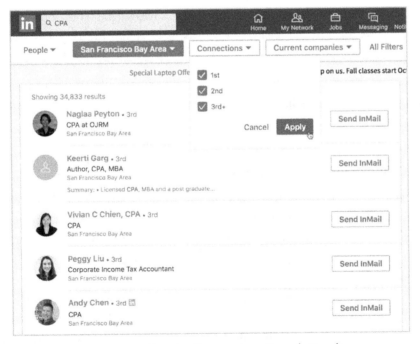

FIGURE 9–4. Sort by Connections Search Result

LINKEDIN RANKING FACTORS

My clients and students frequently ask me what determines their search rankings on LinkedIn. Some of the ranking factors are obvious, such as using your target keywords in your last name field, profile headline, and summary. However, LinkedIn won't officially reveal exactly what determines our search ranking, partly because it's a proprietary secret and partly because it's more technical than most LinkedIn users want to know.

If you're into technical details, here's what LinkedIn is willing to tell us. (More on search rankings can be found at https://www.linkedin.com/help/linkedin/answer/4447.)

According to LinkedIn, the site "uses proprietary algorithms to rank and order the results you get when you search for people on the site." The site notes three main points about how the algorithm works:

1. You will not see one rank for LinkedIn search. Instead, the site generates unique "relevance scores" for each member. The order of each query is determined by several factors, including profile, activity, and connections of the person searching. It's a good idea to track your profile views to see how they affect your ranking. You can learn more about how to do this on the Who's Viewed Your Profile section of your homepage.

2. Searcher relevance, a proprietary algorithm, is based on several factors, including the searcher's activity on LinkedIn, query profile results, and the history of other members who have run similar searches.

3. Choose your keywords wisely. LinkedIn advises that you "only include the keywords, including repeated keywords, in your profile that best reflect your expertise and experience."

LinkedIn rewards you with All Star status when you fill out each profile section including Background, Skills, Accomplishments and Additional Information which includes some Recommendations from your LinkedIn network.

LINKEDIN HASHTAG COMMUNITIES

Another way to bump up your discoverability is by using hashtags. Hashtags are back on LinkedIn in a big way. Over the years, LinkedIn has gone back and forth on recognizing hashtags as a way to associate your content with specific niches and topics. In 2018, LinkedIn announced hashtag communities as the replacement for LinkedIn Topics. Confused? Me too!

Let me go back in time to explain the evolution of Topics and hashtags. In 2013, LinkedIn acquired Pulse, which was an app that let you subscribe to various content on the internet. Newsfeed apps like Pulse let you create your own personal newspaper with custom content. You could subscribe to content from *The New York Times*, CNBC, *USA Today*, and any other popular online news source. You could also subscribe to your favorite blogs and see your custom newsfeed on the Pulse app.

As LinkedIn integrated Pulse into its system, you could also follow Influencers and other LinkedIn members on Pulse by subscribing to their content. After LinkedIn encouraged its members to start posting articles, content distribution exploded. Today, more than 100,000 articles are published on LinkedIn every day.

At the end of every article you posted on LinkedIn, you could add tags, which evolved into hashtags simply by adding # at the beginning. The more hashtags you added to an article, the more viewers you might attract. LinkedIn eventually added the ability for us to follow tags, which became known as Topics.

LinkedIn then eliminated Topics and replaced them with good old hashtags. Who knows why LinkedIn keeps changing the terminology, but the concept remains the same. You can follow people and hashtags related to the type of content you want to see in your newsfeed.

Figure 9–5 below shows some LinkedIn communities based on hashtag topics. LinkedIn initially assigns you some specific hashtags or content based on your previous activity; then you can adjust the content you want to follow. Select the pencil icon next to Your Communities and pin your favorite hashtags by clicking on the pin icon.

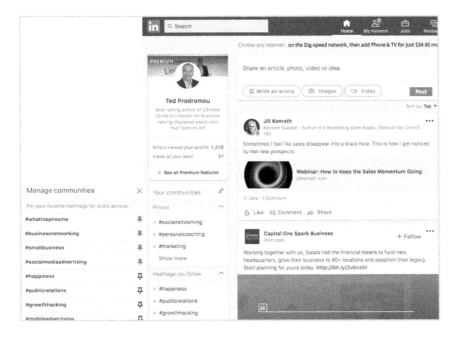

FIGURE 9–5. LinkedIn Hashtag Communities

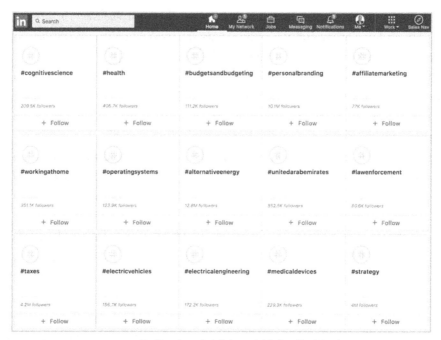

FIGURE 9–6. Following Additional LinkedIn Hashtags

Figure 9-6 shows you how to follow additional hashtags. They won't be pinned to the top of your hashtag list, but relevant content will still appear in your newsfeed. If you don't see relevant hashtags in this list, go back to the main Search box at the top of the page and type # followed by keywords or skills related to your niche. For example, type #coaching to bring up all coaching-related hashtags and follow the appropriate ones as they appear.

LINKEDIN TOPICS

As I mentioned earlier, LinkedIn keeps flip-flopping on the terminology, but the concept doesn't change. Whether you call them keywords, skills, topics, tags, or hashtags, people want to keep up with trending news about their industry and hone their skills to remain in demand.

I love to dig into the LinkedIn website and often find hidden treasures that way. One of these is a complete directory of the Topics on LinkedIn. I don't know why it doesn't publicize this (maybe it's because LinkedIn replaced the Topics tags with regular old hashtags and wanted to avoid confusion), but I'm going to show you how to use this to your advantage. You can see the full directory at www.linkedin.com/directory/topics. Figure 9-7 on page 101 gives you a quick snapshot.

Topics Directory

Browse by name # A B C D E F G H I J K L M N O P Q R S T U V W X Y Z

Featured Topics

Games	Marketing	Oracle	Android
SAP	Java	Microsoft	PHP
IPhone	Data	Google	VOIP
Social Media	Big Data	Leadership	IOS
IPad	Resume	Business	Agriculture
SQL	Linux	SEO	Facebook
ECommerce	Construction	Small Business	SharePoint
Music	Healthcare	Entrepreneur	Javascript
Hadoop	Windows	Mobile Games	Project Management
Web Development	Analytics	Wine	Supply Chain
Biotechnology	WordPress	Cloud	Fashion
Digital Marketing	Customer	Procurement	Telecom
Cloud Computing	Interview Questions	Graphic Design	Mobile
Sales	PMP	Electronics	Python
Outsourcing	Logistics	SMS	Energy
H1B	Advertising	Solar	Call Center
FMCG	Social Media Marketing	Six Sigma	Developer
Aerospace	Health	Packaging	Strategy
HVAC	Data Center	ITIL	Forex
Manufacturing	E-Commerce	Private Equity	LED
PMI	Semiconductor	Mobile Apps	3D Printing
CIO	Internet Of Things	Selenium	Copper
Franchise	Chemicals	Restaurant	Oil
Business Intelligence	Cosmetics	Online Marketing	Security
HTML5	Agile	Change Management	Magento

FIGURE 9–7. LinkedIn Topics Directory

Let's dig deeper into the Social Media Marketing Topic, shown in Figure 9–8 on page 102. On the initial screen, LinkedIn shows the top companies that provide social media marketing. As you can see, there are a total of 10,466,744 LinkedIn members—including 82,498 freelancers—who focus on social media marketing or have that skill and/or keyword in their profile. That's a lot of competition.

How do you position yourself as an expert in social media marketing? Look at the Top Skills below the Social Media Marketing at a Glance diagrams. These are the skills you need to be a top social media marketer, including email marketing, social media measurement, pay-per-click (PPC), mobile marketing, online advertising, and more. You can scroll to the right to see additional skills you need.

LinkedIn also shows you the top universities where you can learn these skills and a broad breakdown of the skills your competitors display in their profiles, including social media, marketing, marketing strategy, customer service, and Microsoft Office.

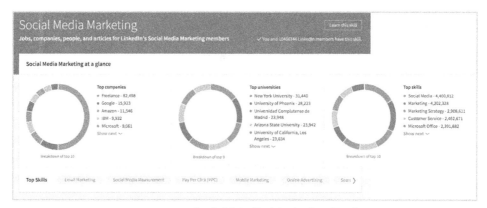

FIGURE 9–8. Social Media Marketing Topic

LINKEDIN PROFINDER

If you aren't interested in learning how to do social media marketing (or any other field of expertise), you can hire a professional with those skills using LinkedIn ProFinder. Chances are you aren't familiar with LinkedIn ProFinder unless you are a freelancer. You can create a profile for your business to promote your services, and LinkedIn adds you to the LinkedIn ProFinder directory. When people search for the kind of skills you offer, they will see your profile and may reach out to you to see if you are a good fit for their project. Figure 9-9 on page 103 shows what LinkedIn ProFinder looks like.

Companies looking to hire someone locally with a specific skill like social media marketing can create a ProFinder request, which will be sent to local service providers who registered that skill in their profile. If you have a ProFinder profile and match with a request, you will receive a message in your Notifications that there is a new ProFinder request. But you have to act fast—only five service providers can submit a proposal to the potential client, which can happen within minutes.

LinkedIn ProFinder is a great idea and is improving as LinkedIn gathers feedback from both service providers and businesses. When ProFinder was first released, you had to submit your hourly rate or a flat fee for a request, which was difficult if you had to submit a detailed quote for a request that only stated "I need ongoing marketing services." The service does work well with well-defined requests, such as when someone asks for a LinkedIn profile makeover, which is a one-time service with a flat fee.

Initially, I created my ProFinder profile to offer online marketing and social media marketing, and I received some requests, but as I mentioned above, the project descriptions were very vague so I never successfully landed any new clients. After I changed my services offered to resume writing/LinkedIn profile makeover and career/leadership

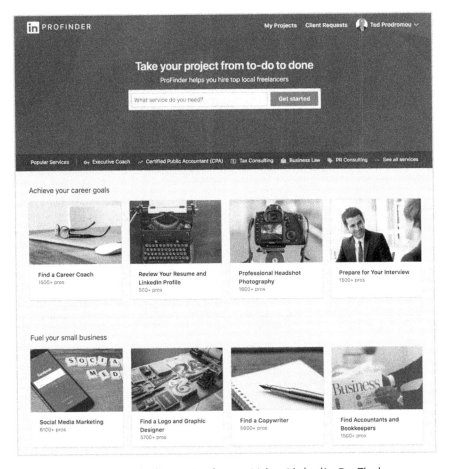

FIGURE 9–9. Finding a Freelancer Using LinkedIn ProFinder

coaching the floodgates opened. I was receiving 30 to 40 resume requests a day and at least a dozen career coaching requests every day. Since I don't do resume makeovers, I removed that service from my profile and I'm receiving up to 20 career coaching requests every day.

You can register your company on ProFinder or search for local service providers at https://www.linkedin.com/profinder.

CONCLUSION

Use your target keyword phrases frequently when you fill out your LinkedIn profile, but don't overdo it. The rest of your search ranking comes from the size and composition of your LinkedIn network, how active you are on LinkedIn, the relevance of the content you post and interact with, and other factors determined by the LinkedIn algorithm.

The bottom line is, you need to be active on LinkedIn on a regular basis by posting new content and interacting with other people and their content to rank well.

You can also be found on LinkedIn by following popular hashtags and adding them to your status updates and articles. A third strategy is to register with LinkedIn ProFinder so you will be included in the directory for your top skills. The fourth way to be found on LinkedIn is through LinkedIn advertising, which you will read about in Chapter 20.

In the next chapter, I'll show you the best way to give and receive recommendations, which are an essential part of your LinkedIn profile.

For additional updates and how-to videos, visit
https://tedprodromou.com/UltimateGuideUpdates/.

Chapter 10

Giving and Receiving LinkedIn Recommendations

The evolution of the internet and social media has changed the way we make buying decisions. *Social proof* (when we make decisions based on what others recommend) existed long before the internet, but the ability to submit and view online reviews for products and services has revolutionized our purchasing behavior. In a matter of minutes, we can tap into the collective opinions of hundreds—even thousands—of people who have already purchased a product or service. You can see how many fans are gushing about the product or how many disgruntled customers want their money back. With the evolution of mobile apps, we can scan a bar code on a product with our phone to compare prices and read product reviews right in the store.

Today, there's no hiding if you're offering an inferior product or service. If you read a lot of negative reviews online, you probably won't complete the purchase. On the other hand, when you see a lot of positive reviews, you won't hesitate to spend more for the latest version of the product if others recommend it. Your chances of buyer's remorse also diminish significantly because social proof has justified the purchase in your mind.

In the past, social proof was primarily word-of-mouth or through print media, so word spread slowly. Today, a good or bad review can be seen or heard by millions of people around the world instantaneously. Let's go back a few years to an example of social proof before the digital era. Say your best friend went to a movie last night and can't stop raving about it. They're gushing with enthusiasm and want to tell you every detail, but they resist because they don't want to ruin the movie for you. You can tell it was one of the best movies they've seen in years.

Based on this, will you go? Of course you will—probably tonight! This is classic old-school social proof.

When someone you trust tells you they like a movie, you want to see it as soon as possible. If your trusted friend tells you the movie sucks, you won't see it, and you'll probably tell your other friends to avoid it as well—even though you haven't seen it yourself. Negative social proof spreads exponentially based on what people say, even if they didn't have a negative experience themselves.

The key to social proof is that you act on someone else's advice—without question—if you trust that person. If you don't know the person well enough or don't trust them, you'll probably take the advice with a grain of salt and seek advice from a trusted source instead. We all have a circle of friends and colleagues we depend on when we need to make decisions. The bigger the decision, the more trusted opinions we will seek. We all want to feel certain that we are making the right choice. So we like to bounce ideas off people we trust. Discussing the issues with others makes us feel confident, even if they just listen to our concerns.

Today, online social proof has evolved from online forums to websites like Yelp, where you can post reviews about local businesses. On Yelp, the business owner doesn't have control over the reviews. A few positive reviews can send your sales through the roof, but an angry customer can write a scathing review and damage the reputation of a business. The business owner can respond to the criticism online, but the negative comments remain. These unmoderated comments make social proof more credible because everyone knows that every business occasionally has dissatisfied customers. A series of negative reviews should be a red flag telling you to avoid that business. Chances are it won't survive if it doesn't address the negative comments head-on and change its business practices.

Facebook created its own form of social proof with the "Like" button. You "vote" for comments, pictures, and companies you like on Facebook. Unlike Yelp, which posts positive and negative comments, Facebook only registers positive votes. Facebook likes have taken off, and it has become a significant measure of success if your Facebook company page receives a lot of likes. It has the same effect as great reviews on Yelp.

Today, Google is focused on local businesses claiming their business on Google Maps and people writing reviews like Yelp.

So what does social proof have to do with LinkedIn, anyway? Essentially, you are marketing and selling yourself on LinkedIn. Your profile, job experience, skills, expertise in Groups, and recommendations are your marketing collateral that people read to get to know your product—which is you!

HOW CAN SOCIAL PROOF GET YOU HIRED IN TODAY'S ECONOMY?

You and a few million other people are looking for jobs these days. You can spend hours every day on Craigslist and hope you can be one of the first to submit your resume when a new job listing is posted. If you don't submit your resume within the first few minutes, it will go unnoticed because often hundreds of people apply in the first hour.

You can spend the day searching Glassdoor.com, Indeed.com, and other job websites and pray your resume will be noticed. You can apply for hundreds of jobs, but rarely will you receive any acknowledgment that they even got your resume.

I remember how frustrating it was looking for jobs in the past, especially when you know you are qualified, but you can't cut through the noise and get noticed. You can resort to making one of those crazy YouTube videos to catch their attention, but your chances of getting the job are still minimal.

Finding a job online is very similar to cold calling. You are a complete stranger to each company, so getting past the gatekeepers is a huge challenge. You need to get very creative to get your resume in front of the hiring manager, which seems nearly impossible.

Now let's look at the other side of the coin. Say you work in the human resources department and you've posted some jobs online. Within minutes, you have more than 100 resumes for one open position. You scan through a few of them and very few are qualified, even though you clearly spelled out the requirements in the job posting.

People are so desperate that they're applying for any job, even if they aren't qualified. They hope to catch the attention of the HR department or the hiring manager, so they can get hired for a more appropriate position. HR is overwhelmed and spends hours digging through resumes to find a handful of people to interview. There has to be a better way!

So how do you find good candidates in today's economy, with millions of qualified workers looking for jobs?

Most jobs are filled through word-of-mouth recommendations, not by sifting through hundreds of resumes. It's much easier and more reliable to hire someone who comes highly recommended by a trusted colleague. The old adage "It's not what you know; it's who you know" is more powerful than ever, and you can get to know the right people by leveraging social proof.

Again, the key is building your network and keeping in touch with them so they are there when you need them. Once you establish your core network of 100 to 150 people, you can reach out to them and tap their expertise or their own network to solve your problem. If they can't help you, they'll introduce you to someone else who can. If you suddenly lose your job and you don't have a stable professional network, you have to spend months building your network and gaining their trust before you can reach out to them for help.

You build a strong professional network by creating a solid online reputation with a lot of social proof. When someone searches LinkedIn (or any other search engine) for your name, you want a lot of very positive social proof to appear. When people see pages and pages of positive social proof about you, they will pursue you to join their professional network. You will be in demand, and your professional network will be full of A-list players. One way to achieve that is by getting recommendations.

WHAT ARE LINKEDIN RECOMMENDATIONS?

LinkedIn has created its own version of social proof called recommendations, which is a reputation manager for professionals. When someone writes a recommendation for you on LinkedIn, it's the online version of the recommendation letters you used to receive from instructors and former employers. The good news is that you control the recommendations that are posted on your LinkedIn profile, so you won't see any negative comments.

Recommendations are not just useful for the person receiving them. The person writing the recommendation can display the recommendations they write on their own profile as well. Writing strong recommendations for others adds to your credibility because it shows other LinkedIn members that you have strong connections in your professional network.

Think of LinkedIn as a reputation engine for business professionals. Your LinkedIn activity paints a picture of you and your business. Your profile is more than an online resumé with a list of your jobs, education, and accomplishments. Your professional reputation includes the people you associate with, the Groups you belong to, the associations and clubs you join, and how much you interact with your network. You can think of all these factors combined as your LinkedIn persona.

If you are a small-business owner looking to hire new employees, recommendations can help you determine if a potential employee will be a good fit. Recruiters and hiring managers at large companies also take your recommendations into account when deciding if you are the right person for the job. Recommendations add value to your overall LinkedIn profile, and the more recommendations you have, the better. Later in this chapter, I will show you some sample recommendations that are so powerful they can influence a manager's decision to hire a person. These are the type of recommendations you want to look for when you are searching for new employees.

Savvy LinkedIn members can tell if you are actively networking or if you are a passive LinkedIn member with a static profile and no networking activity. If you are not active on LinkedIn, it doesn't mean you are not good at what you do. It just means you are not actively building your professional network as well as you could be. Ideally, you should spend a few hours every week networking on LinkedIn so you can quickly land on your feet if you lose your job (and chances are it will happen at some point in your career).

Jobs, companies, and even industries come and go quickly in today's fast-paced business world, and you will most likely have to change jobs or careers sometime in the next few years. My 20-year career as a network engineer in the 1980s and 1990s doesn't exist today, and I had to learn new skills. Now I manage Google AdWords and social media and do search engine optimization for a living. None of these jobs existed in their current form a decade ago. A few years from now, AdWords will evolve into some other form of online advertising, social media will have a new name, and who knows what search engines will look like. We're already seeing big changes with voice-activated searches on smartphones, virtual assistants, and even remotest on some cable service providers.

By keeping my LinkedIn profile current, participating in LinkedIn Groups, and publishing and sharing great content, I can tell potential employers more about me than they could ever learn by just reading my resume. The icing on the cake is the recommendations, which provide third-party verification of my skills. Each online activity is like a piece of a puzzle; recommendations are the glue that holds the puzzle together. When you are looking for new employees on LinkedIn, you want members who have a complete, updated profile with lots of great recommendations.

Recommendations are a huge part of your image on LinkedIn. Obviously, it's good to have a lot of recommendations—but what really matters is that they are *quality* recommendations. These days you can hire people to write fake recommendations for you. You can have hundreds of hollow recommendations in a matter of days for less than a hundred bucks. It's better to have a dozen high-quality recommendations than hundreds of low-quality, suspicious ones.

WHY DO I NEED LINKEDIN RECOMMENDATIONS?

People rarely provide written recommendations or testimonial letters when they apply for jobs these days, so why bother getting recommendations on LinkedIn?

First of all, your LinkedIn profile will not be complete until you have at least three recommendations. Getting to the All-Star level on your profile is a huge accomplishment and adds a lot of credibility to your LinkedIn presence, and you can only do that by adding recommendations.

The second reason is because recommendations are the only way you can prove that your LinkedIn profile is genuine. When you enter your profile information, including your education, work history, and accomplishments, there is no way for others to verify this information. But when people recommend you on LinkedIn, it's a written testimonial of your abilities. It's very important to have that third-party verification of your LinkedIn profile, especially if you are a consultant or independent service provider. Your potential customers will use your recommendations to help determine the quality of your work and your expertise before they'll hire you or trust your product.

Third, when it comes to the LinkedIn search rankings, the more recommendations you have, the higher you can rank in LinkedIn searches. If your recommendations contain the same keywords you want to rank for, your search ranking should rise as your recommendations increase. However, don't try to get recommendations stuffed with your keywords just to improve your search ranking. Be genuine and nurture good recommendations, and your search results will take care of themselves.

HOW MANY LINKEDIN RECOMMENDATIONS SHOULD I HAVE?

There is no right or wrong answer to this question. I see some LinkedIn profiles with just a few excellent recommendations that go a long way toward highlighting the person's expertise. I see other profiles with page after page of hollow recommendations that don't convince me the person is someone I would hire.

How many recommendations are right for you? I would suggest at least one for every year you've worked at a job. If you've been at your current company for five years, I think you should have at least five recommendations for that company. I have no scientific proof to back up this formula, but don't you think you have at least one great accomplishment at work every year?

When you accomplish something great at work, ask someone who benefited from that achievement to write you a recommendation. When you benefit from someone else's accomplishment, write that person a recommendation. Don't wait for them to ask you—just do it!

WHAT MAKES A LINKEDIN RECOMMENDATION GREAT?

People want to read relevant recommendations that are clear and concise and add value to their assessment of a person's professional skills and capabilities. Recommendations are a form of social proof that express your personal and/or professional opinion of the person you are recommending.

Recommendations should go beyond letting people know someone is a whiz at Excel or a social media aficionado. Every recommendation should be personalized and detail why you think this person is worthy of your recommendation. When you recommend a person, it impacts your reputation as much as his. If you create a bunch of meaningless recommendations for people who are not worthy of them, it negatively affects your reputation.

Say your friend Joe calls you up one day asking if you know a good plumber. The last time you hired a plumber, they didn't do a very good job for you, but they are the only plumber you know. You give Joe the plumber's name and the plumber goes out to Joe's house to fix his leaking pipe. But instead of stopping the leak, the plumber breaks the pipe, causing a huge flood at Joe's house. Joe is furious and wonders why you would ever recommend this incompetent person. Your reputation has taken a huge hit with Joe, and it could even end your friendship.

Recommending people on a professional level is no different. If for any reason you don't feel comfortable recommending someone, you shouldn't write a recommendation. Remember, your reputation is at stake here, too. If one of your connections hires someone based on your recommendation and it doesn't turn out well, then your connection is going to lose faith in you and your credibility will suffer.

You need to carefully craft your recommendations so you are always telling the truth and not exaggerating. If the people you are recommending are the "best of the best" in their field, you can say that. If they are not, then you shouldn't "highly recommend" them. You can always phrase your recommendation in a different way, so you are not stretching the truth but are still highlighting their strengths and giving them a positive recommendation.

WHAT TO SAY IN YOUR RECOMMENDATIONS

Here's a sample recommendation I found in a profile of one of my connections:

Joe is always a pleasure to work with! He is extremely knowledgeable, personable, communicative, and highly effective.

So what do you think about that recommendation? Are you going to hire Joe? Do you even know what Joe does for a living or what he is extremely knowledgeable about? Since Joe is my friend and I know he is very good at what he does, I know this recommendation is completely true.

But if you don't know Joe, this recommendation isn't going to help you decide if Joe is the right person to hire for your project. You know Joe is a pleasure to work with, which is always a good trait if you are looking to hire some help. But what did Joe do for this person when they worked together? What skills did he use? Was it a big project or a small one? How many times did Joe work with this person? What challenges did he overcome while working on the project? These are the things you need to mention when writing a review for someone, so you can paint a complete picture for the person reading the recommendation.

Unfortunately, the above recommendation doesn't help Joe or the person who wrote it. If you are going to take the time to write a recommendation, make sure you write a thoughtful, thorough summary that speaks to a person's specific skill set, so others will know exactly what kind of person you are recommending.

Now take a look at this recommendation:

Melanie has been one of the biggest influencers on me in my career. I knew the first time I saw her speak at a conference that she was someone I needed to meet and model myself after. She's incredible at seeing the big picture in order to make the necessary changes needed to create a well-oiled machine out of an organization, program, or process, while still understanding the details of the minutiae involved.

We were at different enterprise-level companies with the same challenges when I met Melanie, and the things I learned from her about how the organization needs to be set up for success, properly measuring success, creating accountability, getting the right pieces in place for all moving parts to work together to get to an end goal, and getting around the bullshit were fundamental *insights for me, that truthfully, I just didn't hear from other people in the industry.*

She's a born leader, she's bright, she's quick, she's motivated, and *she's fun to be around. One of the true top players in the entire industry, who I will always intend to continue to learn from. —April 17, 2011*

—Laura Lippay, Director of Technical Marketing, Yahoo!

Wow! Now *that* is an incredible recommendation. What do we learn about Melanie from just one recommendation? She had a big influence on Laura's career, and Laura wanted to meet her because Melanie was her role model. (My guess is that Melanie has had a big influence on many careers.) We know that Melanie has the unique skill of being able to see the big picture while understanding the details. It's rare to find one person with both abilities.

Laura was encountering the same problems in her organization as Melanie was in hers, so they had a lot in common. By connecting with Melanie, Laura learned how to change the direction of her organization by modeling what Melanie did.

The last paragraph sums up Laura's opinion of Melanie: a born leader, bright, motivated, and fun. With all those attributes, it's no wonder Melanie is one of the top players in her industry. From my personal experience, I would second what Laura said about Melanie: She definitely is one of the top players in the search marketing industry.

Laura's entire recommendation was only 186 words long, but look at what we learned about Melanie in just three short paragraphs. Wouldn't you love to have a powerful recommendation like this in your LinkedIn profile? Melanie has dozens of other recommendations just like this one, providing a ton of social proof that she is an A-list player. There's nothing more powerful than your peers writing glowing recommendations about you to build up your reputation and let others know you are a true leader in your field.

WHOM SHOULD I RECOMMEND?

The best way to get started is to recommend others. If you work for a company, recommend co-workers whom you respect and appreciate. You can also write recommendations for your boss if you want to score some brownie points—just kidding! Write one only if they are a mentor to you and if you really respect the work they do.

If you own your own business, you can write recommendations for your customers or the vendors you do business with. When your IT consultant comes in and fixes your server that was down and affecting your entire operation, take a few minutes and write them a glowing recommendation. Talk about how they responded to your call for help in minutes, isolated the problem in no time, and had you up and running in less than an hour. Highlight their responsiveness, troubleshooting skills, and beaming personality. They will appreciate your thoughtfulness in taking the time to do this, as it will do wonders for their business. Someday, they may return the favor when you least expect it.

If you are a consultant, write recommendations for other consultants you work with. Let's say you're a web designer and you work with a graphic designer, who creates the beautiful graphics for your websites. You can talk about the different projects you've collaborated on and highlight their design skills, creativity, timeliness, and passion for the work. Provide as many details as you can, so you can fully demonstrate the range of their talents and expertise.

The best time to write a recommendation for someone is right after you've completed a successful project that you worked on together. You know that fantastic feeling of accomplishment you have after you finish a long project? You and your co-workers work long days for many months, riding the emotional highs and lows of a difficult project. Some days you don't think it will ever end, and then you suddenly have a breakthrough that takes you to the next stage. The breakthroughs come when you work together, combining all your strengths to create a powerful team.

It's easy to write a recommendation for someone after struggling through a long project together. You know their strengths, emotions, leadership ability, and motivations. As we saw with Laura's recommendation for Melanie, you can write a very powerful recommendation in less than 200 words. If you write the recommendation while you're still riding the high of project completion, it will be authentic and meaningful, which has a powerful effect on the reader. I don't know this for sure, but I would guess that Laura wrote Melanie's recommendation shortly after seeing her speak at an event, while she was still feeling the emotional impact of the speech.

When you are ready to write a recommendation for a colleague, you can simply go to their profile, click on the More button, and then click the Recommend link. You must be connected to a person before you can recommend them. Once you click the Recommend link, you will see the screen as shown in Figure 10–1.

Choose the appropriate option, and you will be prompted with a few questions to help customize your recommendation. LinkedIn will typically ask you to identify your relationship with the person you're recommending based on experiences like whether

FIGURE 10–1. Make a Recommendation

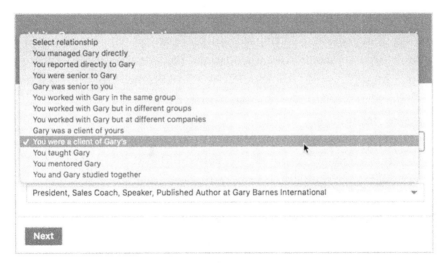

FIGURE 10–2. Create Your Recommendation

you were their client, they were your client, you reported to that person, they reported to you, etc. Figure 10-2 shows the complete list of choices.

Next select the Position at the time of the recommendation. The drop-down list will display all the titles he has listed in their profile.

Figure 10–3 shows the next screen, where you write your recommendation. After you finish, click Send, and the person you are recommending will be notified that you have written a recommendation for them. The recommendation will not be posted in their profile until they approve it. A few things can occur at this point, all of them fairly common: They can send it back to you for revision if they would like you to change

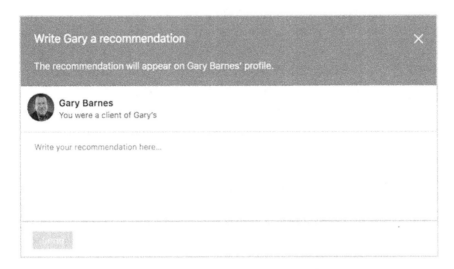

FIGURE 10–3. Enter Your Recommendation

it; they can approve it as is; or they can reject it if they don't want a recommendation from you for some reason. Remember, your professional reputation is at stake here, so you don't need to accept recommendations just for the sake of having a lot of recommendations. If you feel you should reject a recommendation from someone, it's probably a sign you shouldn't be connected with that person on LinkedIn.

After you recommend someone, LinkedIn will ask that individual if they want to recommend you in return. There's an ongoing debate about reciprocal recommendations. Some LinkedIn experts contend that they have less value than one-way recommendations, comparing it to sharing website links on the internet. To rank highly in Google, you need a lot of links from high-quality websites to your website. In the past, webmasters would trade links so both sites benefited. Eventually, Google figured out people were sharing links to improve their search rankings and lowered the value of the links on both sites.

Some experts say sharing recommendations has the same effect on your LinkedIn reputation. Since LinkedIn automatically prompts you to reciprocate, they argue you can get a lot of recommendations by writing a lot of them, which devalues them. Occasionally, I have felt that someone recommended me just so I would write a recommendation for them. I can tell if they are sincere and writing a recommendation for me because they value the work I did for them. I do know a few people who are just looking for recommendations for themselves. After working with many different people over many years, you get a feel for who is sincere and who isn't.

Some LinkedIn members feel a positive recommendation is a good thing, whether or not it is reciprocal. If someone feels you are worthy of a recommendation and takes the time to write it, that adds value to your LinkedIn reputation.

I'll leave it up to you whether you want recommendations only from people who you haven't recommended or if you want to do reciprocal recommendations. Personally, I write recommendations for people I feel are worthy of them. It doesn't matter if they ask me to write a recommendation for them or if it's a reciprocal recommendation.

I frequently receive requests from former employees to write recommendations, which appear in their profile under the company we worked for at the time. Again, if I don't feel they were a good employee or not worthy of a recommendation for the work they did for me, I politely decline.

HOW TO ASK FOR RECOMMENDATIONS

I don't generally ask people for recommendations. It's not that I'm afraid to ask for them; I just feel that if I do a great job for them, they will write one. If I were going to ask someone for a recommendation, it would be from someone I worked closely with and respected a great deal. I would have a close professional relationship with this person, who would be among the 150 people in my network with whom I keep in touch on a regular basis.

I would write a recommendation for this person not because I want a reciprocal recommendation from them, but because I strongly respect their professional ability. Most of the time, I receive a strong recommendation in return. If the individual doesn't reciprocate, I don't take it personally; I just assume they don't have time to write recommendations on LinkedIn.

If you want to ask for a recommendation, do it in a professional way. Don't use a standard request message in LinkedIn; instead, write a thoughtful, personalized message and explain why you are asking for a recommendation at this time. You can say you are looking for a new job, for example, and you would appreciate a recommendation.

Don't ask for a recommendation from someone you don't know well or haven't worked with in a long time. A recommendation about your technical skills from someone you worked with in 2003 isn't relevant today and will have very little impact. But if that co-worker is now a CTO at a large company, you could ask them to write a recommendation focusing on your customer service skills or your work ethic. That would carry a lot of weight in your profile.

When you ask for a recommendation, mention a specific project or job you worked on together. Explain why you think that project succeeded and how well you worked together. Tell the connection what you think their strengths were on the project and ask them what they thought you did well. Also ask them to mention the specific skills or traits you demonstrated on that project and others on which you worked together.

Be very clear when you ask for a recommendation. Tell them exactly what position you are applying for and what skill set and experience it requires. You can even include a link to the job description (if you don't think they would be interested in the job!), so they can write a recommendation that fits its requirements.

For example, if you are applying for a position as a software project manager that requires Scrum experience and knowledge of LAMP, ask the person writing your recommendation to include those skills and knowledge in the recommendation if they are familiar with your skill set. Obviously, you should not ask someone to write a recommendation for you if they aren't familiar with your specific skills. Have them focus the recommendation on the skills they know you excel at.

Here is an example of a recommendation for a director of development for an internet business. Notice how the writer highlighted Michael's skills in project management, software development, and technical programming languages. This recommendation clearly demonstrates Michael's well-rounded skill set.

I worked with Michael at GS1 Canada. Michael is an excellent development director with in-depth knowledge of current software development technologies and keen sense of how to apply technology to maximize business applications. I worked with Michael on several projects. Michael is very capable at any level of software development: analysis, design, development, and support. Michael has excellent knowledge of .NET and Java development environment. At GS1 Canada, Michael made significant contributions to several strategic projects, including GDSN integration with 1SYNC. I would highly recommend Michael for any development director role.

Note how the person writing the recommendation focused on two skills: Michael's knowledge of the products in his industry, and his ability to form partnerships to develop new streams of revenue. It's clear this person worked with Michael and knows his strengths and skills.

If you want great recommendations like this, don't be afraid to reach out and ask for what you want. You have more control over what the person will write when you specify what you are looking for in the recommendation. Unsolicited recommendations are usually thin in content and written in very general terms. I actually think I just convinced myself to change my personal policy of not asking for recommendations and start asking for *great* recommendations!

LINKEDIN ENDORSEMENTS

In 2013, LinkedIn added a new feature called endorsements, which are often confused with recommendations. The primary difference is endorsements come from the keywords you used when you added skills to your profile. Recommendations are individually written testimonials, while endorsements can be done by simply clicking on a pop-up message that appears when you view a profile.

Figure 10–4 on page 119 shows the Skills & Endorsements section of Eric Jan van Putten's profile. If you feel Eric deserves an endorsement for any of the skills on his list, you can click on the + button next to that skill. Notice Eric's profile prominently features his top three skills, followed by a list of many other skills. LinkedIn has added categories for the skills in your profile. The categories are Top Skills, Industry Knowledge, Tools & Technologies, Interpersonal Skills, Languages, and Other Skills. LinkedIn will automatically categorize your skills once you enter them into your profile. As I mentioned previously, you can enter up to 50 skills, so use all of them to increase your chances of being found in LinkedIn searches.

Now Eric's list of skills will have one more vote for each one you selected to endorse. The more votes you have for each of your skills, the higher you may rank for the skill in LinkedIn searches.

In Figure 10–4, you can see Eric's colleagues feel he's very skilled in online marketing, SEO, email marketing, and digital marketing. He has the majority of his votes in these

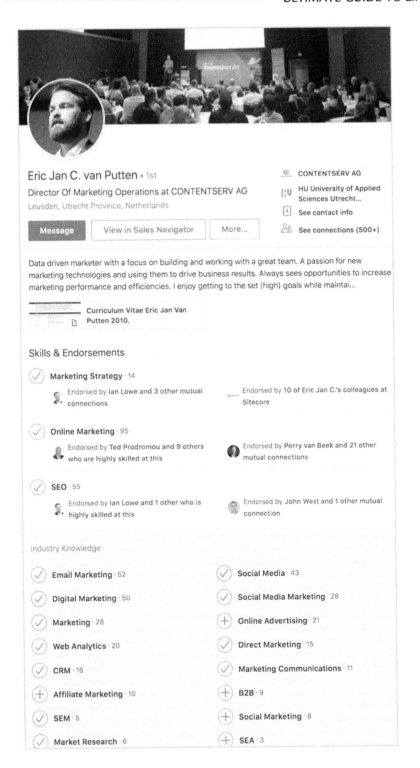

FIGURE 10–4. Make an Endorsement

skills. If Eric changes his career focus and no longer does those tasks as his primary job focus, he can rearrange the list of skills in his profile by dragging them. I did this in my personal profile when I stopped doing SEO, which used to be my top-ranked skill. I moved it near the bottom of my skills list because I wanted to show that while I was knowledgeable in SEO, it was no longer my job focus.

CONCLUSION

As you can see, recommendations are a form of social proof, validating your work history and expertise, and can be a very powerful addition to your LinkedIn profile. I strongly suggest you focus on a smaller number of quality recommendations instead of many lower-quality recommendations. Get at least five quality recommendations for each position you've held. Take time to recommend co-workers and colleagues, which adds credibility to your profile.

People will endorse you for skills because LinkedIn automatically prompts them to do it when they visit your profile. Make sure to keep your skills list updated and ordered properly so you receive appropriate endorsements.

In the next chapter, I'll show you how to connect with others on LinkedIn so you can build a powerful professional network.

**For additional updates and how-to videos, visit
https://tedprodromou.com/UltimateGuideUpdates/.**

Connecting with Others

ow many connections should you have on LinkedIn? People ask me that frequently, but there is no magic number that works for everyone. LinkedIn isn't a popularity contest, where the person with the most connections wins, and it isn't like Twitter, where Lady Gaga has more than 77 million followers but has no idea who they are. LinkedIn is about building one-on-one relationships and connecting with individuals, which is very different from the mass communication of Twitter.

There are two distinct approaches to networking on LinkedIn. The first, which is used by most members, is called *strategic networking*, where you focus on quality, not quantity. Strategic networkers usually have less than 500 people in their network and keep in touch with about 100 to 150 of them. They have a deep connection with a small number of people.

The other approach, which is often used by sales representatives and recruiters, is called *open networking*; this is where you cast a very wide net. Open networkers often have thousands of connections in their network because their business is a numbers game. The more people you have in your network, the easier it is to find someone to fill an open position or outreach to customers for a sale. As an open networker, you have a limited connection with a lot of people. Let's take a look at both.

STRATEGIC NETWORKING

How many people do you think are in your professional network now? Most business people know hundreds of people and often have more than 500 contacts in their online address book. But the real question is how many of those contacts do you correspond with on a regular basis? Some people apply the 80/20 rule and estimate they correspond with about 20 percent of their professional network on a regular basis. But if you have more than 500 people in your network, you don't have time to regularly correspond with even 20 percent of them.

A number of studies—such as "In Your 20s it's Quantity, in Your 30s it's Quality: The Prognostic Value of Social Activity Across 30 Years of Adulthood" Cheryl L. Carmichael, Harry T. Reis, and Paul R. Duberstein (Psychology and Aging, 2015), and "Sorry You May Have Gone Over Your Limit of Network Friends," by Carl Bialik (*The Wall Street Journal*, Nov. 16, 2007)—have been conducted over the years trying to determine the optimal size of a professional network. The studies vary dramatically, with some concluding we can only maintain a stable social network of 100 people, while others suggest we can manage up to 300.

Maintaining a stable social network means we know everyone in our network and maintain regular contact with each and every individual. Maintaining a larger network requires more restrictive rules, laws, and enforced norms, so essentially you are almost being forced to maintain these relationships, which is not natural.

A widely accepted, landmark study by Robin Dunbar in 1992 and reconfirmed in 2007 resulted in the formulation of Dunbar's Number, which suggests the theoretical cognitive limit to the number of people with whom one can maintain stable relationships is between 100 and 230. Dunbar did not specify an exact number because there are so many variables, but the generally accepted number is 150. Dunbar concluded, "This limit is a direct function of relative neocortex size, and that this in turn limits group size . . . the limit imposed by neocortical processing capacity is simply on the number of individuals with whom a stable interpersonal relationship can be maintained."

Do you maintain a regular relationship with 150 people? If you work for a medium- to large-sized company and count your co-workers, you probably do. If you work for a small company, you may not. If you own your own business, you should be communicating with at least that many people on a regular basis to generate leads or find opportunities.

When you view someone's profile who has more than 500 connections, you will only see "500+." Once you are connected, you can view the complete list and connect with any of their connections because you will now have a 2nd-degree relationship with all of them. A great way to expand your network is by connecting with appropriate 2nd-degree relationships.

OPEN NETWORKING

Open networkers on LinkedIn are often called LIONs (an acronym for LinkedIn Open Networkers). LIONs seek to actively increase their connections by freely sending out and accepting connection invitations. LIONs generally accept invites from anyone, so it's relatively risk-free to invite a LION into your network.

Most LIONs take pride in touting their large number of connections, much like the way celebrities compete to have the most Twitter followers. LIONs believe that bigger is better and that large networks lead to more opportunity. I don't see as many people promoting themselves as LIONs these days, but it's still a "thing" on LinkedIn.

How Do You Become a LION?

LION is an unofficial designation coined by people willing to connect with anyone to grow their network as large as possible. The official LinkedIn response in the Help Center is that LION is not a term endorsed by LinkedIn, but is a designation used in some user-created Groups and individual members to show that they are highly open to connecting with members they do not necessarily know, thus the acronym LION (LinkedIn Open Networker).

If you want to be recognized as a LinkedIn LION, you can add "LION" to the end of your name or your headline in your profile, as seen in Figure 11–1. Notice all the LIONs in the People Also Viewed sidebar.

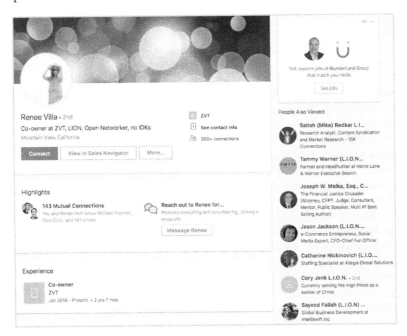

FIGURE 11–1. How to Identify a LION

Being a LION can have its drawbacks. As with any website or online tool that gets popular, people start abusing its popularity. On Twitter, people have automated their tweets so they can send an endless stream of tweets 24/7. There's also been a steady stream of Twitter spam where people create thousands of fake profiles that automatically retweet posts from popular users, adding fake links that lead to automated blogs intended to sell affiliate products. You can see this spam whenever you follow a popular celebrity on Twitter because you will see a hundred retweets in a few seconds from fake profiles all using the same profile picture.

We're now seeing similar tricks with fake profiles on LinkedIn. Be cautious if you receive an invitation from:

- Someone who has no or just a few LinkedIn connections. LinkedIn now warns those who don't have any connections or are new to LinkedIn.
- Profiles with no picture—one of my pet peeves, the incomplete profile
- Profiles with company logos as their profile picture, which is a violation of the LinkedIn terms of service
- Personal profiles with company names instead of a person's name. We connect with people, not companies, on LinkedIn!
- Profiles that use partial names or symbols in their names so they look machine generated
- Profiles that have an SEO-optimized name, a phone number, email address, or their website URL
- A keyword-stuffed title or summary

Do not connect with these people because they're probably machine-generated profiles or on LinkedIn for the wrong reasons. If someone is not willing to provide their complete name and fill out their complete profile properly, they are not fit for your network.

ARE YOUR LINKEDIN CONNECTIONS REAL PEOPLE?

Let's say you promote your business online using SEO and paid advertising. You connect with a lot of SEO experts and online marketers on LinkedIn to find great service providers.

One day you receive an invitation from someone who has SEO in their job title; this looks inviting to you because you are looking for SEO experts to hire. This person claims they are an SEO expert (their job title and professional headline tell me) and have 127 connections. On first glance, this looks like a good fit for your network because they rank #1 when I search for "SEO expert" on LinkedIn.

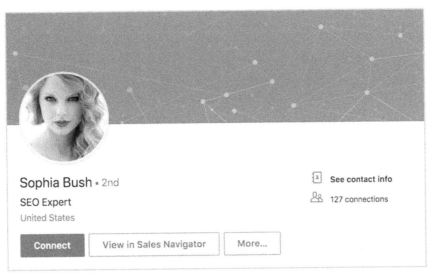

FIGURE 11–2. The Profile Headline of an SEO Expert

Should you connect with this person after reading the profile headline in Figure 11–2?

If you said "no," good for you! Let's take a closer look at this person's profile, shown in Figure 11–3 on page 125, and I'll show you why they probably aren't a good fit for your network.

This is an example of an SEO-optimized profile that contains very little information about the individual. This person claims to be an SEO expert, but there is no description in their job title under Experience. There are no recommendations, no summary, no education, and nothing that would make me want to hire this person to help me with my SEO. If the person were a legitimate SEO expert, they would at least claim their LinkedIn personal URL, add a summary with keywords, add SEO-related skills, and get at least a dozen recommendations. This person is gaming the system. I highly recommend ignoring or declining requests like this. Better yet, report them as spam so we can keep LinkedIn as professional as possible.

By the way, the first red flag? Her profile picture is a photo of Taylor Swift, and her name is listed as another celebrity, actress Sophia Bush. I really doubt Taylor Swift (or Sophia Bush, for that matter) does SEO in her spare time!

CONNECTION INVITATION ETIQUETTE

As your network grows, you will begin to receive invitations to connect from people you don't know. When you join Groups and participate in conversations, more people will reach out to you inviting you to join their networks. What should you do?

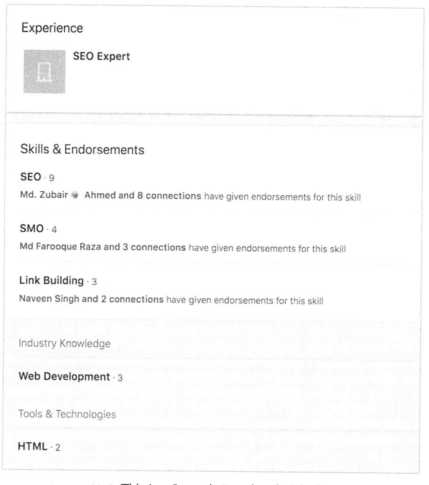

FIGURE 11–3. This Is a Sparsely Populated LinkedIn Profile

LinkedIn has simplified the process, and now you have three options when you receive an invitation instead of six. Your options are:

1. *Accept.* The person will immediately become a 1st-degree connection in your network.

2. *Reply.* You can reply to the person who invited you to connect if you are not sure you want them to become a 1st-degree connection at this time. If you just met someone at a networking event or in a LinkedIn Group but don't know much about them, you can reply to the invitation and set up a meeting or phone call to get to know each other. I also review the profile in detail to see if they will add value to my network. After that, I will know if I want to add them as a 1st-degree connection.

3. *Ignore.* You have two options here: You can select "I don't know them" or "Report as spam." If you select "Report as spam" a message will be sent to LinkedIn so they can review this person's profile and potentially suspend their account.

REMOVING A CONNECTION

Sometimes you connect with someone thinking she will be perfect for your network, but it turns out they are not a good fit. Sometimes your connections are overzealous, with constant invitations to webinars or live events they're hosting. Don't get me wrong. I love to see people actively promoting their businesses and events. I don't mind occasional invitations if the events are interesting and related to my current position. I do mind people inviting me to weekly events and sometimes daily—especially if the events are irrelevant to my job.

If you are connected with someone you feel is taking advantage of your LinkedIn relationship, contact them and ask them to slow down or even remove you from their invitation list. Most people will get the message and stop sending frequent invitations. Unfortunately, there are those who will keep spamming you, so you will have to remove them as a connection.

You can remove a connection by going to My Network on the toolbar/menu, click See All, click on the ellipsis on the right side of the connection's profile, and click on Remove Connection. This will remove the connection from your network without notifying them (similar to the unfriending feature on Facebook).

CONCLUSION

You now know the essentials of connecting with others on LinkedIn. It's up to you to decide if you will build a smaller, high-quality network or become a LION and build a massive network. You know how to vet your connection invitations, so you can create the professional network that best suits your business needs.

In the next chapter, you're going to learn about LinkedIn's InMail, a powerful tool that will help you connect with people who are not in your 1st-degree or 2nd-degree networks.

**For additional updates and how-to videos, visit
https://tedprodromou.com/UltimateGuideUpdates/.**

Chapter 12

Using LinkedIn InMail to Reach Out

There are several ways to contact people through LinkedIn. Each has its nuances, depending on whether the people are in or out of your network. LinkedIn is built to respect users' privacy, so people can pick and choose who becomes part of their network and avoid being barraged by spam or people who will disrupt their business. Of course, the site does want to encourage positive connections, so it has devised a number of tools, such as InMail and Introductions, that allow users to communicate without invading anyone's privacy.

INMAIL VS. INTRODUCTIONS

LinkedIn has changed the way InMail works and continues to adjust it in response to its users. To see the latest updates on InMail visit LinkedIn help at https://www.linkedin.com/help/linkedin.

If you have a basic (free) LinkedIn account, you need to upgrade to a premium account to send up to 30 InMail messages every month.

LinkedIn has a number of features to help you connect with people outside your network. The best way is via an Introduction by someone already in your network (only available on the mobile app at the time of this writing, though they may be made available to desktop users at a later date). A virtual Introduction increases your chances of connecting with that person because there is a level of trust between you and your connection and between your connection and the person you want to meet. The trust is essentially passed from connection to connection.

Introductions are free to all users. If you want to contact someone who is one or two degrees away from you, you can request an Introduction on the mobile app through one of your mutual connections who has a 1st-degree connection with that person.

WHAT IS INMAIL?

When you send email to someone you don't know, it can be perceived as spam or inappropriate if you aren't careful. Reaching out to people who don't know you through normal email channels usually has a very high failure rate. How do *you* respond when you receive an unsolicited email from a stranger who wants to meet with you or sell you something? I rarely respond to unsolicited emails, unless something in the subject line or first sentence catches my eye. There has to be some benefit to me to make me respond.

Reaching out to someone you don't know in a trusted community like LinkedIn is a different story. Most members of LinkedIn are reputable business professionals. You don't expect them to bother you with emails unless they can provide value to you. Even though LinkedIn is a trusted network, it understands not all members will respect others' privacy and may abuse the privilege of being able to reach out to one another. It designed InMail so members can contact each other while still protecting their privacy.

There are several ways to get and pay for InMail if you have a premium account (it's no longer available if you have a basic account). If you have a LinkedIn Premium Business subscription, you receive 30 InMail credits per month. I have a legacy premium account, so I receive 10 InMail credits each month, which roll over to the next month if I don't use them. I can accumulate up to 15 credits in my account. The Sales Navigator Professional subscription gives you 30 credits per month, depending on your subscription level.

What Are the Benefits of InMail?

In addition to helping you outreach and connect with people while respecting their privacy, InMail offers several valuable benefits.

First, it helps you reach out to passive job candidates. For example, let's say you're looking for a new network engineer and you read some great responses from a really sharp network engineer in the Groups section of LinkedIn. You want to contact this person because they'd be a perfect fit for your company. They're not actively looking for a new job, but you see that they have Career Opportunities listed in the See Contact Info section in the right column of their member profile page. They are not in your network, and you don't have any connections in common, so you can't connect with them, but you can still reach out with a personal message through InMail to see if they'd be interested in your network engineer position. Compliment some accomplishments you found in their profile, so they'll feel honored that you know so much about them. This will make them more responsive to your InMail.

You can also reach out to active candidates who listed Career Opportunities in the Contact Settings section at the bottom of the member Profile or have written that they are actively looking for a new opportunity. If they have LinkedIn Premium Career accounts, this will be noted by badges in their profiles so you know to reach out to them using InMail.

Say you are writing an article about social media and are looking for experts to interview. You search for social media experts on LinkedIn and find a few who seem to fit your criteria. You have no connections in your network to make Introductions, and they are not in any Groups with you. Even if you were in a Group with them, they don't allow emails from other group members unless you are already connected with them because they value their privacy. You can still use InMail to reach out to them even though you do not have a relationship with them.

You don't have to be a premium member to receive or respond to InMails. A few times, people have sent me InMails to see if I was interested in an opportunity. I didn't know them, but it didn't feel intrusive because they included some personal details, like "I see you actively participate in the Social Media Managers Group." It's important to break the ice in the subject line or the first line of the email to create a level of trust or familiarity.

Finally, when someone responds to your InMail within 90 days, you will receive an InMail credit so you can send another InMail. If they don't respond, you lose that InMail credit forever.

Sending an InMail

You can send an InMail by clicking the Message button on the left side of a member's profile page or from the search results. If you have a premium account, you will receive a specified number of InMail credits every month depending on your subscription. You can also check to see how many InMail credits you have remaining at the bottom of the new message from this screen, as shown in Figure 12–1 on page 132.

InMail credits can be used up to 90 days after they are issued. Once they expire, they are not renewable, so make sure you use them in a timely manner.

While InMail isn't available for basic accounts, you can still message connections. You don't need to use InMail to send messages to your 1st-degree connections or to open networkers. Just click Send a Message in the upper right of your connection's profile, and you can send them a message for free. You can also send up to 15 free

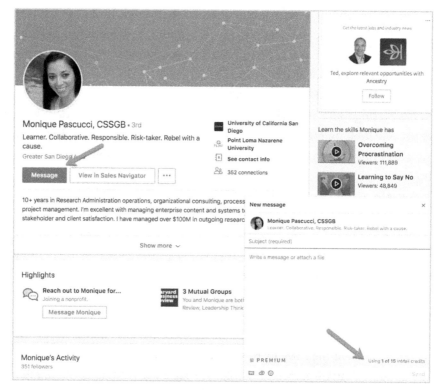

FIGURE 12–1. Sending InMails

messages per month to other group members, even if they aren't connected to you, as long as they accept messages from other group members. If you don't want to receive messages from other group members with whom you are not connected, see Chapter 5 for how to modify your preferences. I don't recommend trying to prevent people from contacting you on LinkedIn because the purpose of the site is to connect with others, and you never know why someone will want to reach you; it could be an opportunity that would lead to additional revenue.

InMail Credits

If you send an InMail message and you don't receive a response, you will not get credited back. If the recipient responds to your InMail message within 90 days of the send date, you will receive an InMail credit. You cannot send a second InMail to someone until they respond to the first InMail message. A reminder is sent to the person within three days if they fail to respond to your InMail message, and this is the only reminder they will receive. Many times, the reminders get buried in my Notifications tab because I am very active on LinkedIn.

LinkedIn added autoreplies to InMail messages to make it easier to respond. Clicking on an autoreply counts as a response. The autoreplies include "Interested" and "Maybe later," which are reflected as accepted messages, while "Not interested" is recorded as declined. Once they click on a response or manually reply to your InMail, you will receive the credit back immediately.

Opting Out of InMail and Sponsored InMail

LinkedIn lets you opt out of receiving both InMail and Sponsored InMail. If you aren't familiar with Sponsored InMail, it's a type of ad you can use to reach your target audience. You can read more about Sponsored InMail in Chapter 20.

If you don't want to receive InMail, you can opt out from your Settings & Privacy page. See Figure 12–2 below. Here's how you do it:

1. Click the Me icon with your profile photo at the top of your LinkedIn homepage.
2. Click Settings & Privacy.
3. Select the Communications tab at the top of the page.
4. In the Preferences section, click Change next to Messages From Members and Partners.
5. Under Allow LinkedIn Partners to Show You Sponsored InMail?, click the toggle to No.
6. If you want to opt out of InMail as well, you can click the toggle under Allow Others to Send You InMail? to No.

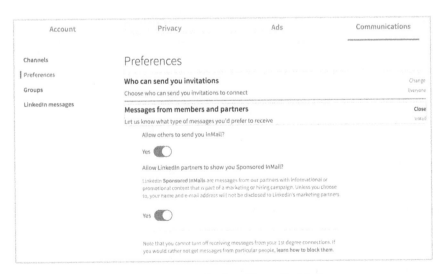

FIGURE 12–2. Opting Out of InMail

TIPS FOR WRITING INMAILS TO INCREASE YOUR RESPONSE RATES

It's important to carefully structure your InMail so the recipient will open it and respond. If they don't, you lose a credit. Your goal is to get them to at least respond to the InMail, even if they aren't interested, so you will be credited back.

If you are familiar with email marketing, you know what I'm talking about, except that there, if they don't open your email, your only penalty is that your open rate decreases.

According to a study by Constant Contact®, an email marketing company, the average open rate of direct-marketing emails sent through their software platform was around 18 percent as of April 2018, as you can see in Figure 12–3 below. The open rates vary by industry, but the overall average has been decreasing because we are overwhelmed with hundreds of messages each day and it's getting harder to deliver email though spam filters. But look at the engagement from mobile devices. A whopping 61 percent of the emails you receive on your mobile device are opened.

FIGURE 12–3. Email Open Rates

The good news is that InMail open rates are much higher if you structure your message properly. If the open rate of InMails were only 18 percent, it would be a very expensive way to reach out. You would have to spend around $40 to get one person to just open your InMail, and opening the message does not guarantee anyone will respond to your request; you might easily shell out more than $100 to get one response.

LinkedIn doesn't provide template options for InMail, which is a good thing. If it did, InMail messages would all start to look the same and people would stop paying attention. It's hard enough to get someone's attention these days when everyone is constantly being bombarded with messages and promotions.

As with all email marketing, your subject line is the most important part of your message. Some email-marketing experts claim the subject line is 90 percent of your message. If you don't catch your recipient's attention in the subject line, they'll never open the email and see what you have to say. Many copywriters spend more time crafting the subject line than they do writing the rest of the email.

Here are some tips for creating a powerful subject line for your InMail:

- Arouse curiosity by asking a provocative question.
- Promise answers to a question or solutions to a problem.
- Include a key benefit for the recipient.
- Ask for advice or an opinion.

You want your subject line to be brief and to the point, catching their attention without giving away the details of your message. On TV, news programs have mastered the technique of teasing upcoming stories to keep us tuned in. Many times, the actual story is nowhere near as exciting as the teasers made it sound. The subject line in an email is like a TV news teaser, a headline in sales copy, or even the title of a book. Its sole purpose is to grab our attention and make us want to learn more.

Remember, your goal is to get the recipient to open your InMail so he'll read your message and start a dialogue with you. You want him to be unable to resist opening your message. Don't overhype your subject line or deceive them , but grab their attention enough to want to open it.

Here are some basic guidelines for composing your InMail that will help increase your response rates:

- Design your InMail as a conversation starter. You don't ask someone out on a date the second you meet them. You strike up a conversation first and get to know them before moving to the next level. The same holds true when you're establishing a new business relationship. If you are too aggressive like a used-car salesman, they will naturally back away.
- The goal of sending the InMail is to discuss and explore an opportunity—not seal the deal immediately. Again, don't be too aggressive. You just want to establish a channel of communication.
- Mention the profile content that prompted you to write. If you were impressed by their education or a specific project, mention it in the first sentence or paragraph of your message.
- Adopt a conversational, enthusiastic tone like you would if you were having a cup of coffee with them at Starbucks. Don't use a form-letter approach with boring, scripted text. Be friendly and inviting so they'll want to get to know you.
- Be yourself. Choose words that reflect your personal voice. Write your message in a natural tone, like you're speaking with your colleagues. Don't use words you wouldn't use in everyday conversation; it will sound unnatural.
- Express interest in helping them achieve their goals, rather than your need to fill a position (if you're looking to hire). As Brian Tracy says, people are always thinking *What's in it for me?* You have to approach them from that perspective.

- Get to the point so you don't waste anyone's time. If you write a long, drawn-out message, they'll lose interest because people tend to scan content quickly from their mobile device.
- Don't share too much. If you do, they may not feel a need to reply. Remember, your only goal is to get a response to begin a conversation.
- Focus on finding out their availability and interest in a job or networking opportunity.
- Express your objective clearly so they know exactly why you reached out. Give them a reason to reply by asking for advice, opinions, or referrals. Don't send a message with a subject line like "Look at this job and tell me if you're interested." It will be ignored 99 percent of the time, wasting your valuable InMail credits. A better subject line would be, "Are you interested in joining the #1 consulting company in the world?"

Every InMail you send should be a very personal message with a unique subject line containing something you read in their LinkedIn profile. Don't cut and paste subject lines and email content; it's too impersonal and won't grab their attention. If you are recruiting for a position, write individual messages mentioning specific skills or accomplishments in their profiles and include a link to the job description. Do not include the entire job description in the InMail.

The same holds true if you are using InMail for networking. Each message and subject line should be unique and let the recipient know your objective in the first sentence or paragraph. If you met them at a conference, mention the conference and why you want to keep in touch. Explain what you read in their profile that made you want to reach out to this person. People love it when others notice their accomplishments. Play to someone's ego, and you'll have a friend for life!

Personally, I don't use InMail to network; I prefer LinkedIn messages. When people catch my eye, I reach out in a Group or comment on their content. Most of the time, they are very responsive to connecting.

CONCLUSION

InMail is a great, unobtrusive way to reach out to people who are not part of your immediate network. It has a very high success rate because LinkedIn's rules ensure that people don't abuse the system. If people don't respond to your InMails, you waste your credits, so you must take the time to craft meaningful messages to your recipients. InMail is a unique tool that makes it relatively easy for you to connect with key decision-makers who are outside your network.

In the next chapter, we're going to learn about LinkedIn Groups, which are niche communities within the larger LinkedIn community. I'll show you how to effectively connect with subject-matter experts in your industry and how you can become a recognized thought leader in your field.

For additional updates and how-to videos, visit
https://tedprodromou.com/UltimateGuideUpdates/.

Chapter 13

LinkedIn Groups

inkedIn Groups are forums or discussion boards where LinkedIn members can talk to each other to find solutions to their problems or share relevant information about a product, service, or topic related to their industry or niche.

Groups can be open, allowing anyone to join (which is now called Standard), or your group can be Unlisted, meaning you have to be approved by the group manager before you can participate. Standard group members can invite others to join, which can help grow your Group faster. In the past, only the manager could invite people to join.

Keeping your Group unlisted can keep the discussions focused and cut down on the unwelcome comments that plague many open social networking sites. This means your group discussions will generally be of higher quality and will be more relevant to members, since a group manager must approve all members. The manager can moderate discussions and remove inappropriate posts or comments, as well as remove people from the Group if they are disruptive or out of line.

When used properly, LinkedIn Groups can be a powerful tool to help grow your business or professional network. Groups can give you the connections you need to reach new industries or markets. You can participate in existing groups as an individual, or you can start your own Group.

In order to create an effective Group, you need to understand how they work and determine the purpose for your Group. Some companies use Groups to support their products, while others use them to build a relationship with prospects or solidify relationships with existing customers.

LINKEDIN GROUPS AREN'T WHAT THEY USED TO BE

Before we continue, I must warn you that the quality of most LinkedIn Groups has declined significantly since I wrote *Ultimate Guide to LinkedIn for Business, Second Edition*. Many Groups have become "spam buckets" and provide little value. Aggressive marketers discovered they could blast articles into multiple Groups every day, giving them exposure and generating business. Over time, they taught this technique to their clients, so now we have Groups with lots of new content every day and almost no interaction between group members.

This is the opposite of what LinkedIn envisioned when it created Groups. The purpose of Groups is to encourage interaction among members so they can help each other out. In 2013, LinkedIn changed the rules and began encouraging group managers to moderate self-promotional content in an effort to curb this behavior, but I am seeing more self-promotional content than ever. Some Groups have hundreds of new posts every day and absolutely no comments, likes, or shares. It's sad to see a valuable resource overwhelmed by aggressive marketers.

The result is many LinkedIn Groups have thousands of members but very little discussion. Most members have stopped participating in Groups. That said, you can still start and manage a successful Group that will generate lots of leads and new clients for your business if you follow my advice. There are plenty of well-managed Groups on LinkedIn where you can still find value.

The good news is LinkedIn is actively trying to resurrect Groups at the time of this writing. Groups you belong to are now displayed in a small widget on your LinkedIn home page in the left column. I'm a member of the LinkedIn Advisors program. I provide input and feedback to LinkedIn features, and there is talk of letting you display new Group posts right in your LinkedIn newsfeed. This hasn't been officially released but I think it would be a great way to increase interaction in Groups.

FINDING QUALITY GROUPS

How many groups should I join? This is one of the most common questions I get about LinkedIn. There are approximately 2 million Groups on LinkedIn at the time of this writing—surprisingly about the same number as when I wrote *Ultimate Guide to LinkedIn for Business, Second Edition*. You may join up to 100 Groups. The problem with joining too many Groups is that you just don't have time to participate in all of them. Another issue with joining a lot of Groups is that you may receive daily or weekly email updates from each one. If you belong to 30 Groups, your inbox will be full of updates that you won't have time to read. You can turn off email notifications from Groups, but then you would have to visit each Group manually to see new discussions.

It comes down to quantity and quality. I believe you can expand your network reach by joining many relevant Groups and by participating in the ones with active conversations. People can see if you are actively participating in a Group, which helps build your reputation and searchability in LinkedIn.

I have to be honest: I belong to at least 40 Groups, but I'm only active in about five. I belong to the others to expand the reach of my network and give me access to people who are 3rd-degree connections. Remember, when you are in a Group, you can message other members even if you aren't 1st-degree connections. However, LinkedIn now limits you to 15 messages per month to group members who are not your 1st-degree connections. That isn't 15 messages per Group—it's 15 messages per month, period.

To keep your membership focused, you can join a Group if you want to learn about a specific subject and leave once you receive the information you need. For example, if you're looking for a new social media monitoring tool, you can join a social media Group and see which products the members are recommending. Ask a few questions so you can make an informed decision when it's time to buy. Once you make the purchase and get the software running properly, leave the Group, since you're unlikely to need their advice again.

Finding Groups

You can search for Groups using the search box in the top toolbar by Groups under the More filter. You can also look under Advanced Search and select Groups to find Groups related to your niche.

LinkedIn has changed the way we search for Groups, and to be honest, it's now harder to find Groups related to your job, position, industry, or skill set. Using LinkedIn Search, you have no way to select keywords related to the Groups and will only see the top Groups when you perform a search with the Groups filter.

To find Groups, you can "enter through the back door," as I call it. From the LinkedIn main menu, select Work and then click on the Groups

LINKEDIN SEARCH TIP

To find the most popular Groups on LinkedIn, click on the empty search box and then the magnifying glass icon. Under the More menu item, select Groups. This will display the most popular LinkedIn Groups and the number of members in each Group, as you can see in Figure 13–1 on page 142.

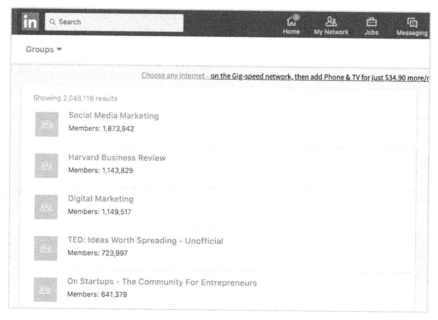

FIGURE 13–1. Search to Find Popular Groups

icon. If you aren't a member of any Groups, LinkedIn will prompt you to Discover some Groups. If you already belong to some, you will see your most active Groups, as shown in Figure 13–2 below.

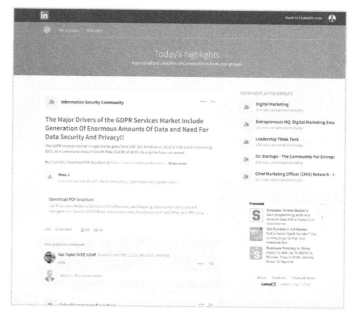

FIGURE 13–2. Accessing Your Groups

Notice many of the Groups seen in Figure 13–2 have a significant number of new conversations today (shown in the right-hand column). The post from the Information Security Community, on the left, has 53 likes and 10 comments in the first week of being posted. This is good news, and I have been seeing more interaction in Groups since LinkedIn announced in February 2018 that it was reintegrating Groups back into the core user experience. Groups are now accessible from the homepage on both desktop and mobile, and as I mentioned above, content shared in Groups may be soon appearing in the main newsfeed.

The new Groups on LinkedIn will feature improved communication tools, including the ability to @ mention other members in conversations (similar to how you would @ mention on Twitter). Whether group owners and managers will have expanded capabilities to monitor conversations remains to be seen at the time of this writing. Expanded content options in Groups, including native video, will also be available.

Evaluating Groups

To effectively use Groups, don't just join the first one that looks interesting. When it comes to professional Groups on LinkedIn, there will usually be several options to choose from, and you need to research the available Groups to find the top three to five in a particular area. If you want to see a directory of every Group on LinkedIn, visit https://www.linkedin.com/groups/. Remember, there are approximately 2 million Groups on LinkedIn, so this directory may seem overwhelming, but it's an easy way to get started.

First, make sure the Group is active. See how many members it has, and check out some of their profiles to see if you know any of them or would want to add them to your network. I believe it's better to join a small Group with the right members than a very large one with people you wouldn't want to connect to.

LinkedIn used to let you preview a Group's discussions before asking to join, which was very useful. Today, you can only see the number of members, a brief description and statement of purpose, the admins, and any of your connections who are in the Group. You have to join the Group to evaluate the content and level of interaction then leave the Group if it's not what you are looking for. Figure 13–3 on page 144 shows a snapshot of the Learning, Education and Training Professionals Group before asking to join.

This Group has 214,076 members. I personally know one of the admins and know all my connections who are in this Group (these are friends, not just LinkedIn connections I've never met). Since this is a large Group and I already know many people, it would be a good choice for me.

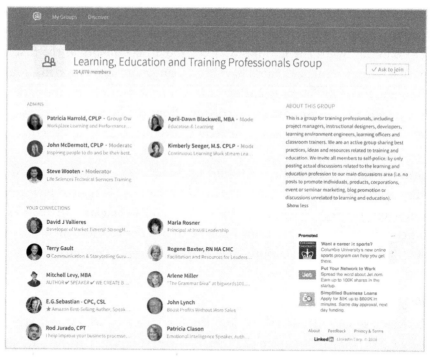

FIGURE 13-3. Details of the Learning, Education and Training Professionals Group

Joining a Group

When you find a Group you want to join, simply click on the Ask to Join button on the listing. A message like the one in Figure 13-4 below will appear, acknowledging your request.

FIGURE 13-4. Automated Response Message

In some cases, you may not be accepted to the Group if you don't meet their membership criteria. For example, let's say you are a marketer and request access to a group of chiropractors. Your goal as a marketer is to meet chiropractors to help them market their business, but the purpose of the Group is for chiropractors to network with each other. Your application to join the Group will probably be rejected.

If you are accepted into the Group, you can adjust your communications preferences by clicking on the three dots next to the group name in the top right corner of your page, then select Update for your settings. See Figure 13-5 on page 145 for your options.

Settings for Group Media & Marketing Professionals Worldwide

Messaging
Choose whether group members in your extended network can message you.

Yes

Display group on profile
This is a standard group. Choose whether this group will appear on your profile for non group members. Learn more

Yes

Communication settings

Emails for all groups ›

In-app notifications for all groups ›

FIGURE 13–5. Email Frequency Settings for Groups

Let's briefly go through each option in Figure 13–5 above so you can optimally configure your group communication settings:

- *Messaging.* You can allow or prevent other group members from messaging you if they are not 1st-degree connections.
- *Display Group on profile.* You can choose whether or not to display this Group in your profile under Interests. I personally display all of my Groups in my profile. If you are actively looking for a new job and you join a job search Group, you can choose not to display this in your profile so your boss doesn't notice.
- *Communications settings.* The next two settings, Email for all groups and in-app notifications for all groups, will redirect you to your Communications settings under Settings & Privacy in your global settings. To reach these settings from the LinkedIn home page, select Me in the main menu. Next, select Settings & Privacy, Communications, Channels, Email Frequency, then Updates from your groups. Choose the Group you want to modify.
- *In-app notifications for all groups:* There are three notification options you can turn on or off. You can be notified in your Notifications tab when your group membership has been approved, when you are invited by another LinkedIn member to join a group, or when posts are shared in a group you belong to. I recommend turning off all three of these notifications so your Notifications tab doesn't get flooded with messages. You can always change the frequency of your Group updates as you see in Figure 13–6 on page 145.

Also choose whether you want to receive group announcements and if you want to be notified of new discussions. Once you save changes, you will be ready to participate (and receive approval from the group manager if it's an Unlisted Group).

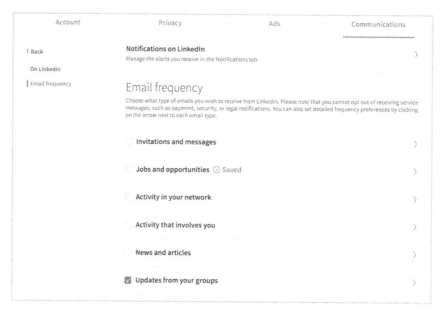

FIGURE 13-6. Global Email Frequency Settings for Groups

WHAT IS THE BEST WAY TO USE GROUPS?

Visiting and following up on your Groups regularly is the only way to effectively use LinkedIn to build your professional network. You need to make frequent and regular appearances within your Group to maximize your exposure. One of the best ways to make sure you are seen is to target the most popular discussions and then be a regular and beneficial contributor to those discussions.

Once you feel comfortable with how a Group works, the next step is to start your own discussion. Choose a topic you are knowledgeable about so you can keep the conversation going. When you start a new discussion, you want it to be as engaging as possible. You can look at a few of the extended conversations in your Group and see how they started. Starting a discussion isn't always about asking a question. You can ask for advice about a specific scenario or post information that would be useful to the target market you are looking to attract. Once you get the conversation started and others are joining in, be sure to reply in a timely fashion. This is when you can change your settings to the daily digest so you know when the conversations are active. Also check in on your discussion a few times a day so you can jump into the conversation when someone comments.

Visit your Groups regularly and participate whenever you can add value to a discussion and keep the conversation going. You can follow people in your Group if you find them interesting; after a while, you can invite them to join your network if you decide they are a good fit.

If you are interested in a particular discussion, you can like it. Your profile picture and a link to your profile will appear below the discussion, showing people you are interested in the topic.

COMMUNICATING WITH GROUP MEMBERS

You can send a message to a group member without being connected and adjust your Messaging settings from within the Group. Here are the rules you can read about on LinkedIn Help:

1. You can send 15 free private messages to fellow group members each month, inclusive of all Groups you are in. If you go over the limit, you'll get an error message. *This means you can't send 15 messages to members of the Real Estate Crowdfunding group and 15 more messages to the Real Estate Investors group. You can only send 15 messages per month total.*

   ▪ Unsent messages don't roll over to the next month. *Use it or lose it!*

   ▪ Only the original message counts toward the limit. Any follow-up replies from either party don't count toward the 15-message allotment. *Message conversations count as one message.*

   ▪ If you need to send more messages for recruiting, promoting, or connecting with members outside your network, LinkedIn offers many alternatives. Please check out the Premium accounts or Recruiter product options, which include InMail messages and recruiting tools to make the most of LinkedIn.

2. You have to be a member of a Group for at least four days. *This is to prevent people from joining a Group and aggressively marketing immediately. The four-day waiting period allows the new member to see what the Group is talking about and get to know some of the members before reaching out through the Group. Of course, you can join a Group, invite a member to connect, and then send them messages through normal LinkedIn Messages.*

3. You have to be a member of LinkedIn for at least 30 days in order to send messages to fellow Group members. *Again, this prevents people from creating a brand-new LinkedIn account and messaging people in Groups immediately.*

Follow these guidelines, and you should be in a good place to connect directly within a Group. But why be satisfied with joining a Group when you can start your own?

HOW TO START A GROUP

Before you start your own Group, you need to decide if you are willing to commit the time to make it a success. Starting a Group is easy, but growing it and keeping it active can take a lot of work, especially in the beginning. I highly recommend you create a team of people who can share in the management and promotion of your Group. As it grows, you can invite a few of the most active members to become Group managers. Most of them will feel honored by the invitation.

The topics you choose to focus on will determine how appealing your Group is and how many members will be interested in joining. Before starting your Group, you should research topics within your niche that generate interest and choose the top two or three as the basis for your Group. Don't just create a carbon copy of exisiting Groups. Find a niche and focus your Group on the niche so you will attract targeted members.

When you start a new Group, you will need to create a profile and a description of the Group, including keywords that will help generate interest in it. Look at some popular LinkedIn Groups, and see how they worded their descriptions, which will help you determine what to say in your group description.

For example, here is the description for the Leadership Think Tank Group, which as of this writing has more than 282,000 members:

About this Group

Leadership Think Tank is a Community committed to collaborating for the improvement of leadership concepts and practices. Our world has entered a new era of relationship between leaders and followers, which very clearly calls for new leaders and a new brand of Leadership in Life and Business.

Gathering a successful community of people is not only helpful, it's necessary to the pursuit of this goal.

So to guide you in this daunting task of picking the right people to join The Leadership Think Tank, I'm going to share with you a four-part checklist:

- *Number One*: Your history. Everyone has something to say. Everyone has something to share. We want to learn from you.
- *Number Two*: Your interest level. If you are interested in improving yourself and others, you are probably a good prospect. Sometimes people can fake their interest, but we have enough members who will be a able to judge whether you are merely pretending.
- *Number Three*: Your responses. Response tells us a lot about someone's integrity, character, and skills. A person's responses are good indications of his or her character. Our attitudes reflect our inner selves, so even if we can fool others for a while, eventually our true selves will emerge.
- *Number Four*: Your results. The name of the game is results. How else can we effectively judge an individual's performance? The final judge must be results. So share yours!

Remember, building a good community will be one of our most challenging tasks, but it will bring multiple rewards for a long time to come.

As you see, they clearly state the purpose and vision of their community. They describe the perfect member of the Group and encourage members to invite other leaders to join the Group.

Group Settings

LinkedIn streamlined its Group settings and removed the moderation tools. Group settings options are shown in Figure 13–7. By clicking on the three dots next to each member's name, the Group administrator or manager can connect with that member if they aren't connected, promote them to manager status, or remove and/ or block them from the Group if they are disruptive. There is no way to moderate content, but the administrator or manager can remove content and/or disable comments on a post.

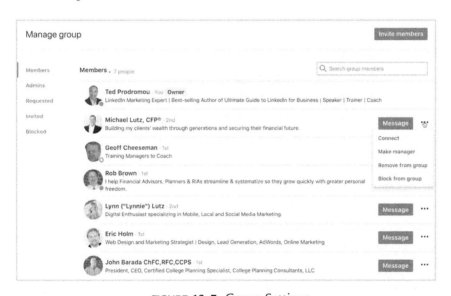

FIGURE 13–7. Group Settings

In my experience, standard Groups with thousands of members can become unfocused if the group manager doesn't participate actively. A good group manager can keep the Group focused by starting new discussions, featuring popular discussions that are relevant to the topic, and privately contacting members who are posting off-topic discussions. It also helps to have multiple managers for a large, standard Group.

Engaging Your Group with Focused Discussions

There are all sorts of ways to keep your Group active using discussions as a way to connect. For example, the discussions in product-related communities are amazingly focused and on topic. You don't see many people asking questions about other Adobe products or competitors' products in the Photoshop communities because the members are knowledgeable enough to keep the discussions focused. If someone does start a discussion that is not relevant to the Group, a group member or manager will often respond and suggest a better place to post that question. These Groups are often self-policing and self-supporting, which makes the community much stronger and more vibrant.

Unlisted Groups, on the other hand, are by nature smaller and more focused, since every member is manually approved by the group manager. You usually don't have as many new discussions or comments, but the discussions are very focused. You also have a small community of experts who are very knowledgeable about specific products or topics.

Open Vs. Closed Groups

It's up to you to decide if your Group will be open (standard) or closed (unlisted). You can start a standard Group and change it to unlisted or vice versa. Groups often start out open or closed and later decide to switch. Here are some questions that may help you decide how to structure your Group:

- What is your Group's purpose (e.g., building loyalty, providing support, networking)?
- Is your product or service mainstream or is it a niche product/service?
- How many members do you estimate your Group will have? If your company has 2,000 current customers, you wouldn't expect your Group to have 10,000 members.
- How many group managers will you have?
- How many new discussions and comments per week do you expect?
- How fast do you expect your Group to grow?
- How will you promote your Group?

There are a lot of factors that come into play when deciding how to structure your Group, and it's imperative to have a plan and a goal before you begin. Your reputation and your company's reputation are on the line when you create a Group; if it's unfocused or unmanaged, it will reflect poorly on you. Identify your Group's purpose, allocate sufficient resources, and create a detailed plan so it will thrive and provide value to your company.

Promoting the Group

LinkedIn has removed the ability to promote your Group by sending mass messages. Now you have to manually promote it using status updates, running LinkedIn ads, or sending LinkedIn messages to your connections.

The best way to invite people to join is by sending an invitation with a personal message to let them know who you are and why you want them to join the Group.

It is acceptable to encourage your members to invite their friends to join if they use personalized messages. You can then approve or decline new invitations as you see fit.

If you want to grow your Group quickly, you can start promoting it via social media. You can tweet links to your Group, post an invitation on your Facebook wall, and blog about it. Encourage people to join and invite their friends. You can also run ads on LinkedIn to promote your Group. I'll show you how to create effective LinkedIn ads in Chapters 20 and 21.

MANAGING THE GROUP

Consistent management is really the key to a strong Group. A good community manager will monitor, facilitate, and grow their Group.

I highly recommend creating rules for your Group and posting them under Group Rules and in a Featured Discussion in your LinkedIn Group. Establishing the guidelines for posting and displaying them prominently are easy ways to help new members get acquainted with your Group. Such guidelines generally provide users with community contacts, encourage them to post only relevant information, and specify conduct that can get them banned. (These usually include things like spamming, excessive self-promotion, abusing other members, and other rules that will keep your Group safe for all members.)

Here is an example of a well-crafted set of rules from Leadership Think Tank Group:

1. We hope the conversations that take place on Leadership Think Tank will be energetic, constructive, free-wheeling, and provocative. To make sure we all stay on-topic, posts might be reviewed by our editors.

2. We ask that you adhere to the following guidelines: No ad hominem attacks. These are conversations in which we debate ideas. Criticize ideas, not the people behind them.

3. It is our challenge to find good people to help us accomplish and make Leadership Think Tank a great place. So gathering the right people is not only helpful, but necessary.

4. Remember, building a great environment will be one of our most challenging tasks. It will bring multiple rewards for a long time to come.

5. Make sure your conversations are in the right place—anything regarding JOBS goes in the JOBS section—anything regarding LEADERSHIP goes in the DISCUS-SIONS section.

6. All conversations placed in the wrong section will be flagged and deleted. You may also lose your membership.

7. Group settings:

   - Discussions and new features are enabled to all members
   - LinkedIn is allowed to move discussions automatically to job
   - Members of Leadership Think Tank are free to post
   - Anyone on LinkedIn is free to post comments and submit discussions for approval; submissions are reviewed periodically
   - New group members require moderation during 1 day
   - New people on LinkedIn require moderation for 5 days
   - People with few or no connections require moderation and approval
   - Content is automatically removed when flagged as inappropriate by group members. Number of flags: 5 flags. Discussions and comments cannot be retrieved once removed.

8. Let the conversations flow.

As you see, the rules are clear and simple. If you violate them, you will be removed from the Group. This is a great example you can use to create your own rules.

When you add a new member, LinkedIn automatically emails them the group rules. If someone violates the rules for a Group I'm running, I send that person a copy of the rules and point out how they are violating them. If they continue to break the rules, I remove them from the Group and block them from being able to reapply.

As a group manager, you're also responsible for getting discussions started and helping to keep them going. As you read earlier in the chapter, discussions keep your members actively engaged.

Group Etiquette

Most LinkedIn members joined to expand their professional network, gain social influence, and increase the visibility of their business. For this reason, people generally follow the rules to present a professional image to their peers and prospects. As group manager, you are empowered to resolve difficulties with any members who decide they do not want to follow the rules. You need to act quickly to resolve issues and ensure that your members have an enjoyable experience as a part of your LinkedIn Group.

You set the tone for the discussions. If you do not want to see a certain kind of language used, you need to make that clear in the rules. The ideal tone for discussions in a Group—especially a business-related one—should be professional. Most of the time this is the case, but there will be occasional exceptions. If you see inappropriate conduct, remove the post immediately and contact the offender. Explain why their post was offensive and remove them from your Group if they refuse to obey the rules.

CONCLUSION

Remember: The image of your Group reflects directly upon you and your company. You need to maintain a high standard and a high-quality reputation.

If you are not the group manager, it is also important to respect that role. If both group managers and members follow the rules, the LinkedIn Group experience can be rewarding for all.

In the next chapter, we will learn how to manage your LinkedIn connections and remain top of mind with key decision-makers.

**For additional updates and how-to videos, visit
https://tedprodromou.com/UltimateGuideUpdates/.**

Managing Your LinkedIn Connections

A s your LinkedIn network grows, you will want to keep track of the people being added. LinkedIn provides some great tools to help you monitor your network. You can see a snapshot of your LinkedIn network, which includes the total number of connections, as well as 2nd- and 3rd-degree connections. With two people joining LinkedIn every second, your network two and three degrees away can grow very quickly. You'll also see the total users you can contact through Introductions.

As you see in Figure 14–1 on page 156, I have 15,867 1st-degree connections in my network. I can reach these professionals through an introduction or an InMail, which is unbelievable. Where else do you have access to so many targeted resources?

Each time I add someone as a 1st-degree connection, my network grows exponentially, because their entire network becomes part of my 2nd-degree connections. LinkedIn used to show us how many people were part of our 2nd- and 3rd-degree connections in a dashboard, but now we have to look this up manually using LinkedIn Search.

To see your entire network, click in the Search box and select People. I have 15,867 1st-degree connections, and my total network size is 8,819,876 people, as you see in Figure 14–2 on page 157. Now, I select 2nd under the Connections button and can see that I have 843,818 2nd-degree

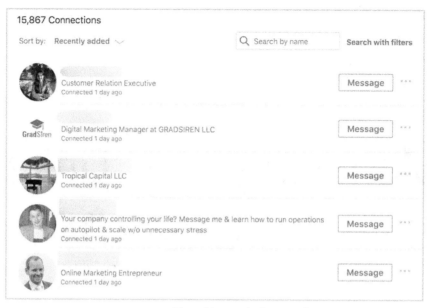

FIGURE 14–1. Your Network Connections

connections. Remember that they are essentially "friends of my friends," so getting introduced to them is relatively easy. That's the power of exponential networking on LinkedIn.

USING NOTIFICATIONS TO ENGAGE YOUR NETWORK

To increase engagement, LinkedIn added a feature where you can congratulate people when they get a new job or when it's their birthday. I log into LinkedIn every morning and spend five to ten minutes congratulating people or saying happy birthday. This may seem trivial, but when you do this, the people are notified that you reached out, and it puts you top of mind with them. I've had students land big deals with people by doing this after not communicating with them for years. You can easily access this feature by navigating to Notifications on your main menu, as you can see in Figure 14–3 on page 158.

SYNCING LINKEDIN WITH GOOGLE CALENDAR AND CONTACTS

Another way to manage your LinkedIn life is to link it. I don't recommend sending mass invitations, but you can automatically sync your Google Calendar and Google Contacts with your LinkedIn account, as you see in Figure 14–4 on page 159. LinkedIn will try to match the email addresses in your Google Contacts with existing LinkedIn members so you can connect with them and maintain a synchronized address book. When you are

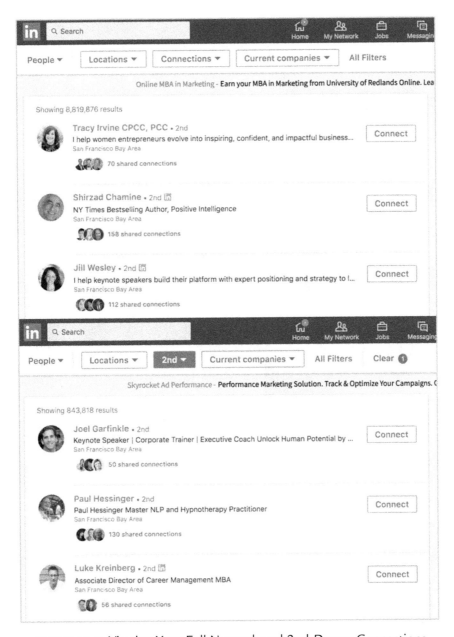

FIGURE 14–2. Viewing Your Full Network and 2nd-Degree Connections

setting up an appointment through LinkedIn Messaging, LinkedIn will automatically look for available appointment times on your Google Calendar and suggest possible times in the message. LinkedIn plans to roll out numerous intelligent "bots" in the near future to automate many of our daily scheduling and messaging tasks. It is also working on extensively integrating the site with Microsoft's flagship Office 365 and Dynamics CRM.

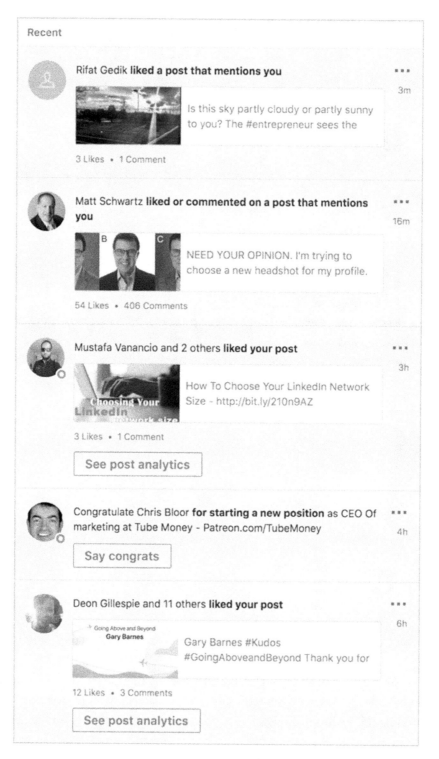

FIGURE 14–3. Your Notifications

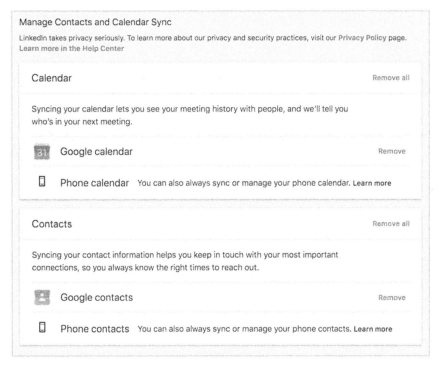

Manage Contacts and Calendar Sync

LinkedIn takes privacy seriously. To learn more about our privacy and security practices, visit our Privacy Policy page. Learn more in the Help Center

Calendar   Remove all

Syncing your calendar lets you see your meeting history with people, and we'll tell you who's in your next meeting.

31   Google calendar   Remove

⎕   Phone calendar   You can also always sync or manage your phone calendar. **Learn more**

Contacts   Remove all

Syncing your contact information helps you keep in touch with your most important connections, so you always know the right times to reach out.

⊟   Google contacts   Remove

⎕   Phone contacts   You can also always sync or manage your phone contacts. **Learn more**

FIGURE 14–4. Google Calendar and Google Contacts Synchronization

You can set up the automated sync, or you can choose to just import your Google Contacts into LinkedIn. This is a quick way to grow your network with people you already know or are doing business with.

Here is how LinkedIn says to sync your contacts:

1. Click the My Network icon at the top of your homepage.
2. Click See All below Your Connections on the left rail.
3. Click Manage Synced and Imported Contacts near the upper right corner of the page.
4. Click Manage Contacts Syncing on the right rail of the Manage Your Contacts page to see your synced sources, or click Sync next to any source you'd like to sync from the pop-up window.

To import a contacts file:

1. Click the My Network icon at the top of your LinkedIn homepage.
2. Click See All below Your Connections on the left rail.
3. Click More Options below the Continue button on the right rail.
4. Click Upload a File on the right rail.
5. Select the file you'd like to upload and click Open.

Your contacts will be imported into LinkedIn and you will be able to easily connect with these contacts if they are not already part of your network.

CONCLUSION

The power of networking on LinkedIn is limitless. There is no other resource that lets you reach so many business professionals with a few clicks of your mouse. The Notification feature prompts you when your connections share content, have birthdays, or change jobs so you can quickly reach out to them and remain top of mind.

In the next chapter, we'll explore publishing and content marketing, so you can share your expertise with your network, company followers, and everyone else on LinkedIn.

For additional updates and how-to videos, visit
https://tedprodromou.com/UltimateGuideUpdates/.

Chapter 15

The Definitive Publishing Platform

I n a 2014 interview on CNBC, LinkedIn CEO Jeff Weiner stated that, at the time, LinkedIn wanted to maintain focus on the company's "core value propositions, professional identity, and making sure that the profile meets the needs of all of our members." He also made it clear that one of his goals was to make LinkedIn more than just a site for connection, but rather, "the definitive professional publishing platform."

LinkedIn has since delivered on that promise. Today, more than 100,000 unique articles and pieces of multimedia content are shared on LinkedIn every day. This content appears in the LinkedIn newsfeed as well as in Google search results. LinkedIn pushes the content to its partner networks as well, so the article you share on LinkedIn is now appearing all over the internet.

LinkedIn's transition to focusing on becoming a world-class content publishing platform and creating a better user experience resulted in the complete overhaul of its desktop and mobile applications beginning in late 2016. LinkedIn wanted to make it easier for users to see relevant content and filter out content that didn't interest them. That meant big changes for LinkedIn, starting with Pulse.

LinkedIn bought the news app Pulse in 2013 for $90 million, integrating its content into the desktop version and using it to enhance the mobile app. Pulse was a very popular news aggregating app that let you create customized newsfeeds. You could quickly and easily scan the app to see breaking news, industry-related content, and entertainment. You could subscribe to your favorite news sources, like *The New York Times, The Wall Street Journal,* ESPN, and other major news outlets. You could even subscribe to specific content channels like Entrepreneur Media so you always saw only content relevant to you.

Pulse was relatively short-lived. As part of the overhaul, LinkedIn Pulse and the Pulse app were retired in May 2017. If you post an article on LinkedIn now, it appears in your connections' newsfeeds. In 2018, LinkedIn expanded the reach of your content, so it can also be seen by anyone on LinkedIn and their partner networks, as well as Google. People no longer need to be a 1st-degree connection to view your content.

The elimination of Pulse was part of LinkedIn's consolidation of its numerous apps, which were integrated into its core user experience. The mobile app was expanded so the primary functions of networking, messaging, and your newsfeed were easily accessible. In the past, LinkedIn had up to six different apps performing very specific tasks, which confused many users, so the new integration was a needed improvement. The move paid off. After the launch of the new mobile app, LinkedIn messaging increased 83 percent in the first year.

Now, with everything integrated, you have even more control over what you publish, where you publish it, and—most importantly—who can see it.

CONTROLLING YOUR CONTENT

In addition to controlling which content you see on the LinkedIn newsfeed, you can now control who sees the content you share as status updates or as articles.

When you post a status update, an article, or a video, you can control who can see it by using the drop-down menu, which magically appears below the your name as you type your update. You can select: Public, Public + Twitter, or Connections.

If you choose Public, your post will appear on:

1. The newsfeed of your 1st-degree connections
2. The newsfeed of your 2nd- or 3rd-degree connections if one of your 1st-degree connections reshared, commented upon, or liked the post
3. Content search results for keywords contained in the content you've posted
4. Search results for hashtags you've used in posts or in the newsfeed of people subscribed to those hashtags
5. Your Activity page, which you see when you click on Who's Viewed Your Posts
6. Your public profile, which is also visible to people who are not signed in to LinkedIn and in Google search results

7. Other sites off LinkedIn, which is called the Partner Network. This includes sites like Bing, Google, and Yahoo!

8. Your followers' feeds. Followers can see your content and activity like a 1st-degree connection, but they cannot message you without using InMail

Your connections' feeds are personalized for them based on people they follow, their connections, and their engagement on LinkedIn. Posts that are professionally relevant will benefit from organic distribution through your network with community engagement, such as likes, comments, and shares, allowing your content to reach the largest group of professionals. One of the most organic ways you can reach your intended audience is with your status updates.

STATUS UPDATES

LinkedIn status updates are a quick way for you to share short updates or article snippets with links to the full article. LinkedIn prompts you to "Share an article, photo, video, or idea" in the status update box, as shown in Figure 15-1.

FIGURE 15-1. LinkedIn Status Update

The character limit for a status update is 1,300 characters, which includes links, hashtags, and tagging other LinkedIn members. You can add an image, a link to additional content, a link to a YouTube video, or a native video MP4 file directly to your status update.

LinkedIn wants to keep people on the site, so it is encouraging users to upload video directly into the status update instead of adding a link to a YouTube video. The LinkedIn algorithm also rewards users for not adding external links to their status updates by receiving more views; it may also be shown to relevant 2nd- and 3rd-degree connections.

In Figure 15-2 on page 164, you see a status update by my friend and client, Doreen Hamilton. She uploaded a short video describing her "Seven Secrets to Fearless Speaking," and offered a free PDF if you commented on her post. Doreen also included numerous targeted hashtags, which helps push her status update to everyone who follows those hashtags.

Doreen Hamilton, Ph.D.
Are you afraid to speak up in public? I can show you how to be authentic and confident!
3w • Edited

Please type "7 Secrets" in the comments and I'll send you my 7 Secrets to Fearless Speaking (PDF, no opt-in). *Make sure we are connected so I can message it to you easily.*

My video and the PDF present a unique approach to overcoming the fear of public speaking. Genuine presence and authentic connection keep you calm and centered.

This will help If you hold back from #publicspeaking because of #anxiety #stagefright or if you are in #leadership. The secrets will increase your #confidence. #Managers #Coaches #SmallBusiness #Entrepreneurs #Authenticity #Mindfulness #Psychologist #Introverts #howto #toastmasters #publicspeakingfear #RelationalPresence #authors #sales #CEOs #ExecutivePresence #SpeakingTips

0:24/2:24

FIGURE 15–2. A Sample LinkedIn Status Update with Native Video

The result? At the time of this writing, Doreen has received more than 5,000 video views in just a couple of weeks. More than 300 people requested the PDF, and she has more than 150 new 1st-degree connections who were previously 2nd- or 3rd-degree connections who saw this post thanks to her hashtags. This is a powerful way to let the LinkedIn algorithm get your status updates to your target audience.

ARTICLES

LinkedIn articles are the new Pulse. In the past, articles appeared under the URL www.linkedin.com/pulse, where you could see all your subscribed content on one screen. Today, it appears in your newsfeed. To be honest, I'm not a big fan of the change because I often miss important content in my very busy newsfeed. I would prefer to see my subscribed content on a separate page like the old Pulse page (are you listening, LinkedIn? LOL).

Publishing LinkedIn articles is a great way to establish yourself as an industry leader because millions of people can potentially see your content on LinkedIn and millions more may see it on Google and LinkedIn's partner networks. LinkedIn doesn't specifically say which websites are part of their partner networks, but I do know Bing is one of the bigger sites. I often see LinkedIn articles when I do Google searches on specific topics. This is because Google loves quality content, and it considers LinkedIn a trusted source.

When you add LinkedIn hashtags to your articles, everyone who is subscribed to those hashtags will potentially see your article in their newsfeed, even if they are not 1st-degree connections. For example, if you add the hashtag #publishing to your post, the more than 4.5 million LinkedIn members who are subscribed to that hashtag can potentially see your article. Make sure to use hashtags that are related to your article topic so you are attracting the right readers. When you are ready to publish an article on LinkedIn, click on the Write an Article button in the status update box. See Figure 15–1 on page 163. Here are the character limits for a LinkedIn article:

- Post headline: 150
- Post body text: no limit

I like to add at least one image per page in the body of the article. As people scroll through your article, the image breaks up the text and makes it easier to read. I also like to add my bio with links for additional, related content or a call to action at the end of each article.

Remember, most people are reading on their smartphones, so don't feel you need to write *War and Peace*. I like to write shorter, focused articles and send people to my website if they want more information.

Many of my clients and students ask me what they should write about in their LinkedIn articles. I always ask them what stories or news items they're seeing in their newsfeed. Popular stories will trend upward as they go viral and more people read them. The LinkedIn algorithm detects trending topics and places the stories in the newsfeeds of other members, multiplying the effect. If you can write an article that gets the attention of a high percentage of your 1st-degree connections (with views, likes, and comments), LinkedIn will push it to your 2nd- and 3rd-degree connections.

An easy way to see the most popular content on LinkedIn is to do a search using the Content filter, as shown in Figure 15-3. Sort your search by relevance, and you see a post shared by Susan Cain, which has 2,121 likes and 144 comments. If this content is relevant to your niche, you can write a similar article, since you know your network is interested in this topic.

You can also do a content search and add keyword phrases to narrow your search to your niche. If cloud computing is your niche, enter "cloud computing" in the search box and select the Content filter. You will now see cloud computing–related content being shared by your network. You can also enter popular hashtags in the search box to see new and popular content related to that hashtag.

Don't forget to keep an eye on What People Are Talking About Now in the right column of your homepage. These are trending national and international stories. When you write relevant articles related to breaking news, you can often piggyback off that trending topic.

WHO'S VIEWED YOUR UPDATES

In the past, we posted status updates and articles but had no idea how many people viewed them or if they were engaging. With the new site analytics, we can see how many people viewed, liked, shared, and commented on our updates and articles. I love this feature because I know exactly what content my network is engaging with so I can create more of it.

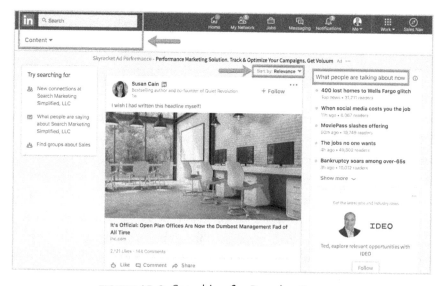

FIGURE 15-3. Searching for Popular Content

FIGURE 15–4. Who's Viewed Your Updates

To see Who's Viewed Your Updates, go to the LinkedIn homepage and click on Views of Your Post, which is in the left column. You will then see who is interacting with your articles, posts, and all other activity, as you see in Figure 15–4.

NATIVE VIDEO

Native video is video you have created and uploaded directly to LinkedIn. In the past, we had to upload our video to YouTube or other video websites and then include a YouTube link in our LinkedIn posts to share with our network. LinkedIn now prefers native video directly uploaded to its site.

According to a 2017 survey by social media marketing website Social Media Examiner, 73 percent of marketers plan to use video in their marketing. Marketers love video because it naturally does what all content should do: It shows instead of tells.

Video boosts your storytelling ability using visuals, text, and audio. Marketers can now harness the power of sight, sound, and motion to get across their messages on LinkedIn. The newsfeed is an attractive format for a range of videos, such as product demos, interviews, industry event coverage, how-to videos, and more.

Video helps you stand out on the newsfeed because it naturally attracts the eye. People cannot resist sight, sound, and motion, so use it to your advantage by posting native videos. Using LinkedIn analytics, you can measure engagement of your videos. You can see the top companies, job titles, and locations of your viewers. You can also see how many views, likes, and comments your videos are receiving.

Most of us will be creating and uploading MP4 files using our phones or video cameras, so we don't usually need to worry about the other formats below.

But if you are a professional videographer and doing advanced video creation, LinkedIn videos can also be ASF, AVI, FLV, MPEG-1, MPEG-4, MKV, QuickTime, WebM, H264/AVC, VP8, VP9, WMV2, and WMV3. You can also upload the following audio extensions: AAC, MP3, and Vorbis.

What are the file requirements for the video? Here's a quick look at the specs listed on LinkedIn:

1. Max file size: 5GB
2. Minimum file size: 75KB
3. Max video duration: 10 minutes
4. Minimum video duration: 3 seconds
5. Resolution range: 256x144 to 4096x2304
6. Aspect ratio: 1:2.4–2.4:1
7. Frame rates: 10fps–60 fps
8. Bit rates: 192 kbps–30 Mbps

Remember, people have short attention spans so it's a good idea to keep your videos shorter than three minutes.

Add text (up to 700 characters) to your update to describe your video. (You can do this before or after you upload the video.) Be sure to include talking points to encourage people to watch. For example, outline the steps for a how-to video, or write a short update that teases the content and links to a longer blog or a LinkedIn article.

To upload a native video from your desktop, click on the Video button in the status update box (which you saw in Figure 15–1, where you read about posting status updates), browse to your file location, select your video (or audio for podcasters), add your descriptive text and hashtags, and click Post.

To publish a native video from your mobile device, open the LinkedIn app. In the share box on the home screen, tap the video camera icon, as shown in Figure 15–5 on page 170. On the next screen, choose a prerecorded video from your camera roll or click Video to record a video on the spot (your video will automatically be saved to your camera roll).

BROADCASTING LIVE VIDEO

Uploaded video can be useful, but to really capture the zeitgeist of the moment, go live. You can now create live video broadcasts from the LinkedIn mobile app, just like Facebook Live videos. At the time of this writing, live video is not available from the desktop version of LinkedIn and is only available to LinkedIn Influencers on the mobile app. Eventually everyone will be able to share live video.

When live video is available to everyone, you can start your own live video broadcast in the LinkedIn mobile app. Look for the share box at the top of the feed (iOS) or the Post button (Android) and tap on the video icon (see Figure 15–5 on page 170). You can record a video in the app or upload something you recorded earlier.

After you post a video, you can see audience insights, such as the top companies, titles, and locations of your viewers, as well as how many views, likes, and comments your videos are receiving. With these insights, you can begin to understand if you're reaching the people and companies that matter to you. You can find audience insights in the dashboard section of your LinkedIn profile on both mobile and desktop. You'll learn more about LinkedIn mobile apps in the next chapter.

CONCLUSION

Jeff Weiner has delivered on his promise to make LinkedIn the largest content publishing platform on the internet. Today, more than 100,000 articles and videos are

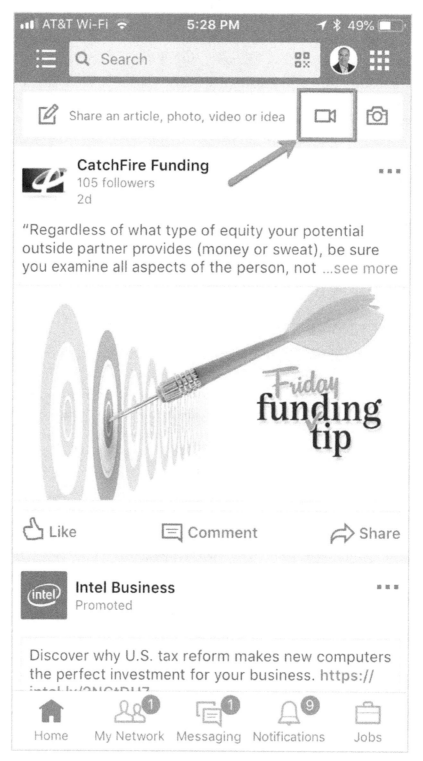

FIGURE 15–5. Uploading Video from Your Mobile Device

shared on LinkedIn every day. You can create and share content that can be seen by your target audience on LinkedIn and throughout the internet via partner networks and Google.

In the next chapter, we will explore LinkedIn Mobile and LinkedIn's flagship app for mobile access.

**For additional updates and how-to videos, visit
https://tedprodromou.com/UltimateGuideUpdates/.**

LinkedIn Mobile

As the world migrates to mobile computing, LinkedIn has been developing apps to meet the demand. According to LinkedIn, more than 60 percent of their members use the mobile app to access the site. This is a huge shift from just a couple of years ago, when people spent most of their time on desktop computers.

LinkedIn has been shifting back and forth with its mobile app strategy. When I wrote the first edition of *Ultimate Guide to LinkedIn for Business*, there were numerous third-party apps that competed with LinkedIn's first attempt at a mobile app. The LinkedIn app was bloated and slow because it tried to provide access to all its tools. The result was that very few people used it.

Next, LinkedIn created multiple apps that provided access to very specific functions of the desktop version. Pulse, Groups, Connected, Students, Card Munch, Blog Link, Projects, and Reading List were just a few of the available apps. The vast number of apps confused users.

In 2017, LinkedIn redesigned the desktop version and mobile app to focus on the core user experience. Most people use LinkedIn to catch up on industry news, interact with other members via messaging, keep in touch with past and current clients, and see what their network is up to.

This new focus has increased usage of LinkedIn. Easy accessibility and the clean design give people a reason to come back to LinkedIn every day. More than 50 percent of Facebook's users log in every day, with the highest traffic occurring between 1 and 3 P.M. LinkedIn aims to match this incredible user engagement. According to a LinkedIn presentation, one year after the new app was released, there was a 30 percent increase in daily mobile app activity, a 40 percent increase in engaged newsfeed sessions, and a 240 percent increase in messages sent from the mobile app. You can view the presentation at https://www.slideshare.net/linkedin/accelerating-linkedins-vision-through-innovation-66309292.

In this chapter, I'll introduce you to a few of the most popular mobile LinkedIn tools. All these apps are free to download and will enhance your LinkedIn experience.

LINKEDIN MOBILE APP

LinkedIn has developed apps for the iPhone and Android smartphones. (The Blackberry and Windows versions are officially retired.) The LinkedIn app is free and connects you seamlessly to your LinkedIn account from your phone. See Figure 16–1 on page 175 to see what LinkedIn mobile app looks like on your iPhone and iPad.

The app is well-designed, fast, and easy to use. It lets you check messages, invite people to connect, review updates, and send messages to your connections.

At the bottom of the screen, you have easy access to your primary LinkedIn functions: Home, My Network, Messaging, Notifications, and Jobs. This is about 80 percent of what I use LinkedIn for. When I'm on Home, I scan my newsfeed to see what's happening with my network, breaking industry news, and content from people and companies I follow. On the My Network tab, I see new invitations to connect, potential new connections under People You May Know, and my total number of connections, as you can see in the left graphic of Figure 16–2 on page 176. When I'm at a live event, I can also turn on Find Nearby, which looks for other people at the conference or event who have this feature turned on. You can connect with other conference attendees instantly. Don't worry about your privacy: People will not see your location if you don't enable this feature.

As you see in the middle graphic of Figure 16–2, LinkedIn Messaging is a powerful way to start conversations with connections who could become clients or great referral partners. In the right graphic is Notifications, where you see who's interacting with your posts, accepting your connection invitations, and having job anniversaries or birthdays.

ULTIMATE GUIDE TO LINKEDIN FOR BUSINESS

FIGURE 16–1. The LinkedIn Mobile App

CHAPTER 16 / LINKEDIN MOBILE   **175**

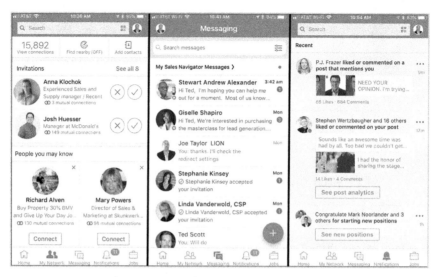

FIGURE 16–2. The My Network, Messaging, and Notifications Tabs

The app also lets you update your profile and see your network statistics, including Who's Viewed Your Profile, Post Views, and the number of times you appeared in searches. In Figure 16–3 on page 177 you can see how to edit different sections of your profile by clicking on the pencil icon in each section.

LINKEDIN JOB SEARCH

Approximately two-thirds of LinkedIn's revenue comes from job postings and recruiter's subscriptions, so, of course, it has an app to help you find a job. LinkedIn Job Search is one separate app that is successful, so it's not going away any time soon. This app lets you easily search for great jobs, see who you know at that company, and apply in one click using the data from your LinkedIn profile. You will also receive notifications when new jobs that fit your search criteria are posted so you can get a jump on your competitors.

While applying via the app is easy, it's not 100 percent hands-off in terms of being able to simply link to your profile. Not all job postings will let you apply through LinkedIn. The employer chooses whether to let you apply through LinkedIn or redirect you to their external website. However, the Job Search app will let you save the job posting so you can apply when you get back to your desktop computer, which is easier than filling out an application on your phone. Check out Figure 16–4 on page 178 for a look at the Job Search app.

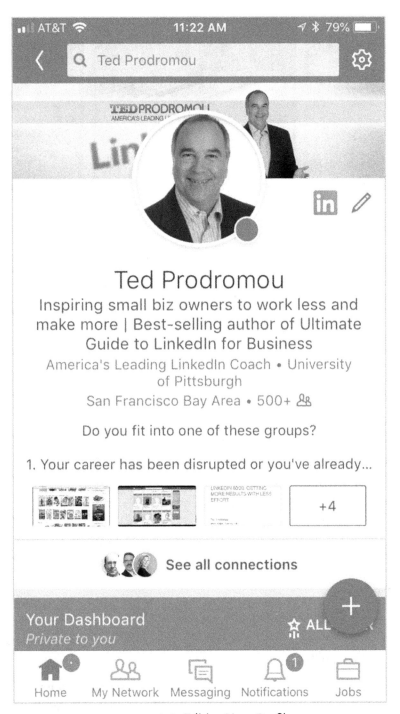

FIGURE 16–3. Editing Your Profile

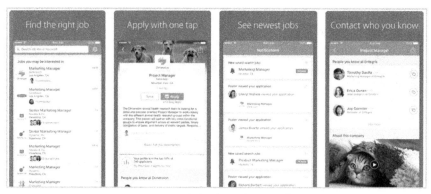

FIGURE 16–4. LinkedIn Job Search App

LINKEDIN SLIDESHARE

Another one of LinkedIn's hidden gems that works well on mobile is SlideShare. SlideShare is an app and a website where you can upload PowerPoint slide decks, infographics, PDFs, and documents. Here are the accepted formats according to LinkedIn:

Presentations

- Adobe PDF (.pdf)
- OpenOffice Presentation Document (.odp)
- Microsoft PowerPoint (.ppt/.pps/.pptx/.ppsx/.pot/.potx)

Documents

- Adobe PDF (.pdf)
- Microsoft Word (.doc/ .docx/ .rtf)
- OpenOffice Documents (.odt)
- Most .txt files

Infographics

- Adobe PDF (.pdf)

You can also upload video if it's included in your presentation, but you can't upload video directly to SlideShare. Figure 16–5 on page 179 shows you a sample of the content available to view and download from the SlideShare app.

FIGURE 16-5. The SlideShare App

LINKEDIN LEARNING

LinkedIn acquired online learning platform Lynda.com in April 2015 for $1.5 billion and integrated its content into LinkedIn Learning in 2017. LinkedIn Learning has thousands of online courses and videos covering every aspect of business. Content is categorized under Subjects, Software, and Learning Paths. Figure 16–6 shows you just some of the training available on LinkedIn Learning.

You receive full access to LinkedIn Learning when you have a premium account. If you don't have a premium account, you can subscribe to LinkedIn Learning for $29.95 per month or purchase an annual subscription for $299.88. The Learning app is free to download, but you need a premium account or a subscription to access the content.

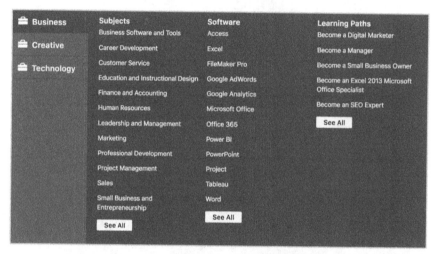

FIGURE 16–6. A Sample of What You Can Learn on LinkedIn Learning

You can stream courses or download them for offline viewing from the mobile app. I often download classes and watch them when I'm traveling to speaking engagements.

PREMIUM APPS

LinkedIn also has several premium apps that are worth checking out (and that may be worth paying the cost of premium for, depending on your needs). These apps work only with the appropriate paid subscriptions, so be sure to check their terms.

LinkedIn Recruiter

The Recruiter app lets you access the tools in your LinkedIn Recruiter subscription. The app lets you search and review the profiles of potential hires, respond quickly to

FIGURE 16–7. The LinkedIn Recruiter App

candidates, and stay organized with projects. While it is not a replacement for the full desktop version of Recruiter, it allows you to stay in touch while you are away from your computer. Figure 16–7 shows you some screenshots from the LinkedIn Recruiter app so you can see what the interface looks like.

LinkedIn Sales Navigator

Sales Navigator is LinkedIn's flagship tool for sales professionals, which helps you find leads and accounts in your target market, connect or send messages to prospects, and get real-time updates while you are on the road. In Chapter 19, I'll go deep into the possibilities of the full Sales Navigator subscription, one of the most powerful tools out there for salespeople. For now, take a look at Figure 16–8 below to see the top features of the app.

With Sales Navigator, you can follow targeted companies and key members of those organizations so you hear instantly about breaking news or key personnel changes.

FIGURE 16–8. The Sales Navigator App

You can quickly reach out with InMail if you're not connected or send free LinkedIn messages to check in with them.

You can also create targeted LinkedIn searches with expanded search fields that run 24/7 and alert you once a day when they find an ideal prospect. Simply open the alert and view the potential client's LinkedIn profile to decide if you want to connect and begin a business relationship.

You need a paid subscription to Sales Navigator to use this app. LinkedIn offers a professional version for individual users at around $80 per month and a version for corporate sales teams at around $130 per month per person at the time of this writing. Visit https://business.linkedin.com/sales-solutions/sales-navigator to see the latest service offerings and pricing.

LinkedIn Elevate

LinkedIn Elevate is a tool for large companies that create and share a lot of content on social media. This app is only available to employees at participating companies. Visit https://business.linkedin.com/elevate for more information.

As employees create social media content for your company, they add it to the Elevate app so everyone in the company can share it on their social media accounts. This is a great way to create a viral effect on social media if enough employees share it in a timely manner. With a huge initial boost from your employees, social media networks see the content trending, so they boost the content to millions of other people.

LinkedIn Elevate lets you:

- Receive quality, approved content that you can easily share with your networks
- Help you reach your network at the best time to boost your impact
- See how your network is responding with detailed analytics

See Figure 16–9 to see how LinkedIn Elevate works.

FIGURE 16–9. The LinkedIn Elevate App

CONCLUSION

LinkedIn has spent a lot of time and money redesigning its dashboard and apps to make its user experience easy and engaging. LinkedIn's app strategy has changed a lot over the years, but its recent focus on the core user experience is bringing members back to the website and to its apps more frequently.

In the next chapter, I'll show you how to find and hire great employees using LinkedIn's powerful recruiting tools.

For additional updates and how-to videos, visit
https://tedprodromou.com/UltimateGuideUpdates/.

Chapter 17

Recruiting New Employees

LinkedIn has become a gold mine for recruiting firms and in-house recruiters. Nowhere else can they find millions of businesspeople in one place prominently displaying their experience, skills, education, recommendations, and expertise. A simple search on LinkedIn can locate multiple qualified candidates in seconds. As the site grows, the available talent pool multiplies, allowing companies to pick and choose from among the very best business professionals in the world. No longer is a talent search limited to your local area.

Recruiting new employees isn't limited to unemployed professionals or recent graduates entering the workforce, either. According to a 2015 survey from The Adler Group, 5 to 20 percent of employed professionals are actively pursuing a new opportunity. "Tiptoers" make up around 15 to 20 percent, and another 65 to 75 percent are open to listening to new opportunities. That means at least 85 percent of all employed professionals are willing to listen to you if you have an interesting opportunity for them. Knowing that, you have a pretty good chance of landing some quality candidates for your open positions.

If that isn't enough for you, in a 2017 survey done by LinkedIn, an incredible 88 percent of all Fortune 500 companies said they use LinkedIn as their primary recruiting tool. A commercial for LinkedIn Jobs on a local radio station that said a job is filled every ten seconds with candidates found on LinkedIn.

Knowing that more than 80 percent of all employed professionals are willing to listen to your opportunity, how can you find these candidates? When you do find them, how can you narrow your search to approach only the very best ones?

HARNESS THE POWER OF YOUR SEARCH

In Chapter 8, we covered LinkedIn Search in great detail. Let's take a moment to refresh your memory, so you'll know how to find your ideal candidates in seconds.

Let's say you're an in-house recruiter at a biotech firm, and you're looking for a director of quality to create, implement, and oversee quality systems in your company. Your minimum job requirements are:

- Minimum eight years of experience in quality assurance for a human or animal drug company
- Substantial knowledge of cGMP requirements for multiple dosage forms along with prior experience in supplier qualification
- Additional experience in GDPs and/or GLPs (preferred)
- Excellent communicator and team player with the ability to proactively address and lead resolution of compliance issues internally and with external partners and contractors
- 25 percent travel

I don't have a subscription to LinkedIn Talent Solutions, so let's go to the basic LinkedIn search and see if we can find some candidates. Make sure you are set to people search, and modify the search parameters as follows:

1. In the Title field, enter "Director of Quality" if you are looking for someone who currently holds that position or held it in the past.
2. Change Industries from its default setting of All Industries to just Biotechnology.
3. Leave all other options at their default settings.

Figure 17–1 on page 187 shows what your Advanced Search should look like to get your first pass search results. If you want to narrow your search geographically, you can change Locations to your area or within 50, 100, or 150 miles of your location.

Of course, you can modify your search parameters further to narrow or widen your search, but first take a look at these preliminary results. As you can see in Figure 17–2 on page 187, you have found 1,965 directors of quality in the biotech field with just one

FIGURE 17–1. LinkedIn People Search

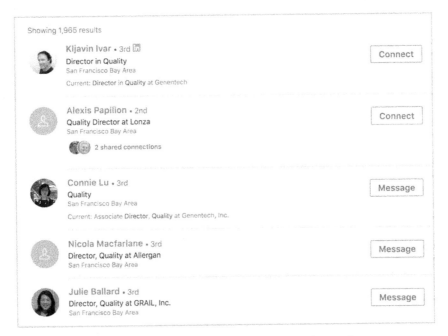

FIGURE 17–2. Biotech Preliminary Search Results

search. Not all of them are looking for a job, but I bet at least a few would be open to a new opportunity if it sounded interesting.

Before you start reaching out to some of these people, try narrowing your search a bit to see if you can pin down the more-qualified candidates. Remember: Your qualifications included eight-plus years of experience and substantial knowledge of cGMP requirements for multiple dosage forms, so try adding "cGMP" to your search criteria in the Keywords field and Director of Quality in the Title field.

Now you have only 376 results, which is much better than having to dig through nearly 2,000 candidates. The next step is to start looking at the profiles of these remaining prospects to see if they are actively looking for work. That information may be displayed in their profile headlines. If you have a subscription to Talent Solutions, you can search for people who have turned on the option in their profile that lets recruiters know you are interested in new positions. To turn this option on in your profile, go to Settings & Privacy, select the Privacy tab, and scroll down to Job Seeking Preferences (see Figure 17–3). Setting Let Recruiters Know You're Open to Opportunities to Yes will not display it publicly on your profile (so your current employer won't know), but recruiters will be able to see it.

If your search returns some LinkedIn members who are interested in career opportunities or who look like a great fit for your job opening, you have a few options at this point:

- Send them InMail to introduce yourself. Don't start out by asking them if they are looking for a new position or you may scare them away—even if their profiles say

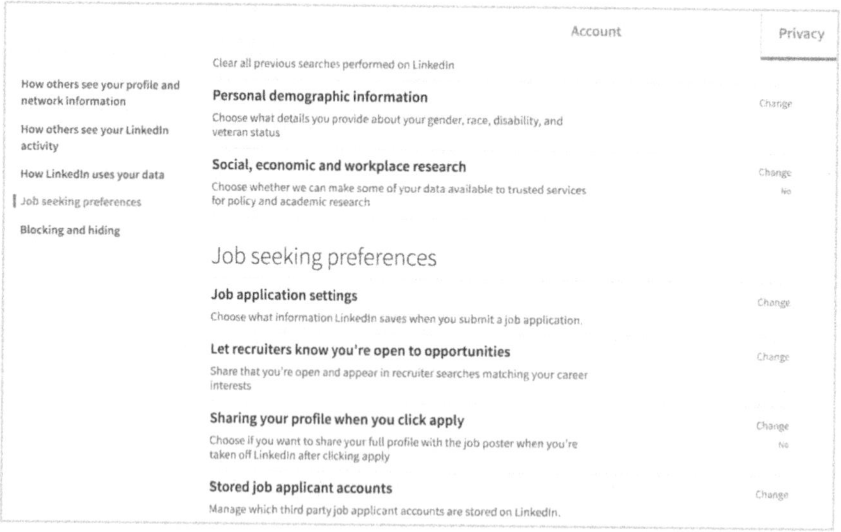

FIGURE 17–3. Changing Your Job Seeking Preferences

they're interested in new opportunities. Tell them you came across their profile and saw something that caught your attention. Find something unique, like an award they won, interesting certifications, schools they attended, etc. You can ask them about it or congratulate them. Try to establish a relationship, so you can get to know them and see if they are a good fit for your organization. If you mention things you have in common, they will be more likely to respond to you.

- Join Groups they belong to so you can send messages directly. At the beginning of the messages, state that you belong to the same Group and you thought they might be interested in an opportunity at your company. If you are a recruiter, I highly recommend joining Groups related to your industry and participating frequently so people get to know your name. If they see you posting regularly in the forum, they are more likely to respond to your messages even if they've never corresponded with you in the past. This is a very effective and inexpensive way for small businesses to recruit new employees.

- If they are 2nd-degree connections of yours, find out who in your network is a 1st-degree connection between you and ask for an introduction. You can also ask your 1st-degree connection what they think of them to help determine if they would be a good fit for your company.

- If they have enabled the Open Profile feature, any LinkedIn member can send regular messages to any Premium member without having to use InMail. Members who use Open Profile are generally open to people reaching out to them with job opportunities. As I've said many times before, you joined LinkedIn to be found, so take full advantage of all the available tools to gain more visibility. Most people join LinkedIn to grow their professional network. Unless your company requires you to limit your visibility, I highly recommend raising your profile as much as you can. No matter how happy you are at your current job, there are always bigger and better opportunities out there, so be open to the possibility, and let LinkedIn help you!

In Chapter 9, I went into great detail about the importance of keywords when searching on LinkedIn and how to choose the best ones for you. Now is a good time to review that section and create a list of keywords that will help you find your ideal candidates. Once you create a search that returns quality candidates, don't forget to save it so you can use it again and again to fill open positions.

TIPS TO HELP YOUR RECRUITING EFFORT

For recruiting tips, look at the LinkedIn Talent Blog at http://talent.linkedin.com/blog. LinkedIn's various blogs teach you more about the solutions the site provides and new features and tools as they are released. Here are some recruiting tips culled from various Talent Blog posts:

- If you are a recruiter looking for talent on LinkedIn, make sure your own profile is in order. Check to see that your profile is at All-Star level, including your three recommendations. When you reach out to candidates, they are going to check out your profile to get to know you and your company, so make sure you give a great first impression.

- Make sure the employees in your company complete their profiles, including their recommendations. When a candidate researches your organization, you want to present a professional image from top to bottom. It makes a great impression on candidates when they see a lot of recommendations on your employees' profiles. Encourage your teams to get as many glowing recommendations as possible so your candidates see that your company hires only top-notch people. Make sure they get a variety from past and current positions, not just from current co-workers, which can look suspicious.

- Create a company page on LinkedIn and fill it out completely. Active candidates will visit your company page to get to know your company and its culture. You can set up a company page for free or invest in a premium account to add more features. See Chapter 7 for more about LinkedIn Pages or go to https://business.linkedin.com/marketing-solutions/linkedin-pages.

- Join Groups related to your business and industry. Be an active participant and have your company's employees do the same. When someone sees a lot of people from one company engaged in intelligent group discussions on LinkedIn, they will get a good impression of your company and the quality of your employees.

- Search posts, Groups, and profiles to find the best candidates. Use the search features to help narrow down your search and save your best search templates in Saved Searches if you have a subscription to Talent Solutions or Sales Navigator. If you are recruiting new employees on a regular basis, invest in a subscription; being able to save your searches will save you a lot of time and effort.

- All these tips are effective whether you are an in-house recruiter or work for a staffing firm. You always want to be on the lookout for quality candidates and keep your pipeline full. The key to success is consistency—whether it's searching through profiles, Groups, and posts for candidates or building your professional network—so you are always just one invitation away from a candidate or hiring manager. As a recruiter, you want to build your network as large as possible to help cast a wider net. It's all about quantity when you are recruiting employees, but you also want to build a network of quality contacts who can send you referrals or introduce you to potential candidates.

Of course, you can manually search LinkedIn and still find great candidates, but it's very tedious and time-consuming. The LinkedIn Recruiter subscription will automate most of your recruiting tasks, saving you precious time, and can filter out the very best candidates based on their work experience and education.

LINKEDIN RECRUITER

This premium subscription is designed for corporate recruiters in large companies who are constantly searching for the best talent. LinkedIn Recruiter is the equivalent of Sales Navigator, the advanced tool for sales professionals. In Recruiter, you can create advanced searches for candidates which run 24/7. As Recruiter learns your ideal candidates, it offers Smart Suggestions for similar candidates.

The LinkedIn Recruiter dashboard, as you see in Figure 17–4, provides a comprehensive snapshot of your recruiting activities. The easy-to-navigate menu lets you quickly access your recruiting projects, a clipboard where you create and save job postings and notes, your posted jobs, reports, and more options. In the newsfeed section, you see real-time updates with new applicants, job posting status, and saved search results. In the right column, LinkedIn recommends potential candidates in the People You May Want to Hire widget. You also see Project Activity and Job Activity in separate right-column widgets.

Most of LinkedIn's revenue comes from recruiting, so it's constantly improving the dashboard and adding new features to ensure you're finding the best candidates for your company.

Next we'll explore LinkedIn's dashboard for job seekers. This is where your job postings will appear if you're a recruiter, so it's a great idea to get familiar with it.

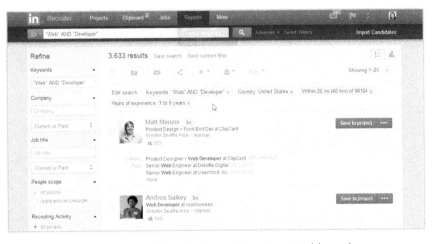

FIGURE 17–4. The LinkedIn Recruiter Dashboard

Here, you see how your postings stack up against your competitors and how appealing your job postings appear to potential job candidates.

FINDING A JOB

When you are looking for a new job, you can select Jobs from the main menu or visit https://www.linkedin.com/jobs/. This is LinkedIn's advanced search tool that helps you find and apply for your new position.

For job seekers, targeted jobs are displayed on the sidebar of their LinkedIn homepage and other LinkedIn pages in the Jobs You May Be Interested In widget, as shown in Figure 17-5. LinkedIn scans your current and previous job titles, companies you've worked for, and the keywords in your profile to automatically match you up with potential jobs.

As I mentioned earlier, according to a 2015 survey from The Adler Group, an average of 18 percent of employed workers are actively looking for a new job. Another 70 percent are willing to explore new opportunities even though they aren't actively looking. By using LinkedIn, companies can expand their search to passive candidates through the Jobs You May Be Interested In widget. Letting LinkedIn members see what other opportunities are out there creates a phenomenon in which your job postings find the best candidates, relieving some of the burden borne by your recruiters.

With job openings constantly but subtly displayed on the LinkedIn sidebar, you can't help but notice and become curious when you see certain job titles or companies you might want to work for. It's almost subliminal advertising: The jobs don't appear in the center of your screen; you just notice them out of the corner of your eye.

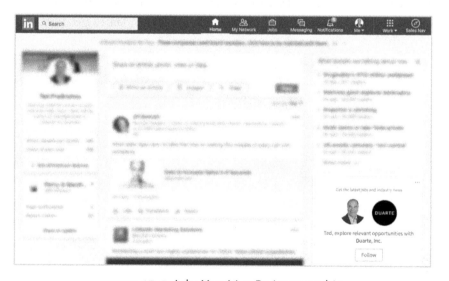

FIGURE 17-5. Jobs You May Be Interested In

As you see jobs that may interest you, you can click on them to see if any are promising enough to investigate further. If you aren't interested but know a friend or colleague who might be, you can forward the job to her LinkedIn inbox—assuming they are a connection—or share the job opening on Facebook or Twitter. This is a huge benefit to companies, giving their job openings publicity at no additional cost. If you post a job opening at your company, it can be seen by millions of people on LinkedIn, Facebook, and Twitter, increasing the chances you will find an outstanding candidate.

Companies that post jobs on LinkedIn can measure their impact through the site's job analytics, which are the equivalent of Google Analytics for your website. When you use Google Analytics to monitor your website, you learn how many visitors you have, how long they stay, what pages they visited, and what they downloaded or purchased. You can also find detailed demographic information like what country, state, city, or ZIP code they live in. This information is invaluable to a website owner. LinkedIn's job analytics help companies understand exactly which types of candidates your job postings are reaching and let you see who's viewing your jobs by role, company, geography, and more to ensure you're reaching the best professionals. If you are not reaching the right people, you can adjust the title, change the wording in the job description, or reconfigure to whom you are targeting in the job search. Without these analytics, you would know you are not attracting the right candidates because their experience or skill sets weren't right for the job, but you wouldn't know why. This will save you a lot of time and help you fill your positions faster with better candidates.

Candidates can find your job postings by searching jobs, but you can also "push" your open positions to qualified candidates using LinkedIn tools like Career Pages and Job Slots.

Spreading the Word About Your Job Postings

You can purchase a recruiting program called LinkedIn Job Slots, which is an automated tool that places your job openings in front of qualified candidates throughout LinkedIn for 30 day periods or until the job is filled. Job slots allow you to:

- Change your job posting as often as you like—even daily, if necessary.
- Easily renew and keep a position open on LinkedIn for longer than 30 days.
- Receive up to 50 real-time candidate recommendations per post.
- Streamline the job posting process with integrated third-party job distributors so your job listing gets maximum exposure on the internet.
- Pull job postings from your website into LinkedIn automatically through Job Wrapping, which is an additional cost. Job Wrapping is a proprietary technology

created by LinkedIn that automatically keeps your job postings in sync on your website and LinkedIn.

- Send applicants straight to your applicant tracking system from LinkedIn. LinkedIn has developed many APIs and plug-ins that let you easily connect your recruiting systems with LinkedIn. You can find out more about the LinkedIn development tools at https://developer.linkedin.com/.
- You can also add a third-party tracking URL to your job posting so you can track your results with your own analytics system, allowing you to easily track the success of your recruiting campaigns.

Have you ever come across the LinkedIn profile of the perfect candidate for one of your open positions or someone who is a "must-hire" for a high-profile role? LinkedIn has a service that lets you create a personalized outreach so that you can woo them to your company. Let's look at LinkedIn Pipeline Builder.

LinkedIn Pipeline Builder

Pipeline Builder is a LinkedIn service that lets you reach out to perfect candidates with customized recruiting pipelines. Here's how it works:

1. Identify a specific candidate and directly reach out to that person with personalized content and targeted ads.
2. The content and ads drive her to your personalized Pipeline Builder page.
3. The content on the Pipeline Builder page is designed to generate interest in your position.
4. Your targeted candidate can express interest in the position by clicking on a link, with no need to fill out an application.
5. You are notified of their interest, so you can reach out to them.

This is a very effective way to reach passive candidates who aren't actively searching for a new position but are open to the possibility of changing jobs. LinkedIn uses a combination of your targeting criteria and data from a person's profile to display your ads to the most qualified candidates. For example, engineers will see only your engineering jobs, and sales professionals will see only your sales jobs—even if they're reading the sports section of an online newspaper.

LINKEDIN CAREER PAGES

One of LinkedIn's premier recruiting packages is called the Career Page. Subscribing to the Silver or Gold Career Page offers many enhancements to your company page that will improve your recruiting experience and build a loyal following for your company. Your Career Page, alongside your company profile, is a powerful tool to educate and inform active and passive job candidates. As potential candidates explore your company page to learn more about your company, they will see your current job openings on the same screen. You can display customized content for each visitor, based on their LinkedIn profile data. If a software engineer visits your Career Page, specific content related to software engineers will be displayed, including open positions that he may be qualified for. This targeted content helps convince candidates that you are the right company for them.

Upgrading to a Career Page will give you more flexibility and let you customize your company page. Some features of the Career Pages include:

- Your messages dynamically adapt to the viewer based on information from her LinkedIn profile.
- Targeted job postings appear for each viewer.
- You can feature employees in the Employees Spotlights module so viewers can get a sense of what type of people work at your company.
- You can add a custom video to your page so viewers get to know your company better.
- You can display a list of benefits of working at your company.
- You can link to additional information on your company website.
- Viewers can contact your recruiters directly.
- You can create three additional customizable modules so viewers can learn more about the culture of your company.

You can also set up ads that run on LinkedIn to drive people to your company page to learn more about your jobs or products and services. (You can prevent ads from other companies from appearing on your company page if you choose the Gold Career Page package.)

The LinkedIn Career Page can help you position your company as an "employer of choice" by providing insight into your company culture and your community of "followers." Candidates are more likely to respond to your recruiting messages when they are familiar with your company and products. The Career Page enhancement also acts as a mini-web portal driving traffic to other important sites, such as your company website, blogs, and social media communities.

WORK WITH US ADS

This is not only one of the simplest recruiting and advertising solutions on LinkedIn but also one of the most effective. The Work With Us Ads let you display your advertising

FIGURE 17–6. Work with Us Ads

on your employees' profile pages and your company page. In Figure 17–6 you can see a Russell Investments ad displayed on the profile page of one of their employees.

To run Work for Us ads, go to https://business.linkedin.com/talent-solutions/job-ads, provide your creative material, and it will automatically place your ads on all your employee profile pages and your LinkedIn Page. If you are only going to run one marketing campaign on LinkedIn, this is the one you need to do to protect your brand.

CONCLUSION

As you've seen in this chapter, LinkedIn gives recruiters a lot of tools to make finding new employees easier and more effective. No matter how big or small your organization is, LinkedIn offers a premium recruiting solution to meet your needs. Of course, you could choose to search for new employees using the free search tools, but the automated solutions will streamline your efforts so you can stay ahead of your competition.

In the next chapter, we'll explore LinkedIn's solutions for sales and marketing professionals. Just as it has tools to help recruiters, the site also offers premium services designed to help sales professionals generate leads for their companies.

**For additional updates and how-to videos, visit
https://tedprodromou.com/UltimateGuideUpdates/.**

Chapter 18

LinkedIn for Sales and Marketing Professionals

I f you're in sales, you have to be licking your chops at the prospect of LinkedIn. With more than 500 million members and a growth rate of two new members per second, it's a golden opportunity for all sales professionals. Whether your product has a long or short sales cycle, LinkedIn provides a perfect networking platform to build lasting relationships with clients and prospects alike. Building and nurturing relationships keeps your sales pipeline full.

We're assuming you're a seasoned sales professional, so we're not going to get into Sales 101 in this chapter. If you're just getting started in sales or are starting your own business, read everything you can about sales, social networking, and social selling to learn the fundamentals. The internet and social media allow salespeople to cast a wide net to find new prospects, if they know how to use these tools properly. The process of selling hasn't changed, but the tools used to find prospects are evolving rapidly, allowing you to reach more prospects with less effort. If you use the internet and social media to find new leads but don't do it strategically, you'll attract lots of leads—but not the ones that lead to relationships and closed deals.

You are probably already aware of the importance of building a strong professional network and contact database. In the old days, salespeople used a Rolodex as their contact "database." I use the term loosely because the Rolodex was just a device that stored specially shaped index cards in alphabetical order. Each contact had their own index card where you wrote their contact information and scribbled reminder notes. If you lost the card, you lost your contact information. The Rolodex was bulky and sat on your desk next to your telephone, so when you traveled to visit your prospects and customers, you didn't have access to your contact database.

Obviously, times have changed. Today we carry our entire contact database on our phones. Our database also resides in our customer relationship management system (CRM), which is accessible from any internet connection. We can now also keep our contacts on LinkedIn, which is accessible from anywhere. The LinkedIn app lets us add new contacts and search existing ones from our smartphones. Today it's easier than ever to build a large electronic database of prospects and customers. Your challenge is to build a *targeted* database—it's easy to fall into the trap of focusing on quantity rather than quality.

BUILDING YOUR LINKEDIN SALES NETWORK

In Chapter 11, I went into great detail about building your network. Now is a good time to briefly review the different networking strategies so you can decide which approach is best for you as a sales professional. There is no right or wrong answer, as there are a lot of variables to consider. Let's review a few LinkedIn networking strategies, discuss the pros and cons of each, and help you decide which one is right for you.

We already talked about the different ways to build your professional network. The first was being an open networker where you connect with everyone who sends you an invitation. This allows you to create a very large network, so you have access to literally millions of connections in your 1st-, 2nd-, and 3rd-degree connections. Open networking is a great option for recruiters, real estate salespeople, and some other sales professionals because you have indirect access to so many LinkedIn members. The downside is that your network is unfocused so you have to spend more time digging through your many connections to find specific contacts or skill sets.

Your other option is to cast a smaller net, which will bring you fewer opportunities but a more focused network. Your audience will be highly targeted, so it's easier to connect with the right people. This requires you to carefully review every invitation to connect and vet every person who wants to join your network, meaning you may have to exclude some of your friends if they don't match your criteria.

How big should your network be? As you read in Chapter 11, studies conclude that it's impossible to effectively manage a network of friends or colleagues if it gets too large. You can communicate with only 100 to 150 people on a regular basis and maintain a strong relationship. If you build a network of 2,000 members on LinkedIn, you will not be able to maintain a strong relationship with everyone because you just don't have enough time.

Does this mean you should limit your network to 150 members? Maybe. It depends on what you are selling and how many people are in your target market. If you are selling a specialty product that is only used by senior bioinformatics scientists in the United States, your target market is very small. It wouldn't make sense to connect with 1,500 other people just for the sake of connecting. Bigger is not always better.

The third option—and the most popular one—is to build a network somewhere in between the niche networker with 150 contacts and the open networker who has the maximum 30,000 connections. While many LinkedIn members have fewer than 500 connections, I see many with somewhere between 500 and 1,000 connections. The longer you've been in the workforce, the more connections you have. I have around 16,000 connections at the time of this writing, many of whom are current and former colleagues. I started aggressively building my network after I was laid off from a corporate job and restarted my own business. I'm constantly looking for quality connections to expand my LinkedIn network in order to generate more leads and, in turn, more sales.

The Pros and Cons of Different-Sized LinkedIn Networks

The size of your network depends on what you are selling, whom you sell to, and how much time you want to spend managing it. Being an open networker gives you a lot of opportunities to connect with others, but you will have to dedicate at least an hour or two a day to accepting invitations to connect and answering emails from your network. Open networkers tend to be aggressive networkers, so they are constantly reaching out to their network and pounding the pavement for new leads.

If you are a recruiter who fills jobs nationally or internationally, you need to build a huge network to keep your pipeline full. As they say, it's all about who you know, not what you know. Many positions are filled because you have a friend who has a friend who's looking for a job. You have to be willing to dedicate up to half your day working your LinkedIn network for leads to fill open positions and for new jobs to post. But there's nothing wrong with spending 20 to 30 hours a week networking on LinkedIn if it's your primary source for job listings and quality candidates.

If you are selling niche products, it probably doesn't make sense for you to spend more than an hour or two a day on LinkedIn. You probably have a few key contacts on LinkedIn who can connect you with the right people, and you know which Groups to participate in.

Most salespeople choose the middle-of-the-road approach. They have a professional network of 5,000 to 10,000 connections, which gives them access to millions of 2nd- and 3rd-degree connections. They also have a smaller core network, with whom they communicate on a regular basis.

Figure 18–1 on page 201 is a table that describes some of the pros and cons of each style of LinkedIn networking. The optimal size of your network depends on many factors that only you can determine. Everyone's situation is different, so weigh the benefits and disadvantages of each networking style and decide which is best for you.

Of course, you can always change your mind if you choose a style that doesn't work for you. If you start out as a niche networker, you can easily switch to build a medium-sized network or become an open networker. It's harder to begin as an open networker and reduce the size of your network. It's a long, tedious process to remove the connections that are not highly targeted. Some people even close their existing LinkedIn account and rebuild their network from scratch with a brand-new account.

Take a look at Figure 18–2 on page 202, which is from my profile. My network consists of 23,401 connections, which includes 15,904 1st-degree connections and 7,497 followers. (You can follow someone on LinkedIn without being a 1st-degree connection.) Look at what happens at the 2nd and 3rd degree. The number of potential connections I have access to grows exponentially. Imagine what these numbers would look like if I were an open networker. Looking at my numbers, it's easy to see why so many sales professionals choose that strategy.

As new members join LinkedIn, I don't even have to add anyone to my 1st-degree connections to expand the reach of my 2nd- and 3rd-degree networks. As more of my 2nd- and 3rd-degree connections connect with others, my network is growing exponentially without my lifting a finger. When I started writing the latest version of this book, my total network had around 4 million members. It has almost doubled in size in the two months it took me to finish, and I've only added around 1,000 1st-degree connections.

LinkedIn's growth shows no signs of slowing down, so by the time this book hits bookstores, my total network could be well over 20 million people. Why would I want to take the time to grow my 1st-degree network when my 2nd- and 3rd-degree networks are growing like crazy all by themselves? If and when I need to reach out for new connections, I can easily tap into those networks.

SHOULD YOU GO ANONYMOUS?

I've seen blog posts and articles from LinkedIn experts recommending a technique where you go stealth by creating an anonymous profile and spy on your competitors.

Network	Pros	Cons
Small Niche Network	1. Targeted audience	1. Limited ability to reach 2nd- and 3rd-degree connections
	2. Less noise/emails from connections	2. You may miss some sales opportunities because you don't have as many 1st-degree connections referring you to new connections
		3. You will not appear in the People Also Viewed sidebar as often as you would if you have a larger network.
Medium-Sized Network	1. You benefit from having a targeted audience and an extended 2nd- and 3rd-degree audience	1. You may be limited when you try to reach out to 3rd-degree connections
	2. More opportunities to connect with prospects when you need Introductions	2. You may receive a lot of connection requests from strangers or people who don't fit your professional profile
	3. More opportunities to receive network referrals from your network	3. You may receive a lot of unsolicited emails from connections
Open Network	1. You have a very wide audience to sell to and to help refer you to prospects	1. Your network is very unfocused so you have to work hard to find targeted prospects
	2. You have access to millions of 2nd- and 3rd-degree connections	2. You will receive a lot of unsolicited emails from your connections
	3. You are never more than two hops from millions of prospects	3. You will have no personal relationship with more than 90 percent of your network
		4. You will receive a lot of requests to recommend people in your network whom you don't know very well

FIGURE 18–1. Pros and Cons of LinkedIn Networking Styles

FIGURE 18–2. My LinkedIn Network

I leave it up to you to ponder the ethical questions. The technique will let you view others' profiles on a limited basis, monitor your competitors' LinkedIn Page and Groups, and essentially be an anonymous LinkedIn member. You do this by creating a second LinkedIn account with a fictitious name and lock down your profile, so members will only see that Anonymous viewed their profiles. You probably won't be able to join your competitors' Groups because they have to approve memberships, but you can still learn a lot about them. LinkedIn changed its policy in 2013, which affects anonymous profiles. If you lock down your profile and do not share profile information with others, LinkedIn limits what you can see on others' profiles. Something people do is use fake names, company names, profile information, and even stock photos as their profile pictures in their stealth accounts to make everything look real.

Again, I'll leave it up to you if you want to use this approach—but personally it's not for me. Oh, by the way, it's also against LinkedIn's terms of service, so if you get caught, you will be removed from LinkedIn.

LEVERAGING YOUR COMPANY PAGE

There are many reasons every B2B company should have a LinkedIn company page—increasing sales being at the top of that list. The obvious reason is that it is the largest business networking site in the world. In Chapter 7, you learned how to set up and manage your LinkedIn company page. If you haven't done it yet, go back and set one up right now.

Assuming you now have a company page or have the right person working on it, let's get back to the benefits of a company page and how you can use it to increase your sales. As I mentioned in Chapter 7, your company page is accessible to others even if they aren't a LinkedIn member. Take a look at https://www.linkedin.com/company/microsoft/jobs/ to see a sample company page. This page is accessible to everyone, LinkedIn member or not. Your company page also shows up in Google search results, giving your company additional exposure online.

LinkedIn Pages allow you to share new product announcements and other news in the Recent Updates section. You can post as many updates as you want. You can also recruit the best talent by posting your open positions in the Jobs section. The best part of the company page for sales professionals is the Showcase Pages section. You can create up to ten Showcase Pages featuring your top products, which will also show up for both members and nonmembers. Your customers can write recommendations for your products, building social proof for your company that you can share with your LinkedIn network. For example, if you were selling the Microsoft Dynamics 365 CRM software, you could post links to the product and to the recommendations as a status update on your LinkedIn profile and in your Groups. Here's a link to the Dynamics 365 Showcase Page so you can see what it looks like: https://www.linkedin.com/company/microsoft-dynamics?trk=biz-brand-tree-co-name.

LinkedIn Pages are like mini-websites for your company that you can share with your LinkedIn network. When people see your products and recommendations, they can reach out to you on LinkedIn or visit your website to learn more. Companies can now share their employees' best LinkedIn posts on their LinkedIn page so all of their company followers will see the article or video.

LEVERAGING A COMPANY GROUP

LinkedIn Groups can allow you to build an online community for your company within the larger LinkedIn community. Since most of your customers and prospects are already on LinkedIn, it makes perfect sense to give them access to the Group as well. There they can ask questions, find resources, and get to know your company better. The discussions on your Group can give you insight into what your customers are struggling with and what they want more of. They'll also tell you what they like and dislike about your products, and they'll even help other customers by answering their questions.

Sales professionals should always monitor their company's online communities to keep their finger on the pulse of their customers. If customers are complaining about the performance of your product, you can reach out to them or get the right people involved to help them. Being proactive and helping dissatisfied customers is a great way to build strong relationships and show prospective customers that your company provides excellent service.

PROSPECTING ON LINKEDIN

Imagine a Rolodex with more than 500 million names at your fingertips. In addition to the names of the top business professionals in the world, you have a list of the employees of every major business segmented by the companies they work for. You have access to the top employees of such companies as Google, Facebook, IBM, Costco, Target, and every other Fortune 500 company. If you don't sell to large companies, you have access to thousands of small and medium-sized businesses instead. You even have access to consultants, coaches, and other solopreneurs who are members of LinkedIn.

Never before has prospecting been so easy for a salesperson. In the past, you would have to purchase lists from list brokers and cold-call hundreds or thousands of people. Most of the time you reached a gatekeeper and spent countless hours on the phone trying to get five minutes of the decision-maker's time to persuade them to meet with you for 15 minutes.

If you weren't buying lists, you were scouring the phone book or business directories, looking for the contact numbers of your target businesses. Prospecting was a lot of work and not for the faint of heart. You were essentially a telemarketer with a 99 percent rejection rate when you reached out to prospects.

LinkedIn makes prospecting a lot easier. Using the Advanced Search features, you can find your target audience in seconds. Advanced Search is a fantastic tool, but there are even more ways to find new prospects on LinkedIn. By learning how to use other tools like publishing and Groups, you'll learn your prospects' frustrations and hot buttons so you'll know exactly how to approach them and get their attention.

The key to successfully prospecting on LinkedIn is to network the same way you do in person. Listen before you talk. Get to know someone who is struggling or frustrated and could benefit from your product or service. You'll know how to approach them with your solution when the time is right. The key is to stay in the background and observe before reaching out.

Prospecting in LinkedIn Groups

You can use Groups to find prospects because they have discussion boards where people reach out for support. The discussion boards in Groups are similar to the now-defunct LinkedIn Answers, but the discussions are more focused. Since Groups are often dedicated to companies or specific products made by a company, the questions and discussions go much deeper.

For example, someone might ask a basic question about Photoshop on a marketing-related Group, such as "How do I crop a photo in Photoshop?" However, if you join the Photoshop Group, the questions will be about the more advanced features of Photoshop, and the answers will be very detailed. You may get three or four great answers that show you how to accomplish the same task using different techniques. A typical question in that Group might be something like: "JPG and RAW, of course we all know the advantages of RAW. Is there anyone out there who will still use JPG format for professional work?" This question received 251 comments in one month—with many varying opinions—and continued without any signs of slowing down. You see active discussions like this frequently on the Groups focused on specialties and specific products. I highly recommend joining the Groups related to your product, industry, and the vertical markets that use your product or service so you can get a bird's-eye view of what people in your industry are talking about.

You can also learn about industry trends and your competitors' advances in Groups. Companies often use LinkedIn Groups to announce new products and services and to gather feedback from customers by conducting surveys. LinkedIn no longer uses its

Polls feature, but you can post a question and lead people to an external survey tool like SurveyMonkey.

The same prospecting rules apply here as when networking in person. Be genuinely interested in helping others, and spend time listening to their issues before you reach out. You can also monitor the Groups to find top professionals in your industry. If you notice a certain person reaching out consistently and providing excellent advice, you can contact that person to see if they want to connect on LinkedIn. If they are located in your area, you could invite them to meet for coffee or lunch to talk about industry trends or to see if they want to join a local networking group you belong to. Building relationships with other experts helps extend your professional network, which will help you gain more sales.

LINKEDIN COMPANY GROUPS

In addition to Groups related to specific topics and products, most companies have Groups dedicated to the company along with their company page, so join both if you can. You can learn a lot about your competitors, your industry, and the vertical markets where your product or service is used. People always ask me if it's appropriate to join your competitors' Group. Now that all requests to join a Group must be approved by the manager, they will deny our membership request if they are paying attention. Occasionally, you can slip through the cracks, and they will grant you access. If that happens, I recommend being a silent participant and just observing so you can learn as much as possible about the issues your competitors are having with their products or services. You can use this when selling against your competitors, which gives you a huge advantage. If you start participating in discussions, they will become aware that you are a competitor and will remove you from the Group.

You should be able to join industry-related Groups and vertical market Groups without difficulty. If you aren't monitoring those Groups, you are missing out on a lot of relevant discussions that will help you discover potential sales opportunities. Remember, LinkedIn is one of the largest business intelligence databases available to you, so use it to your advantage to gather competitive information.

LinkedIn Pages

I've already mentioned LinkedIn Pages several times, but it's worth noting that you can use them as much for sales goals as for personal or hiring tasks. LinkedIn lets you "follow" companies similar to how you can "like" a company page on Facebook. Once you follow a company on LinkedIn, anything it posts on its company page will be visible on your newsfeed. This is an easy way for you to monitor prospective companies (and your competitors) to learn about new product announcements and other news. If one of your prospective companies hires a new CIO, it may be a perfect opportunity to get your foot in the door because that often means a clean slate, open to new vendors.

You can also monitor their LinkedIn Page to see what job openings they have. If you see a lot of new job openings or promotions in a certain department, it may be a great time to test the waters, as the company and the new hires might be looking for new products or services.

You can infer a ton of great information from LinkedIn Pages, if you take the time to dig into the job postings, news items, and new product announcements with a sales-oriented set of goals in mind.

LinkedIn Jobs

I touched on this in the previous section, but you can learn a lot about a company's strategic direction by monitoring their job postings. You know your target companies and perhaps even their key decision-makers. Spend a few hours a week (or have your assistant do it) monitoring their job postings. Use the Advanced Job Search feature to home in on the current job openings in the departments you sell to. When you see new job postings for key positions or a lot of listings for similar positions, it's a sign that you may have an opportunity to sell. If they are suddenly hiring 50 new C++ programmers, there must be a huge new product being developed that could mean a big opportunity for you. With a Sales Navigator account, you can save your search criteria in Saved Searches so you can easily replicate your best searches on a regular basis.

LinkedIn Newsfeed

The newsfeed is where you can subscribe to popular news sources such as *The New York Times*, *The Wall Street Journal*, and industry-specific news. You can also follow LinkedIn Influencers, who frequently post industry-related articles. I never logged into LinkedIn on a daily basis until it added features like Pulse, which has now evolved into the newsfeed. Now I can see the latest industry and financial news and keep up with my professional network from my LinkedIn homepage.

I use the newsfeed to learn about the latest trends in my industry and business news in general. When I see a breaking news item, I add my commentary and share it with my network, which makes them think of me as a trusted source of information. When I regularly share other people's content, they subconsciously associate me with those people.

LinkedIn Mobile

The LinkedIn mobile app has improved dramatically since it was initially released, as I discussed in Chapter 16. The app lets you easily access your LinkedIn account from your cell phone. Before you meet with a prospect in person, you can quickly review their profile, see the latest news from their company page, and check the latest industry news just before the meeting by searching for content in your newsfeed. You will be well prepared and make a good impression.

Using LinkedIn Ads

You will learn everything you need to know about LinkedIn advertising in Chapter 20, so I won't go into great detail here. But I do want you to know that you can run very targeted ads to promote your business brand and advertise white papers, webinars, videos, and workshops for lead generation. The advanced targeting ability of LinkedIn advertising makes it one of the most efficient advertising platforms online today. Your ads will only be displayed to the appropriate companies, industries, job titles, and keywords, as well as many other advanced targeting options.

LinkedIn Sales Navigator

Of course, LinkedIn provides premium packages designed for business professionals and sales representatives. These are designed to help you generate leads and manage your LinkedIn network. Figure 18–3 on page 209 shows you the features and pricing of the different Sales Navigator packages. I will talk about Sales Navigator in detail in the next chapter.

InMail

I've talked about the pros and cons of InMail throughout this book, so I won't get into the details here. In Chapter 12, you can learn how to use InMail to effectively reach out to your 2nd- and 3rd-degree connections. With Premium Business or Sales Navigator, you can send up to 30 InMails every month, depending on which package you choose. There are many ways to connect with others without using InMail, but sometimes it's easier and faster to just contact them directly via a personalized InMail message.

Premium Business Account

A LinkedIn Premium account offers you significantly more features than a free account. LinkedIn Premium offers two tiers of service, Premium Business and Executive. With Premium Business you receive 15 InMail messages every month and you receive 30

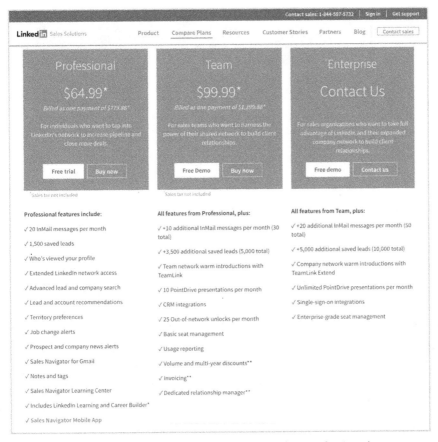

FIGURE 18–3. Premium Packages for Sales Professionals

monthly InMail messages with the Executive account. Business Insights show you detailed demographics about a company including their growth rate and hiring patterns. With your premium account, you also receive full access to the training courses on LinkedIn Learning.

One of my favorite premium tools is Who's Viewed Your Profile which I describe in detail below.

Figure 18–4 on page 210 shows you the other options you will receive with the LinkedIn Premium account.

As you can see, it's worth upgrading to LinkedIn Premium or Sales Navigator just for the additional prospecting tools. Being able to filter and save your searches will save you time and provide more targeted leads.

Who's Viewed Your Profile

This vital feature lets you see who's been viewing your profile, which can tip you off to potential customers. As you participate in Groups and establish yourself as

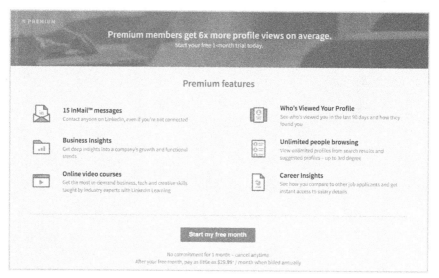

FIGURE 18–4. LinkedIn Premium Account Options

a subject-matter expert, people will click on your profile link to learn more about you. This simple act is better than if they opted in on your website to download a white paper. You'll find out a lot more about a potential client from their LinkedIn profile than you would from the name and email address they provided when they opted in on your site.

More Monthly Searches

I touched on this feature of premium accounts earlier. With a free LinkedIn account you are limited to an unspecified number of searches per month. Nobody knows the exact limit, but some of my clients say it's around 50 per month. With a LinkedIn Premium account, you have no limits.

Let Anyone Message You for Free with Open Profile

You are on LinkedIn to connect with as many prospects and customers as possible. Some people lock down their profiles so it's almost impossible to connect with them, but this completely defeats the purpose of being on a business networking site. As you know, I'm all about opening up my profile so it's easy for people to connect with me and see that I'm an expert in my field. When you get any of the premium subscriptions, you can enable Open Profile, which allows anyone on LinkedIn to send you a message. If you start getting too many unsolicited messages from people you don't want to connect with, you can disable it at any time. I only receive a few messages a month, and most are relevant opportunities. Remember, LinkedIn is a higher-quality network than most online networking websites, so you don't have to worry about being bombarded with spam.

CONCLUSION

LinkedIn offers many free and paid subscription levels. If you are in sales and serious about surpassing your numbers every month, you need to invest in Sales Navigator to get the most out of LinkedIn. As the site continues to grow at a staggering rate, you will need as many automated tools as possible to help you track down qualified leads. The premium accounts are worth the nominal fee, and your ROI will be exponential.

In the next chapter, we'll explore Sales Navigator, LinkedIn's flagship product for sales professionals, in detail. It is a hugely useful tool and has enough moving parts that I wanted to showcase it in its own chapter so you can dig deeply into how it works.

For additional updates and how-to videos, visit
https://tedprodromou.com/UltimateGuideUpdates/.

Sales Navigator

S ales Navigator is LinkedIn on steroids: a completely separate application designed to meet salespeople's needs. Subscriptions range from $64.99 per month for an annual personal subscription to $99.99 per month for an annual team subscription. Some people balk at the price, but even at $1,200 a year, unrestricted access to the entire LinkedIn membership and specialized tools for prospecting and follow-up make it worth the money. Bluntly, if you can't earn at least $1,200 a year from your LinkedIn network, you are in the wrong job.

The heart of Sales Navigator is its advanced search engine, with detailed filters that let you pinpoint your ideal prospects. You can search for leads or for accounts. Figure 19–1 on page 214 shows you the multiple lead search filters available when you do an advanced search. These are the most popular search fields that will help you find an unlimited stream of prospects for your products and services.

To save time, you can set up your sales preferences, or default search settings, under your Sales Navigator Settings. You can set geography, industry, company size, function, and seniority level, as shown in Figure 19–2 on page 215.

Think of sales preferences as your starting point when you are prospecting. They should include the characteristics of your top customers.

FIGURE 19–1. Advanced Lead Search Filters

Once you have created advanced searches that are reliably finding great prospects, you can save them so they are running 24/7. You can be notified of new leads daily, weekly, or monthly, or you can manually check for new leads from those searches.

As you scroll through your list of search results, you have a few options. You can:

- *Save.* This lets you monitor a person to see how active they are on LinkedIn and get notified when they post or share content. You can send them a message without being a 1st-degree connection or using InMail. You can also save their company as an account lead.
- *Connect.* Use this to send the person a personalized invitation to connect on LinkedIn.
- *View Profile.* You can view their profile to see if they are a good fit for your network.
- *View Similar.* LinkedIn's algorithm will show you 99 other professionals who are similar to the person you are looking at. This is a very powerful feature.

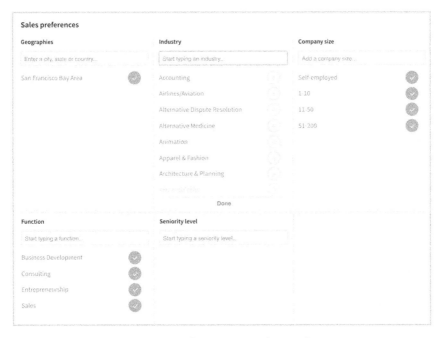

FIGURE 19–2. Defining Your Sales Preferences

- ▨ *Add Tag.* You can flag a prospect using preselected categories like Follow-up, Customer, or Decision Maker, or you can create your own tags like Cold, Warm, or Hot leads.
- ▨ *Message.* You can send a message without using InMail, even if you aren't connected. This is a huge benefit of subscribing to Sales Navigator.

Once you've started growing your sales funnel, it's time to spark up some friendly conversations with your prospects and begin building relationships. I prefer the slow and steady approach, but I'll leave it to you to decide how aggressively you want to move them through your sales funnel. Over the years, it has worked better to slowly build trust through short interactions before engaging in sales conversations. I have many long-term customers and repeat buyers who love to refer me to their networks because I've earned their trust over time.

ENGAGING YOUR LEADS AND CONNECTIONS

Now that you are following some leads, Sales Navigator will give you a lot of great information about their LinkedIn activity. Figure 19–3 on page 216 shows you information about the people in your network. As you can see, 755 people in my 1st-degree network changed jobs in the past 90 days. This gives me an opportunity to

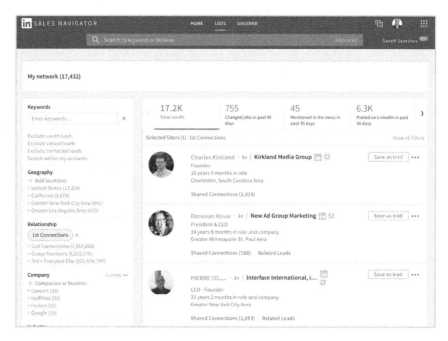

FIGURE 19–3. Engaging Your Network

congratulate them and start a conversation. I could ask them about their new roles, which might lead to an opportunity to help them as a consultant as they are getting established in their new positions.

Forty-five people have been mentioned in the news in the past 30 days. This is another opportunity for me to congratulate them. More than 6,000 posted on LinkedIn in the past 30 days, so I can view their posts and be one of the first to like, comment on, or share their content. I'm always looking for ways to start conversations on LinkedIn, and Sales Navigator offers ways for me to reengage my connections or prospects.

News and updates from your network as well as people and accounts you are following will appear in your Sales Navigator newsfeed. This is similar to your LinkedIn newsfeed, but you will only see information about specific people and accounts you saved as leads.

You can filter the newsfeed data by most important or most recent. You can also sort by sales alerts, job changes, suggested leads, lead news, lead shares, account news, and account shares. You can also display only news and updates by one specific company or person you are following.

Again, engaging quickly with people who appear in these updates is a great way to start a new conversation and get back on their radar.

DISCOVER NEW LEADS AND ACCOUNTS AUTOMATICALLY

The Discover tab on the menu uses LinkedIn's algorithm to view recommended leads and accounts. There's no need for you to waste your time digging for new leads because LinkedIn will do it for you. The site finds people and accounts with similar characteristics to the leads and accounts you are currently following.

TEAM TOOLS

Sales Navigator also has a tool set designed for large sales organizations. The Team version of Sales Navigator lets you connect popular CRM applications like Salesforce and Microsoft Dynamics, so all your Sales Navigator activity is captured in your CRM records. The most powerful tool is called Teamlink, which lets you coordinate your sales activity when selling to large organizations. Let's say you have 20 sales reps who are responsible for managing a large account, like IBM. It would be embarrassing if two of your sales reps from different divisions called the same contact at IBM to sell them services. With Teamlink, your sales reps would know who has been calling that person and what they've been discussing.

SOCIAL SELLING INDEX

LinkedIn also has a tool called the Social Selling Index that assigns you a "score" for your LinkedIn activity (see Figure 19–4 below). Your score is based on how well you:

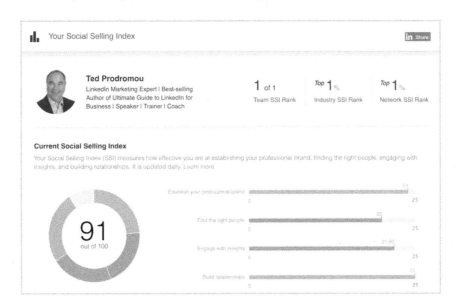

FIGURE 19–4. Social Selling Index

- Establish your professional brand.
- Find the right people.
- Engage with insights.
- Build relationships.

The Social Selling Index gives you an idea of how well LinkedIn thinks you are using the site. The score isn't perfect, but it gives you an idea of what LinkedIn thinks of your daily activity. To learn more about the Social Selling Index and how you can improve your score visit https://business.linkedin.com/sales-solutions/blog/g/get-your-score-linkedin-makes-the-social-selling-index-available-for-everyone.

CONCLUSION

Sales Navigator is a powerful tool for sales professionals who want to generate new business from LinkedIn. Sales Navigator is a must have, mini CRM and prospecting tool that can automate many of your lead-generation tasks. It is by far one of the most powerful and affordable ways to grow your business.

In this chapter, we looked at how to use LinkedIn to find prospective customers to boost your sales. In the next chapter, we will explore a related topic: the world of LinkedIn advertising.

For additional updates and how-to videos, visit
https://tedprodromou.com/UltimateGuideUpdates/.

Chapter 20

LinkedIn Advertising

inkedIn advertising is evolving quickly so some of this chapter may become outdated as new advertising options are released. To see the latest advertising options from LinkedIn, visit https://business.linkedin.com/marketing-solutions/ads or search Google for "LinkedIn advertising."

Internet advertising is bigger than ever. Everyone complains about seeing too many ads online, but obviously they are very effective. In the second quarter of 2014, Facebook's advertising revenue was $2.68 billion. That had ballooned to $13.04 billion by the second quarter of 2018—a 387 percent increase in just four years, with no end in sight. Google's ad revenue was approximately $60 billion in 2014 and as of this writing is expected to exceed $120 billion in 2018.

Advertising on LinkedIn offers a variety of affordable ways to get your message out to a very targeted audience. While some online advertisers consider LinkedIn's average cost per click of around $10 to be high, the cost per acquisition (CPA) of a new client is significantly lower than that of Google and Facebook. Your CPA depends on the market you are targeting, but I personally run LinkedIn ads for a client who acquires a new client for around $350, which turns into an average sale of $50,000. That's a pretty good ROI on your advertising dollar. Nowhere else on the internet can you create such laser-focused advertising at such an affordable price.

The beauty of LinkedIn advertising is its incredible targeting ability. You can display one set of ads to keyword-specific content, display another set to specific Groups, and create targeted InMail ads to designated categories, by job title, by company, and by a host of other options we'll cover in detail in this chapter. Since LinkedIn is already a targeted, business-oriented community, the ability to use precisely targeted advertising stretches your dollar and can produce extraordinary results.

LinkedIn members include highly educated, affluent, executive-level, and influential decision-makers. According to Nielsen's @Plan, almost 27 percent of LinkedIn members are business decision makers and more than 34 percent earn more than $100,000 per year. In case you aren't familiar with @Plan, it is the leading target-marketing platform for internet media planning, buying and selling of online advertising, according to Nielsen. @Plan uses more than 5,000 personal profile data points and 19 profile categories to provide wide-ranging details about the U.S. adult online population. In a nutshell, they know a lot about our online and offline habits, including what we like, what we dislike, where we shop, what brands we like, what entertainment we like, and more.

@Plan also says three out of four LinkedIn members use LinkedIn to keep up with business news and industry trends because they trust the information they read. More than 64 percent of these LinkedIn members believe LinkedIn helps develop business relationships and grow their businesses.

LinkedIn members are the perfect group to market to because they are receptive to relevant advertising and have the authority to take action when they see products and services that will solve their problems.

CONTENT MARKETING

With algorithm changes that help distribute your articles throughout LinkedIn and to external websites, plus advertising options like Sponsored Content, now called Feed Ads, LinkedIn is making it easier than ever to get your content in front of your target audience. You can publish articles, blog posts, presentations, and even video on LinkedIn and then promote it so it appears in the newsfeeds of your ideal clients. Feed Ads and Message Ads are very affordable ways to get your brand in front of millions of potential customers.

ADVERTISING OPTIONS

Your LinkedIn advertising options include:

- Text Ads
- Dynamic Ads
- Feed Ads

- Message Ads
- Display Ads
- Elevate

Each advertising option allows you the flexibility and affordability to reach your target audience, whether you are generating leads, growing your network, recruiting new employees, or attracting followers to your LinkedIn Page.

Let's learn about the different advertising options available to you on LinkedIn, as well as its powerful data-gathering tools, and then in Chapter 21 I'll show you how to create powerful, laser-targeted ads that will convert like crazy.

TEXT ADS

Text Ads are a self-service advertising solution allowing you to create and place ads on prominent pages and locations on the website.

You specify which LinkedIn members view your ads by selecting your target audience: by job title, job function, industry, geography, age, gender, company name, company size, or LinkedIn group.

Here are the components of a self-service ad:

- Headline (up to 25 characters)
- Description (up to 75 characters)
- From (your name or company)
- Image (50 x 50 pixels)
- URL (the website people visit when they click on your ad)

As for location, your Text Ads, as seen in Figure 20–1 on page 222, will be displayed at the top of members' homepages in text-only format and in the right sidebar on certain other pages, such as Groups.

DYNAMIC ADS

Dynamic ads are the ads you see on LinkedIn that are personalized for you. They will display your profile photo and first name in the ad encouraging you to follow a company or to envision yourself working for a company. Dynamic ads can include your name, a company name, job title, or other profile data to grab your attention.

The purpose of Dynamic Ads is to entice people to follow your LinkedIn Page or to increase brand awareness. You can also use Dynamic Ads to generate leads through content downloads, fill your webinars with targeted registrants, or just drive traffic to your website.

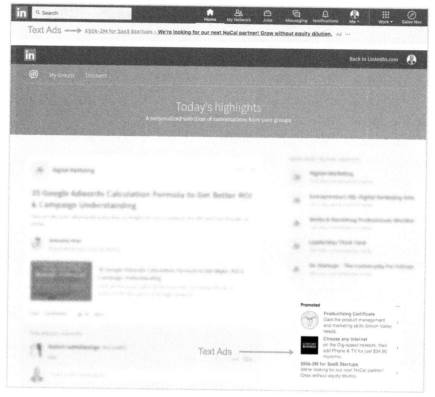

FIGURE 20–1. Text Ads

There are three types of Dynamic Ads:

1. Follower Ads—to increase your LinkedIn Page followers
2. Spotlight Ads—to showcase your products or services, promote a webinar, offer a whitepaper download for lead generation, or drive people to your website
3. Job Ads—to display targeted job opportunities

All three ad types use LinkedIn profile data to personalize the ad to increase engagement.

See Figure 20-2 on page 223 to see an example of a Dynamic Ad from Marketo asking me to Follow their LinkedIn Page to learn more about their career opportunities.

FEED ADS

If you are familiar with Facebook's Sponsored Posts, you'll understand LinkedIn's Feed Ads. If you haven't heard of this concept, you can pay to promote content you have created and posted on your company page. You can also create Direct Sponsored

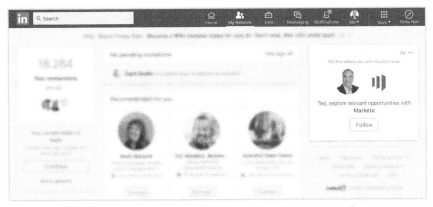

FIGURE 20–2. Dynamic Ad Growing LinkedIn Page Followers

Content, which does not appear on your company page but will be displayed in your ad campaign.

Figure 20–3 on page 224 shows a sample Feed Ads posting appearing in a newsfeed. The first post, from CatchFire Funding, is a normal unsponsored post. The second post is a Feed Ad from Vimeo. Except for the "Promoted" label identifying it as an ad, it looks just like any other post. If you click on the Vimeo logo or the word "Vimeo," you will be redirected to its company page, where you will learn more about the business and can choose to follow the company. If you click on the link, you will be redirected to the blog post being promoted in the ad content.

There are three components to a Feed Ad post. The introductory text at the top, the image, and the headline and URL, as you saw in Figure 20–3.

There are many great online resources for creating successful ads including Google, Facebook, and LinkedIn ad campaigns. Start with a Google search similar to "how to create successful Google ads" or "how to create successful online ads." You will see lots of great examples and tutorials that will help you get started.

As I mentioned earlier, LinkedIn advertising is in constant flux, so as LinkedIn rolls out new Feed Ad features and tools, visit https://business.linkedin.com/marketing-solutions/best-practices/ad-tips/sponsored-content-tips to see their latest recommendations. Here are LinkedIn's most recent tips for high-performing Feed Ad campaigns:

- Write ad headlines that are under 150 characters. Concise headlines lead to more engagement.
- Keep descriptive copy under 70 characters. Note that anything longer than 100 characters could be truncated on desktop.
- Embed larger images instead of standard thumbnails. An image size of 1200 x 627 pixels is recommended. Content with larger visuals tends to get up to 38 percent higher clickthrough rates.

FIGURE 20–3. Feed Ad

- Feature a clear call to action so your audience knows what you want them to do.
- Your image should be a minimum of 400 pixels wide.
- Be specific with ad targeting but not so specific that you narrow your audience. Choose location and two other targeting criteria to start. See Figure 20–4 for targeting options.

FIGURE 20–4. Targeting Options

- Analyze industry news instead of just sharing it. Offering insights and key takeaways will keep your content from feeling generic and help establish thought leadership in your field.
- Add content curation to your plan, and share information that is useful and relevant to your audience, without creating it all yourself. Use the 80/20 content marketing plan: Twenty percent of the content you share is original, and 80 percent is relevant content created by reputable sources. Always credit your source.
- Repurpose your own content. Remember to check your blog, website, and social media channels instead of creating new content every time. Write one blog post for your blog, read your post like a newscaster, and post it on YouTube. Create a PowerPoint presentation from the blog and post it on SlideShare. Take excerpts from the post and tweet them on Twitter. You can also post the same content as an article on LinkedIn and share it via LinkedIn status updates.
- Use rich media (like video, audio, or other elements) by incorporating YouTube, Vimeo, and SlideShare videos. They play right in the LinkedIn feed, so your audience can engage organically.
- Include human interest stories that connect to your brand to help your audience establish an emotional connection. According to LinkedIn research:
  - B2B buyers are **50 percent more likely** to make a purchase if they see emotional value in a product or service (as opposed to functional value).
  - B2B customers are **20 percent more likely** to buy after engaging with video content and social media channels.

- Studies have seen emotive ads generate **twice as much profit** as rational, logic-based ads.
- Internal research suggests LinkedIn's top-performing B2B video ads feature at least one of three emotional drivers: **compelling music, brand-reinforcing colors, or emotive storytelling**.

You will also learn how to create high-performing LinkedIn ads in Chapter 21, "Creating LinkedIn Ads That Convert Like Crazy."

MESSAGE ADS

Message Ads, previously called Sponsored InMail, let you use InMail to deliver highly relevant messages to targeted audience segments. These messages are different from standard InMail because they're designed to deliver a personalized marketing message to the recipient. Ordinarily when you send an InMail to someone, you don't want to include a marketing message. The sole purpose of an InMail is to establish contact.

Message Ad messages are hand-delivered, personalized messages with space for extensive marketing copy on a co-branded landing page, one ad unit, and a call to action. Message Ads are always delivered to the top of the member's LinkedIn inbox, increasing visibility and improving the open rate. LinkedIn members can only receive one partner message every 60 days, so they aren't overwhelmed with unsolicited emails.

When you send a Message Ad, you can create personalized messages to very specific audiences because you can target any facet of the member profile. For this reason, Message Ads have an average open rate of 20 percent and a 20 percent clickthrough rate on the call to action. These are phenomenal rates, well above the industry standard. Figure 20–5 on page 227 shows a sample Sponsored InMail message from LinkedIn offering a guide to help you write more effective recruiting InMails.

DISPLAY ADS

Display Ads or Programmatic Display Ads is considered an *enhanced marketing solution,* and you need to contact the LinkedIn sales team for more information. The starting price for these campaigns is $25,000, but it may be possible to negotiate and start campaigns at lower price points.

According to LinkedIn, there are two ways to purchase display advertising:

1. Purchase LinkedIn Display Ads programmatically. Choose your preferred demand-side platform (DSP) or agency trading desk (ATD) with flexible purchasing and targeting options.

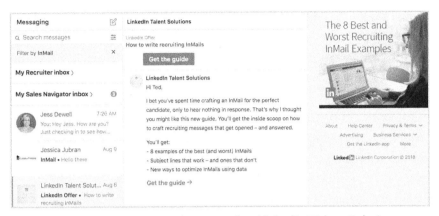

FIGURE 20–5. Message Ads Promoting LinkedIn Talent Solutions

2. Buy your inventory through open or private LinkedIn auctions.

LinkedIn only accepts 300 x 250 ad banners for these ads and the ads will be displayed in the right column of the LinkedIn home page. The placement will be identical to the placement of the Dynamic Ad Growing LinkedIn Page Followers previously shown in Figure 20–2. To be honest, I rarely see these ads as LinkedIn constantly rolls out new advertising options.

LINKEDIN ELEVATE

Elevate is not a traditional advertising product, but it is a paid LinkedIn service that helps drive social media engagement and traffic, so I guess you could call it a paid traffic source. LinkedIn offers Elevate under the Marketing Solutions and Advertising sections of their website.

Elevate empowers all of your employees to be social media advocates for your company. The benefits of social sharing include increased LinkedIn Page followers, filling open positions by attracting top talent through social media, building brand awareness, sharing customer testimonials, and building your other social media followers on Twitter, Facebook, Instagram and other top social media platforms.

LinkedIn Elevate is a social media monitoring and management tool that creates a list of your company's top social sharers and the content they are sharing. Elevate places this popular social content on the LinkedIn newsfeeds of your employees so they can share the content with their social networks. This expands your social media reach exponentially when you have hundreds—if not thousands—of your employees sharing the same content through their personal social media accounts.

Elevate monitors your brand's social media presence through an easy-to-use dashboard. When your social media team sees trending, relevant content on the social media networks, they can share it with your employees so they can amplify the content through their personal networks using the Elevate mobile app or through the LinkedIn desktop application.

According to LinkedIn and their experience with Elevate's customers, content shared by a company's employees has twice as much engagement as content shared by the brand's social media accounts. LinkedIn's research also says sales people who share social content are 45 percent more likely to exceed sales quotas.

To learn more about LinkedIn Elevate and see case studies, visit https://business.linkedin.com/elevate.

DATA TOOLS

LinkedIn provides a variety of tools to help you generate more leads and to monitor your LinkedIn ad campaigns. As I've mentioned numerous times, the LinkedIn advertising platform is evolving faster than any other section of LinkedIn, so you can keep up with the latest updates at https://business.linkedin.com/marketing-solutions/ads.

LinkedIn Lead Gen Forms

LinkedIn created Lead Gen Forms to make it easier for people to register for offers because more than 60 percent of members now access the site on mobile devices. Lead Gen Forms lets users fill out the form automatically using data from their LinkedIn profiles with just one click. This way, forms are always filled with accurate data and opt-in rates soar. For example, Bynder, a software company, used Lead Gen Forms to increase leads from its Sponsored Content by 400 percent and achieved a 20 percent conversion rate.

Figure 20–6 on page 229 shows you how to set up your Lead Gen Form in a Sponsored Content ad campaign.

LinkedIn Conversion Tracking and Matched Audiences

LinkedIn finally created ad tracking and retargeting capabilities in 2017 and continues to enhance these tools today. Before then, there was no way to track your ad campaigns on the site unless you used third-party tools. With the release of Insight Tags and Conversion Tracking, we can track the performance of our campaigns and create Matched Audiences, which allow us to retarget page visitors with follow-up ads.

The first step is to create an Insight Tag and install it on your website. The Insight Tag is a small piece of code that is installed on your website, just like

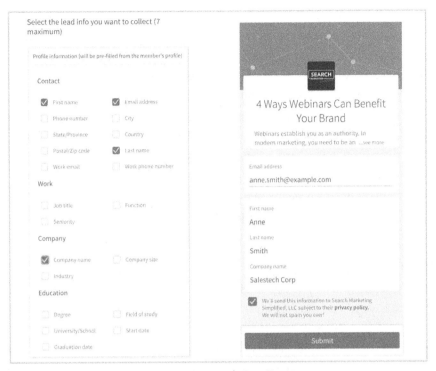

FIGURE 20–6. Lead Gen Forms

you install code to track Google Analytics. Your marketing department and web developers can set this up for you. Log into your Campaign Manager by going to your LinkedIn homepage, select Work and Advertising. Next, select Insight Tag under Account Assets. Once your tag is created, as shown in Figure 20-7, copy the script and install it on your website into the body section of your site's HTML, above

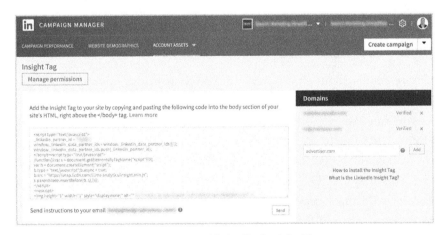

FIGURE 20–7. LinkedIn Insight Tag

the </body> tag. If you use Google Tag Manager, which I highly recommend, you can add the Insight Tag script into your current Google Tag. You can learn more about Google Tag Manager at https://marketingplatform.google.com/about/tag-manager/.

If you have a WordPress website, you can download a free plugin like RO Marketing from Red Olive, which lets you install and manage your Insight Tag, among others. I recommend searching for WordPress plugins for LinkedIn Insights and see how many downloads and positive reviews the plugin has. Here's a URL to view WordPress plugins designed for the Insight Tag: https://wordpress.org/plugins/search/linkedin+insight+tag/.

Once your Insight Tag is installed on your website, add your site's URL in the right column of LinkedIn's Campaign Manager under Domains. LinkedIn will go to your URL and verify the tag is installed properly.

Conversion Tracking

Now that your Insight Tag is installed, you can set up your Conversion Tracking. The tag will track your conversions and manage your Matched Audiences, which I will explain later in this chapter.

To create a new conversion to track, go to Account Assets and Create New Conversion. Figure 20–8 on page 231 shows a sample conversion setup form. Fill out the conversion name and select the type. Your choices are:

- Add to cart
- Download
- Install
- Key page view
- Lead
- Purchase
- Signup
- Other

For more details about the conversion type, visit https://www.linkedin.com/help/linkedin/answer/67515.

Next you can assign a value to the conversion. If you are selling a product, it's easy to know the value of the conversion. If you are offering a whitepaper as a lead generator, you could assign the value of the product or service you hope to eventually sell them. This may not be the best measurement since you will not convert 100 percent of the people who download the whitepaper. For example, if you offer a $5,000 coaching package, you could assign the value of $5,000, but it may be better to assign a value of $50, which would be a 1 percent conversion rate.

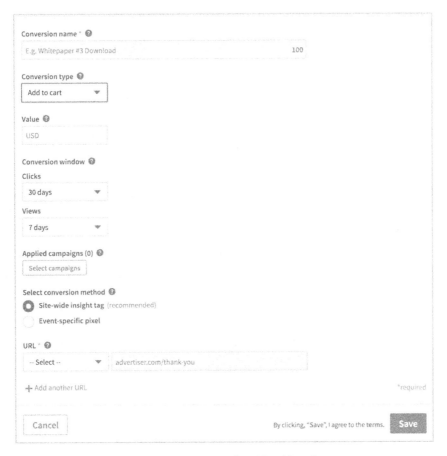

FIGURE 20–8. Conversion Tracking Setup

I leave the Conversion Window at the default settings: Clicks at 30 days, and Views at seven days. This lets you set the amount of time that a conversion can be counted after someone clicks or views your ad.

Select the campaign you want under Applied Campaigns. I usually select Site-Wide Insight Tag unless I'm tracking an event-specific conversion. In that case, I would need to create a separate pixel for that event. To complete the setup, enter the URL where you are sending the traffic from the click. You have three choices: Contains, Starts With, or Exact. If I'm driving traffic to a specific landing page on my website, I select Exact so I know how well that landing page is converting. For example, I would select Exact and enter "https://tedprodromou.com/li-chapter" if I were promoting a free chapter of this book. After you click Save, LinkedIn will verify your conversion to make sure it's set up properly.

Matched Audiences

Now comes the fun part. If you are familiar with Facebook Custom Audiences and Google Audience Targeting, you'll love LinkedIn's Matched Audiences. There are two types of Matched Audiences, pixel-based and list-based.

Pixel-Based Audience

This is one of the most powerful online advertising tools in existence. Once you place the pixel or Insight Tag on your website, you can create a list, or audience, of everyone who visits that page. You can then run follow-up ads to those people if they didn't complete the conversion you want to achieve. Research by HubSpot says people are more likely to convert after they see an ad at least seven to ten times. If they only see your ad once or twice, the likelihood of converting is low.

Let's say I set up a Sponsored Content ad to promote a free chapter of this book, which leads to an offer to buy the book after they download the chapter. Here's the basic marketing funnel:

1. A viewer clicks on my LinkedIn ad and is taken to a landing page, like https://tedprodromou.com/li-chapter.

2. Once he views that page, a cookie is placed in their browser by the Insight Tag, and he is added to the Matched Audience I created for this campaign, called LinkedIn Free Chapter Visitor.

3. If they fill out the web form and downloads the free chapter, a conversion is triggered, and they are placed into a different Matched Audience, called LinkedIn Free Chapter Downloaded and removed from LinkedIn Free Chapter Visitor.

4. If they do not fill out the web form, I can run follow up ads to the LinkedIn Free Chapter Visitor Matched Audience to urge them to download the free chapter.

5. If they do download the chapter, I can run follow-up ads to the LinkedIn Free Chapter Downloaded Audience and offer a video tutorial for $97 about optimizing your LinkedIn profile. (This is how you earn back your advertising costs and move them further down your marketing funnel toward your high-end products.)

6. Once they are on my email list, they are a follow-up email sequence, where I can share free tips and entice them to invest in my Linked Accelerator course or one-on-one coaching.

This basic funnel gets my campaign started. I'll show you how to create high-converting LinkedIn campaigns in the next chapter.

List-Based Audience

Another type of Matched Audience is created by uploading a list of contacts. The most common list upload is your email list. Once you upload your email list into a new Matched Audience, LinkedIn will try to match your email addresses to email addresses in LinkedIn profiles. Once this process is complete, you can run ads to this targeted Matched Audience. These ads can be very effective since they subscribed to your email list at some point and may already be customers. When they see ads from your company, your conversion rates should be very high because they are already familiar with your business.

You can also upload a list of contacts who have purchased a specific product or service from you into a Matched Audience. When you run an ad campaign to promote that product or service, you can prevent those people from seeing your ads. This way you don't waste money showing ads to people who don't need the product.

WEBSITE DEMOGRAPHICS

Another great feature of the Insight Tag is the powerful analytics you receive about your website. In Figure 20–9 below, you can see one of LinkedIn's Website Demographics reports. I placed the Insight Tag on my website, https://tedprodromou.com/, and all visitors there are matched to their LinkedIn profile demographics. This screenshot shows me the LinkedIn job functions of my website visitors from January 2018 until mid-August 2018.

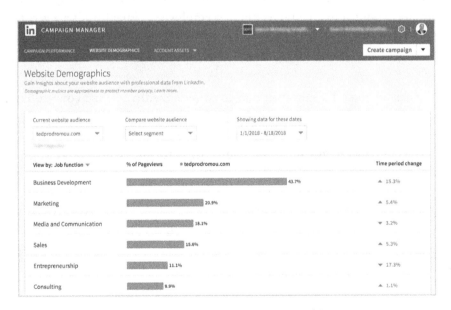

FIGURE 20–9. Website Demographics

Business development professionals made up 43.7 percent of my website visitors during this period and were trending up. This tells me I need to be creating products and services geared toward those professionals. During the same time period, entrepreneurship was declining at only 11.1 percent of my visitors. I should stop writing sales copy targeting entrepreneurs and consultants, the two smallest categories, and focus on business development, marketing, and media and communication people.

I can also break out this data by:

- Company industry
- Job title
- Job seniority
- Company size
- Location
- Country
- Company

Using this data, I know exactly which demographic is visiting my website, which helps me fine-tune my marketing messages. I can create products and services these people need and shorten my sales cycle dramatically.

CONCLUSION

As you can see, LinkedIn provides a variety of advertising solutions to help you generate leads, promote your company, and recruit new employees. LinkedIn ads are very targeted and very effective because you have access to so much demographic data. You can precisely target your advertising, so your conversion rates are often well above industry average.

In the next chapter, I'll show you how to write LinkedIn ads that convert like crazy.

**For additional updates and how-to videos, visit
https://tedprodromou.com/UltimateGuideUpdates/.**

Chapter 21

Creating LinkedIn Ads That Convert Like Crazy

What makes one ad bring in sales better than another? We've all seen ads that grab our attention and make us want to learn more. We've also seen ads that leave us speechless, wondering what the heck the advertiser was trying to say.

What is the difference between an ad that works and an ad that leaves us confused? It's simple. Ads that get our attention aren't visibly trying to sell us anything. Nothing turns us off more than being given the hard sell like a used-car salesman. We like ads that teach us something or entertain us. They turn off our noise filter so the advertiser can start to build a trusting relationship with us.

Apple is one of the very best at this. Just watching an Apple commercial makes you feel like your part of the "in" crowd. Notice that Apple never tries to sell you a phone or a computer in its ads. Instead, it creates an experience where average people just like you and me are enjoying a perfect life, without a care in the world. They just happen to be using an iPad to surf the internet or talking to Siri on their iPhone while they're living that carefree life. This makes us associate Apple products with an ideal lifestyle. As a result, we want to run out and buy an iPad or iPhone so we can be just like the people in the commercial. Who doesn't want to feel like that?

Owning Apple products has become a status symbol, like driving a Mercedes or BMW. Make sure you focus on creating an experience, and people will remember you.

On the other hand, have you ever watched a commercial or seen a banner ad that left you feeling angry or annoyed? Or maybe the ad was so offbeat that you had no idea what company produced it and what product it was promoting?

For example, ads with annoying jingles or irritating characters can turn us off. The ads with Flo from Progressive Insurance—the woman in the white apron, selling insurance like it's a product in a box—are always considered among the most annoying commercials by my friends.

Flashing banner ads with too much rapid movement are also considered ineffective. While the fast, flashy movements catch our eye, they can also turn us off, even if the ad has a great message.

Ads that confuse us often try to sell us something before we even know what the product is. Sometimes the ad does a terrible job explaining how the product can help us, so we get confused and tune out. It may be a product we really need, but it tried to close the sale before we were ready.

So how do we create text and banner ads on LinkedIn that seduce like the Apple ads do?

SELLING THROUGH ADS ON LINKEDIN

When creating ads for LinkedIn or any other online platform, don't sell your product or service through the ad. Perry Marshall, online marketing expert and bestselling author of *Ultimate Guide to Facebook Advertising* and *Ultimate Guide to Google AdWords*, teaches that you are "selling the click," which means your only goal is to get the viewer to click on the ad. Once they do, they are redirected to a landing page where you can continue the conversation you started in the ad. You want to make a connection with the reader and build a long-term relationship.

If you are selling business-to-consumer (B2C) products, like you see on sites such as Amazon or Target, it's OK to sell in your advertising because you can entice people to make impulse purchases. The price point for B2C products is much lower and the buying cycle can be seconds or minutes. LinkedIn isn't a great place to advertise B2C products since it's aimed at a business audience.

B2B products and services have a much higher price point and a longer buying cycle—sometimes up to a year, so you have to build a long-term relationship with the buyer.

On LinkedIn, you may be running ads for many reasons, including:

- Lead generation so your sales reps can follow up with the prospects

- Inviting people to follow your company or join your Group
- Recruiting new employees for your company
- B2B products or services promotions
- Client case studies or success stories promotions
- LinkedIn polls or promotions to gather business intelligence
- Brand promotions so people will become familiar with your company

LinkedIn advertising can be a very powerful tool if used correctly. As with any ad campaign, you need to create a plan and an objective. A well-executed advertising campaign will return huge dividends for your company.

CREATING LASER-FOCUSED CAMPAIGNS

If you are creating an ad campaign to generate leads, focus on generating leads. If you are running a branding campaign to publicize your company name, focus on the branding campaign. Do not try to kill two birds with one stone by combining a lead-gen campaign with a branding campaign. The mixed message will yield terrible results.

When you see an online ad, you should be able to tell if it is meant to promote a brand, advertise a product, generate leads, gather information, recruit new employees, or build relationships. If the ad's intent isn't obvious, it's probably a failure. Remember, people decide in a split second if an ad is relevant and move on if it's not.

Everyone sees thousands of ads every day, so it's hard to break through the clutter and grab someone's attention. You need to interrupt a viewer's thought pattern without being annoying. If you pique their interest, they'll click on your ad to learn more. If you don't grab their attention in a second or two, they move on and can subconsciously block you out in the future. This is why you need to carefully plan your ad campaigns to get the most for your dollar.

LinkedIn has some of the most advanced targeting capabilities of any online advertising platform. You can display specific ads to specific job titles, companies, or Groups. A well-planned LinkedIn ad campaign includes tracking your results so you know which ads and targeting demographics work best for you.

If you are creating ad campaigns for a web content management software company, you can target web developers, IT managers, marketing executives, project managers, and CEOs. You can display technical ads to the developers and IT managers, marketing-focused ads to the marketing executives, project-management-related ads to the project managers, and financial-related ads to the CFO and CEO.

Many advertisers don't take advantage of the site's targeting capabilities, displaying all their ads to all job titles. The web developers thus see ads designed for the CEO, and the CEO may see the technical ads, which results in a lower conversion rate. Creating specific, relevant ads and displaying them to the appropriate target audience will improve your conversion rate significantly while reducing your advertising costs.

WRITING EFFECTIVE ADS

Remember when you were learning to ride a bike? You were probably nervous—maybe even scared—because you didn't know what to expect. You were afraid you would fall and get hurt. Maybe you thought people would laugh at you. At first, you were unsteady and fell a few times. You might have even fallen a lot before you got the hang of it.

But eventually you caught on, and before you knew it, you were bombing down the street on your bike. The more you rode, the better you got, and soon your fear completely disappeared.

Copywriting, like bike riding, is a skill you need to practice regularly to get better. No one is born an expert copywriter. We get good at it by practicing and making mistakes. Fortunately, it doesn't hurt when you make a mistake when writing copy. It just may cost you a few bucks because your ad didn't convert as well as you expected. Like learning to ride a bike, start slow and hone your skills. If you practice consistently and learn from your mistakes, you will get better.

There are many great books that will teach you the basics of copywriting and ad writing. Some of my favorites include:

- *The Ultimate Sales Letter* by Dan S. Kennedy (Adams Media, 2011)
- *Ultimate Guide to Google AdWords* by Perry Marshall, Mike Rhodes, and Bryan Todd (Entrepreneur Press, 2017)
- *Ultimate Guide to Facebook Advertising* by Perry Marshall, Keith Krance, and Thomas Meloche (Entrepreneur Press, 2017)
- *How to Write Copy That Sells* by Ray Edwards (Morgan James Publishing, 2016)
- *The Adweek Copywriting Handbook* by Joseph Sugarman (Wiley, 2006)
- *Breakthrough Advertising* by Eugene M. Schwartz (Bottom Line Books, 2004)

The most important thing you will learn from the above books is how to write sales letters and ads from the customers' perspective. The biggest mistake beginners make when writing copy for ads is that they write from their own perspective. They talk about the features and benefits of their products or services and tell you how wonderful your life will be when you purchase them.

The key to writing successful online ads is to put yourself in the shoes of the people who are reading your ad. Imagine how they are feeling. Find their pain points. Understand why they are frustrated. Once you get into their heads, you can write ads that will instantly grab their attention and make them comfortable with you and your products.

LINKEDIN TEXT ADS

Now you know the basics of writing good ads and have some great resources that will help you become an expert copywriter and ad writer. In the previous chapter, I gave you a brief introduction to LinkedIn Text Ads. Now let's dig deeper into what it takes to write high-converting ads.

LinkedIn Text Ads consist of the following components:

- Headline (up to 25 characters)
- Description (up to 75 characters)
- From (your name or company)
- Image (50 x 50 pixels)
- URL (website people visit when they click on your ad)

The headline and the image are the most important factors in your ad. Most online advertising experts agree and say the headline can account for up to 90 percent of your conversion rate. If you don't grab users' attention with a compelling headline or an eye-catching image, they'll never read the rest of your ad, let alone click on it.

You could say the headline and image in your online ad are very similar to the title and cover of a book. Research has shown that the title is one of the chief reasons people purchase a book. In 1938, Napoleon Hill wrote a book with the controversial title *Outwitting the Devil*. Sales skyrocketed after he retitled it *Think and Grow Rich*. To date it has sold more than 100 million copies.

CREATING ATTENTION-GRABBING HEADLINES

Think back to one of your favorite commercials or ads. Great ads are more than just words. Great ads tell a story or create an unforgettable experience. The ad's headline is the title of the story, which makes you want to read more. In fact, great headlines make you *have* to read more.

High-converting headlines trigger emotions and pique your interest. How many times have you been standing in line at the grocery store and covertly checked out the cover of *Star* or *Cosmopolitan* magazine, hoping nobody you know would see you? These publications are masters at creating attention-getting headlines that *make* you pick up the magazine to read the story behind the headline.

Some sample headers from a recent issue of *Cosmopolitan* include:

- How to turn an office crush into something more
- It drives him wild when I . . .
- Blow his mind every single time
- Five dates that will drive him wild
- The five new ways to lose weight

All these headlines trigger an emotion (positive or negative) or grab your attention. They are provocative, and you can't miss them as you stand there waiting to pay for your groceries.

Of course, it's unlikely your LinkedIn advertising will trigger these same emotions, but you want to create the same effect when people see your ads. When they read your headline, they'll *have* to read the rest of your ad and click to learn more.

FACTORS THAT GENERATE CLICKS

Here are five factors that can make your ads more clickable. Obviously there are other factors to consider, but these five work well in online advertising. Not all of them will result in clicks on ads for your product or service, so you have to test to see which ones convert best for you. They are:

1. Curiosity
2. Benefit
3. Emotion
4. Credibility
5. Expectation

They may seem pretty obvious, but let's explore them so you're clear on how you can use them in your headlines.

Curiosity

We are curious by nature and want to learn more about subjects that interest us. If you start your headline with phrases like "How I . . ." or "How do I . . .," the reader will be curious and want to read the entire headline. You can also use contradictions in your headline to confuse the reader so you'll have their attention. Here are some sample headlines that use curiosity to get attention:

- "How I turned my business around in the worst economy ever . . ."
- "How do I get top search rankings in Google for my business without spending a fortune?"
- "Social media is NOT your only way to get web traffic"

See how easy it is to generate curiosity? Once you've piqued their interest, they will continue reading your ad and discover the benefits you offer them.

Benefit

By providing a clear benefit in your headline, people will click on your ad to find out more. You are implying that they will learn something new that may give them a competitive advantage. Some examples of benefit-driven headlines include:

- "3 Easy Ways to Increase Your Clickthrough Rate by at Least 40%"
- "How to Convert More Web Visitors into Raving Customers"
- "How to Work Less and Earn More"

Benefits are very different from features, so don't confuse them. Features are the distinctive red knobs on my Wolf range or its built-in convection oven. Benefits are the fact that the heavy-duty red knobs make my stove easy to operate, and when I bake in the oven, the heat is distributed evenly, ensuring everything is finished to perfection.

Emotion

People respond to certain words, especially when they trigger an emotion. The right words will make people click on your ads. If you watch an infomercial, you will hear and see a steady stream of emotion-triggering words, like *amazing, incredible, superb, excellent, free*, and on and on. You may hear them say something like, "This amazing formula will help you feel superb, look incredible, and make you completely irresistible." Who wouldn't buy that? Here are some examples of emotional headlines:

- "8 Incredibly Simple Ways to Increase Sales by at Least 25%"
- "Ten Free Social Media Tips That Will Generate More Incredible Comments on Your Blogs"
- "Easily Learn a New Language in Just 20 Minutes a Day!"

Advertising experts know people buy based on emotion and then justify the purchase with logic. According to Michael Harris, author of the 2015 *Harvard Business Review* article "When to Sell with Facts and Figures, and When to Appeal to Emotions," people do not decide logically. The decision to buy is made subconsciously, and these subconscious decisions are based on a "deeply empirical mental processing system" that follows a logic of its own.

Credibility

Most people like concrete or tangible ideas because they are familiar and make sense to them. When you hear "1 + 1 = 2," that is tangible because you know it's true. When you hear "How large is space?," you don't feel comfortable because there is no definitive answer. Including familiar experts is an easy way to make your headline tangible and credible. Some examples of tangible headlines include:

- "Warren Buffett Shows You How to Invest Your Money Wisely"
- "Tony Robbins Shares His Deepest Personal Development Secrets"
- "How to Start a Social Network like Mark Zuckerberg"

We perceive celebrities as experts because we are familiar with them, so we subconsciously trust them. Not many of us know Warren Buffett personally, but we all know he became one of the richest men in the world by becoming an expert stock market investor, so we trust him.

Expectation

It's important to set reasonable expectations in your ad and not over-promise. You can't promise people that you can get them top rankings on Google for all their target keywords or guarantee they will lose at least 20 pounds with your home exercise program unless you really can give them those results. It's just not realistic to promise results that you know everyone won't achieve, and it's illegal to make promises you can't guarantee. You need to provide exactly what you are promising in the headline. If you promise a free white paper showing seven steps to success, then you have to provide all seven steps in the white paper—not just one step and then coax the reader into purchasing the next six.

Here are some reasonable expectation-based ads:

- "Voted Best Restaurant in San Francisco 5 Years in a Row by Sunset Magazine"
- "7 Steps to Setting Up Your WordPress Blog"
- "Learn How to Recruit the Best Employees on LinkedIn"

You might like to create a spreadsheet to track which factors work best with each product. Figure 21–1 on page 243 demonstrates how to track your ads. The best-converting ad is placed in the box that corresponds with the factor and appropriate product. So how do you create attention-grabbing headlines that convert like crazy? In the next sections, I'll walk you through a few techniques to help you get started.

BRAINSTORMING HEADLINES

Top copywriters like Dan Kennedy, Bill Glazer, and John Carlton teach you to sit down with a blank pad of paper and start writing headlines until you run out of ideas. Just put your pen on the paper and write down everything that comes to mind. Don't stop until you have at least 30 headlines. Most of them will be terrible, but by doing a complete brain dump, you will come up with a few good ones to test.

Factor	Product A	Product B	Product C	Product D
Curiosity				How I Turned My Business Around in the Worst Economy Ever . . .
Benefit		How to Convert More Web Visitors into Raving Customers		
Emotion	Easily Learn a New Language in Just 20 Minutes a Day!			
Credibility	Warren Buffett Shows You How to Invest Your Money Wisely			
Expectation			Learn How to Recruit the Best Employees on LinkedIn	

FIGURE 21–1. Tracking Factors of Successful Ad Conversion

THE OLD MAGAZINE RACK TRICK

Another great way to get headline ideas is to go to your nearest bookstore or grocery store and check out the magazines as I did for the *Cosmopolitan* magazine headlines above. Your local bookstore will have huge racks filled with hundreds of magazines in every niche—or you can search online.

Write down the headlines and article summaries that grab your attention and use similar wording to create compelling headlines for your LinkedIn ads.

FIGURE 21–2. Article Titles

Let's say you sell computer security software and want to advertise on LinkedIn. You could create a targeted advertising campaign that is displayed only to IT professionals. You need headlines and ad content, so you check out *PC Magazine* for some ideas. In one issue, you see the following articles related to computer security, as shown in Figure 21–2. You hit the jackpot!

These are article titles and descriptions that could easily be modified to be powerful ads on LinkedIn to promote your products or white papers describing your products. What if the first article was a LinkedIn ad? Would you click on it if you were in the market for a new antivirus program?

Best Antivirus Software

Still not running antivirus protection?

We'll help you choose the best solution.

The headline, "Best Antivirus Software," should catch their eye if people see this ad in a LinkedIn Group. The simple question, "Still not running antivirus protection on your Mac?," will trigger an emotion if they don't have an antivirus program or they're using an inadequate or free version that isn't protecting their computers. They're probably thinking, "I'm so stupid for not protecting my business data," or something to that effect. The last line of the ad, "We'll help you choose the best solution," triggers another emotion: "I'm not in this alone. This expert is going to save my data."

Or you could promote a white paper you created to help people decide which solution is best.

Best Antivirus Software?

We reviewed the 21 best solutions.

Free white paper helps you decide.

This ad works the same as the first one by grabbing attention and triggering emotions. People who respond to this ad probably tried to figure out which antivirus program to buy but were overwhelmed by their choices or got lost in technical jargon. They feel great relief when they read this ad because this white paper will guide them to the best solution.

See how easy it is to create ads that resonate with people who are looking for what you are selling?

CREATE A SWIPE FILE

All copywriters have what is known as a *swipe file*, where they save articles, magazine and newspaper headlines, and direct mail that they use as a source of ideas for their own ads. Those ads you receive in the mail every day are great sources for headlines and ad copy.

Create a file folder where you can save headlines and articles that caught your attention. If you run ads for many different niches or topics, create a separate swipe file for each one. When you're ready to write new ads, pull out the swipe file for that niche and read through the clippings you've collected. After you've gone through all the clippings, do the brainstorming exercise I showed you earlier. Your brain is full of ideas from the swipe file, so you should be able to crank out 30 to 50 headlines in short order.

When I was a personal coach, I purchased a lot of personal development programs from Nightingale-Conant. They are masters of direct marketing, sending daily motivational quotes via email along with a promotion for a related personal development program. The emails have catchy subject lines that act as the headlines. I copy the emails and subject lines into a huge Word document as an electronic swipe file. They are also masters at direct-mail promotion, so I receive at least two promotional postcards or sales letters in the mail every week. Every envelope has a compelling headline that makes you rip it open to read the letter promoting the latest method for improving your life. I save every envelope and sales letter from them in my swipe file so I have content to give me ideas when I'm ready to write ads or web copy.

WRITING YOUR AD COPY

Once you have a headline, it's time to write your ad copy. Remember how I described the Apple ads? The cool stuff you can do with an iPhone and the cheerful people in the ad make you feel happy and part of the crowd. When Apple shows you the cool iPhone tricks, it is visually describing the benefits of the product. Some Apple ads don't even show people. They just show an iPhone in one hand and a finger sliding across the screen doing tricks like a magician. The simple imagery is so powerful and makes the iPhone seem so easy to use, like all Apple products. What a huge benefit for a high-tech product when most people are overwhelmed by the complexity of technology!

Your ad copy should tell a story that triggers an emotion, catching readers' attention so they take your desired action. If you want them to download a white paper, for instance, they won't hesitate to fill out your web form because they know you are going to solve their problem.

Your ad should look like this:

Headline

Describe a benefit of your product or service (paint a picture in the reader's mind).
Provide a solution to a problem in the call to action or offer.

The headline is the title of the story the opening line of the ad should describe a benefit of your product or service, and the last line is your call to action or your offer.

THE POWER OF IMAGES

Images in advertising are as powerful as your headline. Often the image can be the most important aspect of your ad, depending on what you are promoting. The images you use in your ads are like a book cover. An attractive cover design for a book can increase sales exponentially, just like a compelling title.

Advertisers have long realized the importance of images in advertising. Claude Hopkins, one of the great innovators in advertising, was one of the first copywriters to discover that the combination of powerful, benefit-driven copy and relevant images increased response rates significantly. This combination also created a consistency in the response rates that never before existed. Creating ads for products was always a hit-or-miss proposition until Hopkins revolutionized the advertising industry.

Selecting the right image for your ad can be up to 70 percent of the reason that someone clicks on it. Your image will make your ad stand out on LinkedIn and interrupt the viewer's attention. The image you choose must be relevant to your ad and your offer. Deception may get viewers' attention and get them to click on your ad, but they will quickly become disappointed if your offer doesn't match the image.

Images of a real person, from the neck up, convert best on LinkedIn. The image size on the ad is only 50 x 50 pixels, so you don't have much real estate to work with. A simple headshot of a professional facing the camera works best. You don't want to use casual pictures of a person out at the baseball game or making silly faces. You are targeting professional people on a business-oriented website, so choose appropriate photos.

I've done a lot of testing of images on ads in which I gave away white papers, and the results are not surprising. Once I ran the same ad headline and content and just changed the image. One had a picture of an average-looking professional woman. The second had an average-looking professional man—the analyst who had written the white paper, in fact—and a third featured an image of the logo from the white paper. The ad with the woman received four times more clicks than those of the man or the logo. She had nothing to do with the ad or the white paper, but she was far more effective.

The above result may sound sexist, but most of the time people will click on an ad with an image of a woman. However, I recently ran the same three ads again but changed the targeting from executives and managers to just a few LinkedIn Groups. The ad with the picture of the male analyst outperformed the other ads two to one. I'm assuming the people in the Groups were familiar with the analyst, making him a bigger draw.

FOLLOW ADVERTISING GUIDELINES

LinkedIn has a very strict approval process for new ad campaigns and any changes to your existing ad campaigns. Your campaign will not run until a human manually reviews your ad content. It can take 24 to 72 hours for your ads to be approved or re-approved, so you need to plan ahead. Other ad platforms like Google and Facebook will begin running your ads immediately then flag them if they detect inappropriate ad content.

Be sure to adhere to LinkedIn's advertising guidelines so your ads are approved quickly. Use common sense when creating your ad campaigns. To see the guidelines visit https://www.linkedin.com/help/linkedin/answer/727/advertising-guidelines.

Here's a quick list of high-level guidelines for ads:

- Don't deceive or lie.
- Don't use nonstandard spelling, grammar, capitalization, punctuation, or repetition.
- Don't discriminate.
- Don't use inappropriate or unacceptable language.
- Don't deceive, confuse, or otherwise degrade the experience of members who click.
- Don't advertise prohibited products. See the complete list of prohibited products in the advertising guidelines link above.
- Don't use trademarks that you aren't permitted to use or the LinkedIn logo.
- Don't promote sensitive content including illegal products, dating sites, hate or violence.

The guidelines are pretty self-explanatory and easy to adhere to. Of course you never want to deceive or lie in your ads because your reputation could be permanently damaged. LinkedIn will disallow any ads that break these rules, and it can permanently ban you and your company from running ads on the site if you are a repeat offender.

A/B SPLIT TESTING

Above I showed you why it's important to always test your ads and measure the results according to the group you are targeting. You can never be 100 percent certain which headline, ad copy, or image will perform best. There are many factors that determine this, so you have to constantly test your ads and adjust accordingly.

Testing your ad combinations is commonly called *A/B split testing*. You are testing ad A against ad B to determine which one performs best. You always want to split test different combinations of headlines, ad copy, and images until you find the highest-converting combination. Once you do, use that ad as your control ad and run it while you test new combinations. Once you beat your control ad, that combination becomes your new control ad.

You never know what subtle changes will make one ad perform better than another. Sometimes capitalizing every word works; other times changing one word in the headline does the trick. Here are some tips:

1. Create multiple ads for each campaign.
   - Use at least three variations.
   - Try capitalizing every word in the headline and ad copy.
   - Try different calls to action.
2. You can create up to 15 ads per campaign and set different budgets and settings for each ad.
3. You can start to show the ads that do best more often, or you can display all the ads equally.

Make sure you track your ads accurately so you know which ones are performing best. Your goal is to achieve the highest clickthrough rate (CTR) and conversion rate possible. The other important statistic to monitor is the number of impressions, which is the number of times your ads are displayed. You want your ads to be displayed as many times as possible, but they should be displayed to the appropriate audience to raise your CTR, which reduces your cost per click (CPC).

TARGETING YOUR ADS

One of the most powerful features of LinkedIn advertising is your ability to target the audience to whom your ads will be displayed. You can create very specific ads for very specific demographics, so your response rate increases dramatically.

You can target your LinkedIn ads based on any or all of the following criteria:

- Job function
- Job title
- Company
- Company industry
- Job seniority
- Company size
- Location
- Country

It will take some testing to determine the perfect targeting for your ads, but once you nail the demographic of your ideal customer, your ads will generate consistent leads and sales for your business. Be patient, split test your ad campaigns, and measure your results so you know which campaigns are fully optimized.

BIDDING

For each campaign, you set a payment method of cost per click (CPC) or cost per thousand impressions (CPM). In both cases, you also set a bid for the maximum you're willing to pay.

For CPC ads, you can enter a bid that's within the suggested bid range, which is an estimate of the current competing bids by other advertisers. The higher you bid within the range, the more likely it is that your ad will be shown and receive clicks. Once you become more familiar with how the bidding works, you can adjust your bids accordingly.

For CPM bidding, you enter the maximum you are willing to pay for 1,000 impressions of your ad. In CPM bidding, you are paying for ad impressions, not clicks, and with CPC bidding you are paying for each time a person actually clicks on your ad.

You should test CPC against CPM bidding in your campaigns because sometimes you pay less for CPM bidding and get better results. If you are running a branding campaign to give your brand more exposure via maximum impressions and you don't care about the number of clicks, you should use CPM.

HOW TO MEASURE SUCCESS AND IMPROVE YOUR PERFORMANCE

It's important to measure success for every ad campaign so you can tweak how you plan for future campaigns. Knowing your goals and revisiting them during or after

Ad Name	Impressions Clicks	CTR Cost	Cost per Click (CPC) Conversions	ROI
Ad 1				
Ad 2				
Ad 3				
Ad 4				

FIGURE 21–3. Ad Performance Tracking

a campaign will help you know when you've created the right ads, targeted the right audience, optimized the best landing pages, and maximized your revenue. Keep these things in mind:

- *If your goal is to generate traffic to your website landing page,* you can use the Campaign Performance section in the Campaign Manager to track your performance. You can track the number of clicks you've received (the number of visitors to your website) and your total budget spent.

- *If your goal is to generate leads,* you need to track users' actions on your website with a web analytics tool like Google Analytics or with LinkedIn's Conversion Tracking, which is located under Account Assets in the Campaign Manager. Using web analytics and conversion tracking, you can track the number of web visits from LinkedIn, the number of conversions, and the conversion rate.

You can use a chart like the one in Figure 21–3 to manually track your ads and see which perform best. The chart shows you everything you need to know about your campaigns, including the number of conversions and your return on investment.

CONCLUSION

Online ads that convert best are relevant to the target audience and are written with clear, compelling words. Keep the following tips in mind as you create your own LinkedIn ad campaigns:

- Remember to use emotion-triggering words that grab the reader's attention in the headline.
- Make sure the description in your ad clearly outlines the benefits of your offer.
- Use an image that readers will notice and is relevant to your offer.
- Always include a clear call to action in your ad, like "download now" or "try it for 30 days."
- Use special offers, trials, or free reports to entice them to click on your ad.

In the next chapter, we'll meet some people who have had great experiences on LinkedIn and have used it to make long-lasting connections, find employment, and build or enhance their businesses.

For additional updates and how-to videos, visit
https://tedprodromou.com/UltimateGuideUpdates/.

LinkedIn Success Stories

Now that we've talked about all the ways you can use LinkedIn to build your business and brand, it's time to meet some of my clients who have used the site to grow or start their business. All of them created their LinkedIn account years ago but rarely logged in. They didn't realize LinkedIn was the perfect marketing tool to grow their business. I worked with each of them for a few months, and together we applied all the principles I have showed you in this book. Today, LinkedIn has become an essential part of their marketing toolkit. In this chapter, they talk about their successes (and failures) on LinkedIn in their own words. Let's meet them.

GROWING YOUR COACHING PRACTICE
Gary Barnes, The Breakthrough Business Mastery Coach

I have built three successful businesses over the past 40-plus years, personally selling more than $280 million in products and services. I spent the first nine years in real estate before establishing one of the very first financial-planning firms in the United States. I built that firm into the top 3 percent in production as a solo producer and sold it after 30 years.

After that, I founded Gary Barnes International and became known as "The Breakthrough Business Mastery Coach." I am a high-performance business and sales strategist, popular national and international speaker, and award-winning international Amazon bestselling author of nine books. My clients have spanned seven countries, and I have been published in many media outlets, including *The Boston Globe, Los Angeles Daily News, Miami Herald, CBS MoneyWatch, Morningstar,* and *Worth* magazine. I have also been featured on ABC, CBS, NBC, Fox, PBS, and TEDx.

The common element in building all my businesses has been my ability to cultivate personal relationships with my clients. What I lacked when I owned my first two businesses was the power of social media to connect to my perfect client base. The challenge now is creating those personal, high-touch relationships in a high-tech world.

LinkedIn is one of the primary social media platforms that I actively use to build those connections and relationships. I believe one of the major misconceptions in using social media for marketing is that all you need to do is open an account, create your profile, and have a presence. People will then flock to you like magic. In my experience, this couldn't be further from the truth.

Building effective relationships using high-tech platforms like LinkedIn is no different from building relationships in person. The more you know about the person and their needs, the more opportunities you have to provide possible solutions. It isn't about the number of connections you have but rather how relevant you are to those connections.

Since I met Ted, he has helped me use LinkedIn more effectively by creating a unique user profile and strong presence on the site. I invest approximately 15 to 20 minutes every day on my LinkedIn connections. The areas I focus on are:

- *New invitations to connect.* I accept almost all invitations. I take it one step further and send them a welcome message, sharing a little about me and asking them to do the same. I use this to determine whether they really want to build a relationship or whether they're just adding me to their list of connections. If they don't respond, I don't make a judgment about their intention. But if they do, it tells me I need to invest more time in the conversation. When I connect with someone, I have no agenda other than getting to know who they are. This allows us to have open and productive conversations.
- *Birthdays and work anniversaries.* It takes very little time to reach out and say happy birthday or happy anniversary. Many times I will get a response about how meaningful it was to get my greeting and thanking me for taking time out of my busy schedule to reach out. I never use the standard auto-fill but rather their name and a short greeting. If I get a thank-you, I make sure to respond to that as well. I want them to know it is really me that is getting back to them.

- *Responding to messages.* When someone sends me a message, it tells me I have risen to a certain level of significance for that person. Even if it's just about something that they are promoting, I will give them a short reply.
- *Liking and commenting on other people's posts.* When I spend a few minutes looking at the newsfeed, I usually find comments or articles that I can at least like. But what I'm really looking for are posts I can comment on. My comments are not necessarily just opinions but also suggested resources that could be useful.
- *Messaging current connections.* It's important to me to not only build new connections but also to maintain existing relationships. It can be as simple as saying, "I just thought of you and wanted to reach out and say hi. Have a fantastic day!" Again, it is amazing how people will respond when they know you really do want to connect with them.
- *Posting comments and articles.* This is one of the best ways to showcase the benefits of connecting with you. It is not an opportunity to promote and sell your "stuff." If you do that, it will come across as a commercial and people will not see you as a valued resource. This is another area where I have no agenda about converting the reader into buying something.

LinkedIn has meant a lot to my business. I have chosen to use it as a vehicle to showcase who I am and what I do and not as a direct-selling platform. That way, I have shown that I'm a safe person to connect with, someone who really wants a relationship, not just a sale.

That doesn't mean, however, that I have not received revenue from my LinkedIn endeavors. I have had people reach out to engage me as their business coach. I have secured speaking engagements, both locally and nationally. Almost weekly I am asked to be interviewed on radio shows and podcasts, some of them nationally and internationally syndicated.

LinkedIn can be one of the most effective and influential elements of building a successful business. The key to that success is being seen as a unique, relevant resource.

Gary Barnes is The Business Breakthrough Coach. You can connect with Gary at https://www.linkedin.com/in/speakersalescoachgarybarnes/.

SELLING THE DREAM ON LINKEDIN
Paige Collin, Franchise Owner

I'm a franchise owner of Cruise Planners, an American Express Travel Representative. Our franchise also includes land vacations and cruises anywhere in the world. Before my husband and I bought our Cruise Planners franchise, I was the personal assistant to one of the wealthiest men in the world. I traveled to many destinations with him and planned events around the world, which fueled my passion to help others travel.

We purchased our franchise six years ago, and it's the best investment I ever made. My husband and I have traveled extensively, and I thought it was appropriate to share our love of travel and use the skills I learned from my previous job.

LinkedIn has provided me with an entirely new audience that I didn't know existed. The majority of my LinkedIn contacts are between the ages of 25 and 55, and many are very interested in traveling. Most people on LinkedIn are successful business professionals who have enough disposable income to explore the world, which makes them my ideal prospects.

It's very easy for me to engage potential clients on LinkedIn. People at work are running from meeting to meeting, working 50 to 60 hours a week, and their stress level is through the roof. When I post pictures of exotic vacations on my newsfeed, they receive a "mini-mental vacation" between meetings. When they like or comment on my pictures, I engage them in conversation through LinkedIn messages. They ask questions about the picture I posted, and I describe the vacation they can enjoy there. The newsfeed pictures do most of the selling; I simply take the orders.

We design itineraries for our clients based on their needs and wants. We also suggest other options and excursions for our clients to take on their vacations. For example, customers might choose to go horseback riding in countries with gorgeous views, such as Italy, Australia, and Canada. Other interesting ideas are flying to Europe and taking a river cruise in France or Germany. There are so many wonderful options for those who want a different type of vacation. In the past, river cruises were more appealing to older travelers, but things have changed. River cruising is my favorite type of cruise, nice and slow, winding down the many rivers of European countries. These are all perfect getaway options, and I showcase them daily to my LinkedIn connections.

Most important, I met Ted, who has taught me the LinkedIn secrets many people don't know about: the use of hashtags to make my posts go viral, the use of native video, growing my network with my ideal prospects, and engaging new contacts with LinkedIn messages. The site is very important to me and my business. I enjoy making my posts and telling a story about different options for vacations and travel.

■ ■ ■

Paige Collin began her love of travel when she was a little girl. She has become one of the premier travel agents using LinkedIn. You can connect with Paige at https://www.linkedin.com/in/paige-collin-16078165/.

PAVING THE WAY TO A SUCCESSFUL MILITARY TRANSITION
Cedric Crumbley, Author and Marketing Consultant

If it wasn't for LinkedIn, I don't know where I would be. I certainly wouldn't have published a book. I first learned about the power of LinkedIn during a Perry Marshall webinar that featured Ted Prodromou sharing his LinkedIn strategies.

After that webinar, I ordered Ted's first edition of *Ultimate Guide to LinkedIn for Business* and started applying the advice in the book. I started getting some traction, and I was so excited about my results that I sent a message to Ted and told him I appreciated him for writing the book.

Ted responded with a thanks and suggested I fix the headline on my profile, which I immediately did. That's one thing that rings true with LinkedIn. Your headline is like the header on a billboard or the headline in a newspaper. It gets people to stop and read the rest of your profile. If your headline doesn't grab readers, your chances of getting them to engage more with you plummet.

Another good decision I made was to start preparing for a military exit eight years ahead of time. My job in the Army was as an Army recruiter. In the beginning, recruiting was not my favorite thing, but if it had not been for recruiting, I would not have needed to study marketing. And that was what prepared me to live the life I have now.

It turns out there are a lot of people looking for someone on LinkedIn who can help them grow their business. If you can get their attention, you will be the one chosen to solve their problem. LinkedIn became the key to my successful transition from the military to civilian life. Throw in mentorship from Ted, and you have a turbocharged recipe for success.

Ted would give me tasks to learn how I think. At one point he asked me about my life story, and I told him how I went from being a failure to becoming a top producer in Army recruiting. He told me I should write a book about it. I followed his advice, but I was a little skeptical; at the time, I didn't think anyone would want to read a book about an Army recruiter. To my surprise, the Kentucky National Guard purchased 150 copies and invited me to speak at a conference. That changed my life forever and set me on the path for life after the military.

After the book was published, things started taking off. I kept studying marketing and applying different techniques. I decided to experiment on LinkedIn in different markets, and I knew people love reading stories, so I started posting stories on LinkedIn targeting my market. Sure enough, I started getting traction. The key to posting articles on LinkedIn is knowing your audience and what they're struggling with.

After a while, people started reaching out to me for different projects. You can't beat the amount of high-quality connections on LinkedIn. It's the only place I know where you can send a message directly to the CEO of a company and get a response without going through an assistant.

Priceless.

■ ■ ■

Cedric Crumbley is an entrepreneur and marketing consultant. You can connect with Cedric at https://www.linkedin.com/in/cedcrumbley/.

OVERCOME YOUR FEAR OF PUBLIC SPEAKING
Doreen Hamilton, Public Speaking Coach

I had a Ph.D. and a career as a clinical psychologist, but I hid my fear of public speaking. It was easy for me to work one-on-one, but speaking in front of a group made me extremely nervous. What I discovered on my journey to overcome public speaking anxiety was a basic truth—it's not about performance techniques; it's about being comfortable with who you are.

The traditional approaches such as Toastmasters, which are aimed at reducing the fear of being in the spotlight, did not reach the place where I hid my weakness. And if I couldn't back out of giving a presentation, my Ph.D. from Berkeley was a good cover to convince others that I knew what I was talking about. I was always nervous because I was always hiding.

The approach that finally helped me be authentic was Speaking Circles, founded by Lee Glickstein. In these groups, my fear dissolved because I could expose my fear, talk about it, experience it, and watch it dissolve naturally. And at the same time I found a way to connect to my inner voice. Now I know this is the most powerful asset I possess.

My book, *Essential Speaking: The 7-Step Guide to Finding Your Real Voice*, combines the work I've done as a training director, my experience as a psychologist, and my interest in mindfulness. The question I started to ask was how I could reach more people with my signature seven-step process.

LinkedIn was and is the answer. Using the platform, I've been able to fill my groups, workshops, and private coaching schedule.

First, I needed to become very clear on what I offered and to whom. It wasn't a specific demographic. It was a psychographic, meaning that someone who suffers the fear of speaking in public could recognize themselves if I put in the headline a phrase such as, "Are you afraid to speak up in public?" This question elicits a yes or a no. Once I've grabbed the attention of someone who does have that problem and wants to solve it, they can read my LinkedIn summary.

In that summary, the potential client can learn more about me, the struggles I overcame, my programs, and how to take the next step. They can see from the way I've shared my story that I am interested in authenticity. My approach is not about delivering speeches; it's about helping people find the confidence to express themselves in any situation.

To appeal to the kind of person I thought would most benefit from my methods, I searched LinkedIn Groups about public speaking, mental health, and mindfulness. One particularly useful one was Conscious Women in Business. I simply wrote invitations to group members saying that we shared an interest in mindfulness and asked them to connect. This was the first step in finding how LinkedIn could bring together people who share the same values. I scheduled calls with many of these women, and we continue to engage, share each other's content, and refer to each other. I've been asked to be in their newsletters, blog posts, and podcasts.

In addition to Groups, I searched my 1st-degree connections for those I knew had a large audience and shared similar interests in personal and professional development. I then looked at the 2nd-degree connections and sent messages noting that we both were connected to such-and-such and I'd like them to join my network.

Another way I have found great connections is to like, comment on, and share posts by others whose material is relevant to my work or approach. In that way, I start to be known by a wider audience. And I often reach out to that person, say what I liked about their article, and invite them to connect with me.

Posts I make on LinkedIn are scheduled in advance. I make sure to vary them and offer value each time. I post inspirational quotes on images that also have my name and brand on them. I also post quotes from my book on images of my book. I share articles written by others about overcoming fear and speaking authentically. I have video clips of me leading groups.

By far, the most effective and engaging post I have shared has been a two-minute video I made in my office about the "7 Secrets to Fearless Speaking." It has had more than 2,500 views with more than 150 comments. I asked people to simply write "secrets" in the comments and offered to send them my PDF of the "7 Secrets to Fearless Speaking" in exchange. The response has been amazing. I've been having conversations with people who have this specific kind of anxiety. And they want help. They are asking me for answers, and I'm engaging them with steps they can take with me to solve their problem.

My groups and workshops in the San Francisco Bay Area are full. And people are enrolling in both my three-month and six-month private coaching programs. It's been a fun journey to develop what I love and find ways to promote it on LinkedIn.

■ ■ ■

Doreen Hamilton helps business professionals overcome their fear of public speaking and learn how to be heard in meetings. You can connect with Doreen at https://www.linkedin.com/in/drdoreenh/.

LINKEDIN NATIVE VIDEO SUCCESS
Deborah Herman, Book Publishing Professional

My experience with LinkedIn and working with Ted is indeed a success story. There is still a great deal to learn and implement, but his instruction and shared experiences from the group changed my understanding of the benefits of LinkedIn as a professional networking platform and helped me refocus my entire business.

I am the type of person who has education, skills, and valuable experience but is unsure how to present my unique value to a prospective client. Before working with Ted and his group, I was straddling the fence in too many directions. This is the difficulty for those of us with too much creativity and a short attention span. We create avenues where any one of them could be the right one, and then we get stuck in the intersection, waiting for something to propel us forward. I noticed some of the other members in the course facing some of the same challenges.

Ted's mastery of the LinkedIn platform helped me see how to reframe my disparate pieces into a cohesive and simple plan. This was not only beneficial to people seeking what I have to offer, but it also helped me understand how to choose the clients for whom I can be the most effective consultant.

My education began in law school. As is typical for me, halfway through my first year I discovered writing and created a dual degree with the Graduate School of Journalism. My ultimate goal was to write a true crime book, which I finally did in 2017 by co-writing the memoir of the youngest member of the Manson family: *Member of the Family: My Story of Charles Manson, Life Inside His Cult and the Darkness That Ended the Sixties*. This was a breakthrough for me. I had already written 11 other books, but this gave me the experience of being a front list author and confirmed to me that I really do know what I'm doing.

This became my unique selling proposition. As I learned in Ted's course, it takes at least 10,000 hours to become a true expert in a field. I have more than this in all aspects of the publishing industry. As consultants, we can be a bridge for our clients between that 10,000-hour learning curve and their goal. In only a few hours, I can analyze a manuscript to determine what will make it trade competitive. Sometimes it is an immediate instinct.

I began the course with an underused LinkedIn profile. Although I am still making improvements, I had not realized how important each section is in creating an image that will attract an appropriate network of colleagues, as well as generating leads for clients.

The few changes I made over the next several months made significant improvements in my visibility and helped others know immediately what I am about.

I am not unfamiliar with social media strategy and digital marketing. After creating a social network for writers, agents, and editors, I realized I needed to know more about this new way of marketing. Rutgers University offers mini-MBA certifications, and I received one in digital marketing strategy, social media strategy, and entrepreneurship. However, I had not embraced LinkedIn. I thought of it as professional networking, and since I had a business already, I didn't see the benefit.

But when you understand the community on LinkedIn and the protocols of how to network, the results are quick and discernable. I posted a video with a clear explanation of what was in it for others. I followed the advice of Ted and the group, who helped me word the offer in a way that was not too full of hype or obvious sales language. Ted taught me that people on LinkedIn are looking for specific things to assist in their personal or career development. That caused me to shift from focusing on my credentials to how my experience and credentials can help others reach their goals.

The video, which was the first I had done of its kind, got at least 4,000 views, which converted into requests for the PDF I was offering about "the basics of writing your book." I did a second video about "how to get started writing your first book." This one was also well-received, and I am still following up on the leads.

There were many tips and suggestions on how to optimize my profile and ways to automate communication with potential clients. In addition, I connected with people who can continue to help me grow my business. The best thing that came out of the experience is I have been completely redoing my own website to reflect my clearer focus on the three parts of my business, Micro Publishing Media.

The new website is clear about how we offer a team approach for authors on the early side of the learning curve. We can accommodate authors who want to pursue the traditional route of book proposal and submission to agents and large publishers. We can also publish and distribute books that fit in our various imprints. We strive for direct-to-consumer sales from our own ecommerce site, using the latest in digital marketing.

We are also an indie bookstore, like you used to be able to find in out-of-the-way places. I feel wonderful knowing exactly what I have to offer and having the confidence and focus to present it to potential customers and consulting clients. Working with Ted and the LinkedIn platform raised my awareness of my professionalism and the value of my skills that can benefit others.

You can connect with Deborah at https://www.linkedin.com/in/bookpublishingexpert/.

HELPING WOMEN SALES PROFESSIONALS SELL MORE COMFORTABLY AND CONFIDENTLY

Natalie Klun, Sales Expert

I am a sales guide to women business owners, sales professionals, and entrepreneurs with more than 20 years of sales experience. I am passionate about merging purpose with sales. I guide women in sales on how they can create predictable results when selling, know exactly what to say in any sales encounter, and sell with unshakable confidence by overcoming the fear of selling through my signature program, the Sales Spotlight.

LinkedIn was an untapped resource in my business, and I was able to accomplish the goals I had using Ted's Linked Accelerator system and tips from this book.

I started by optimizing my profile, adding clarity on who and how I serve and having clear messaging. I created a profile that is engaging and that spoke directly to my target audience. Afterward, I increased my social selling index by six points, from 71 to 77, and it continues to increase to this day. Prior to optimizing my profile, my social selling index was declining daily and my profile views were declining by as much as 67 percent. Today, my profile views have increased 109 percent.

Before implementing Ted's tips, approximately 35 percent of my 3,246 connections were not my target audience. I lacked a clear LinkedIn networking strategy that fit within my business goals and objectives. I recently added about 100 new connections who are my ideal clients, and many of them have invested in my $97 mini-course after just a few LinkedIn messages.

My goal now is to focus on growing my network with quality connections who are aligned with my business objectives instead of randomly connecting with everyone who sends an invitation. The system I have in place has me on track to grow my LinkedIn network a minimum of 25 percent over the next year with my target audience and/or collaborative partners.

A crucial component of my daily LinkedIn plan is the message feature. I did some testing by sending short messages and questions to my network. Based on the feedback from the people I interacted with, I was able to identify a need within my network, which resulted in a free guide called "7 Steps to Selling with Confidence." I produced a video and shared it with my network to offer the guide. This video had 2,050 views and generated 30 warm leads in just a few days. I'm planning to produce a weekly video and handout, as it has proved to be a valuable lead-generation tool for my LinkedIn network.

The lessons I learned from Ted and his *Ultimate Guide to LinkedIn for Business* are:

1. How to get clear on messaging that will increase engagement from the first point of contact with an optimized profile.
2. Clarity on my target audience and how to find them on LinkedIn.
3. How to virtually network using the tools on LinkedIn—it's about quality, not quantity.

The key for me has been to be proactive and intentional when networking on LinkedIn and other social networks. This has included engaging with connections for feedback and input, gaining insight on what my network needs from me, and then creating value-centered resources to grow my network and my business. These new products have so far engaged more than 20,000 individuals on LinkedIn, Facebook, and Instagram and have increased my email list by 10 percent each week, significantly increasing potential profit to my business in the very near future.

Applying these steps has optimized my profile and taught me to use LinkedIn as part of my daily business-building activities. It has also given me greater clarity on my target audience and helped me connect with them on LinkedIn as valued additions to my network.

Natalie Klun helps women sales professionals sell more comfortably and confidently. You can connect with Natalie at https://www.linkedin.com/in/natalieklun/.

THE ACCIDENTAL ENTREPRENEUR
Linda Lovero-Waterhouse, Social Media and Online Marketing Coach

I never spent a lot of time dreaming about running my own business, but I ended up unexpectedly buying one. It has turned out to be a journey of exceptional personal growth, as well as a way for me to live a life full of the flexibility and freedom I crave.

A few years ago, I was working for a small digital marketing company. The company was a franchise the owner had purchased a few years before, but he hadn't really focused on growing the business until that point. I was hired to update the company websites and do search engine optimization. The owner, Lance, and I were the only employees, and we worked well together. We lost a few clients as we were restructuring our services, but we were gaining momentum. Lance had just signed a lease on some outside office space, we had a plan to acquire new clients, and we were raring to go. Lance's first grandchild had just been born, and he was on a high.

Then the unthinkable happened: Lance died in an accident. Not only did I lose an incredible person, but I was also in limbo about what to do with our remaining customers and my career, since he was the franchise owner.

Lance's widow came to me and asked me to take over the business and continue his legacy. I was very torn. I had three kids in school and felt strongly about having the flexibility to drive them to their activities and be available for them. Being the sole owner of the business sounded like it would take up more time than I wanted to spend working at that point in my life. I didn't know anything about running a business and didn't feel ready to jump into owning one.

But one day, I saw a quote by Sir Richard Branson, "If somebody offers you an amazing opportunity but you are not sure you can do it, say yes—then learn how to do it later!" I had the chance to take over a profitable business with the support of the franchise network. I decided I couldn't pass this up and jumped in with both feet. An accidental entrepreneur was born.

I have learned many lessons over the years since I made that decision—lessons about how to run a business, lessons about how to stay up-to-date in an industry that is constantly evolving, and many, many lessons about perseverance and what kind of person I really am. In previous jobs, I had received many accolades about how self-motivated and independent I was. Working by myself in my house day after day and week after week made me question whether I truly had those qualities. I came to realize that I needed to be around people more than I had originally thought; I also realized that collaboration was very important to my happiness and my success.

One of the most effective ways I found to fulfill those needs was to attend networking events. In addition to the benefit of seeing other people, networking meetings added structure to my day and required me to get out of my entrepreneur's "uniform" of sweatpants and T-shirts. I met potential clients as well as potential partners there.

Because the various aspects of digital marketing kept expanding—website development, SEO, social media marketing, email marketing, online reputation management—it was soon clear that becoming an expert in one area was the only way to keep from being overwhelmed. While contemplating which area I wanted to specialize in, I noticed that most of the people at the networking events only saw the other attendees at the meetings. With once-a-month meetings, it was sometimes many months before people bumped into each other again. How can you develop a relationship with people you see so infrequently? The solution I found was to take face-to-face networking online.

Since LinkedIn is the only social network platform dedicated to professionals, I focused on LinkedIn. Microsoft bought LinkedIn in 2016 and has been revamping the user interface to make it more user-friendly and adding many useful features for professionals to keep in touch. LinkedIn is no longer just for job hunters and recruiters.

Although being part of a franchise system provided a number of advantages—in particular, having a group of people to discuss digital marketing issues with and opportunities for partnerships—I chose not to renew my contract and to branch out on my own, specializing in LinkedIn training. LinkedIn is an ideal platform for professionals to develop and nurture relationships. It can store many different types of content: text, articles, images, presentations, and most recently, videos and audio messages. You can share this content with people in your network to provide value and showcase your expertise.

I teach people how to use LinkedIn to follow up online after face-to-face networking events. Rather than connecting with people and then trying to sell to them right away, I suggest offering free content that they develop or sharing curated content that other people have created. Staying top of mind between in-person meetings is crucial to building the "Know, Like, and Trust" factor that is so essential to a business relationship.

Enhancing relationships with online activity on LinkedIn is a key way to find out whether someone is your ideal client and whether your solution would help someone before you try to sell them your product or service. It can be done anywhere there's an Internet connection and at any time.

Becoming an entrepreneur has allowed me to work *and* to travel to see my family and friends on my own terms. As my daughters settle down in different areas of the country, I foresee visiting grandchildren more frequently than my own working mother was able to do. I couldn't imagine being tied to a corporate job at this point. Sir Richard Branson had it right. I'm glad I took his advice.

■ ■ ■

Linda Lovero-Waterhouse is a social media and online marketing consultant specializing in LinkedIn coaching. You can connect with Linda at https://www.linkedin.com/in/lindalwaterhouse/.

CYBER SECURITY
Craig Petronella, The Petronella Technology Group

The Petronella Technology Group leverages LinkedIn as a powerful lead-generation component of its Unhackable Growth Platform system. Craig Petronella has developed a unique system that blends artificial intelligence, customer relationship management (CRM) software, and a human sales team to create a powerful lead-generating machine.

The AI system leverages LinkedIn to search for customers' ideal clients and build a highly focused LinkedIn network and prospect list. Automated, advanced LinkedIn searches are created in Sales Navigator to search for appropriate job titles, industries, locations, and specific company names.

Petronella Technology Group is a well-known and trusted cybersecurity group that specializes in helping medical practices, health-tech startups, and law firms with security and compliance:

- PCI DSS for credit-card processing
- HIPAA for patient health info
- HITECH for electronic medical records
- GDPR for privacy
- Gramm-Leach-Bliley Act for confidential financial information

There are very specific and complicated cybersecurity requirements for these niches, so the automated searches in Sales Navigator help Craig zero in on his ideal client easily.

When a potential client is found on LinkedIn, we automatically send an invitation to connect to engage interest. When an invitation is accepted, we send follow-up messages to build a relationship with the new connection. We add leads from LinkedIn to our CRM system so they can be nurtured and tracked.

We send LinkedIn messages sharing valuable tips and information to build trust. We also start conversations using short messages to ask questions. As the relationship grows, we suggest scheduling a "get to know you" call with an automated calendar system. My sales team monitors the system and intervenes when necessary to move the prospect through the sales funnel.

■ ■ ■

Craig A. Petronella is the CEO of Petronella Technology Group Inc. (PTG), a well-known and trusted cybersecurity group that specializes in helping law firms with security and compliance. You can connect with Craig at https://www.linkedin.com/in/blockchainsecurity/.

FINANCIAL FITNESS FOR AMERICA
Keith Youngren, CPA and Financial Money Coach

I should have accessed the power of LinkedIn for business marketing and development a long time ago. I decided to take on a 90-day challenge in the summer of 2018 to commit to daily interaction on LinkedIn. I already had a respectable network of approximately 2,500 connections from existing clients and business contacts, but I had not directly worked with them to generate new business. During my 90-day commitment, my LinkedIn database more than doubled to more than 5,000 connections. Interacting with my new contacts as they accepted my invitations to connect created thousands of dollars in new business in just 90 days, with new Financial Money Coach (FMC) memberships and FMC Tax Planning Blueprints developed.

I am excited with my results over this short time period and plan to continue using LinkedIn as a significant part of my marketing strategy. This approach has reached many new potential FMC members and tax-planning clients I previously did not have access to.

Marketing costs using LinkedIn are virtually nonexistent and require only a daily commitment of 20 minutes. The returns have been well worth the effort. I have taken the approach of focusing on a niche market. My CPA tax firm concentrates on clientele in the real estate industry, including real estate market centers, realtors, and real estate investment. It made sense for us to focus our connection invitations on professionals in the real estate industry and others closely associated with this market.

My results have been tremendous since becoming active on LinkedIn daily, and focusing on a niche market created some unexpected additional benefits. We send between 40 to 60 invitations to connect every day. Our acceptance rate has averaged about 50 percent, ranging from 20 to 30 per day. Everyone does not respond the same day, but the pipeline is primed for daily responses from earlier invitations.

We spend only about 15 to 20 minutes each day sending out invitations, usually first thing in the morning or in the evening. It takes another 30 to 45 minutes every day to respond to our new connections with a brief, "Thank you for connecting. Let's keep in touch" message.

LinkedIn has picked up on who my target market is. Fully 80 to 90 percent of its recommendations to connect are real estate industry professionals. Connecting with our niche target market has been made easier by LinkedIn.

I am just beginning to see the fruits of our marketing efforts on LinkedIn. The process takes time to continue interacting with your database, developing relationships and trust, but the journey is well worth the effort. Keeping your pipeline active is the key. Your business will thank you!

■ ■ ■

Keith P. Youngren is a CPA and the owner of Financial Money Coach LLC. You can connect with Keith at https://www.linkedin.com/in/financialmoneycoach/.

Chapter 23

Commencement

Many authors call the last chapter of their books "Conclusion," "Wrapping It Up," or something else to signify that you've successfully reached the end of the book. I prefer to call it "Commencement" because this is a new beginning for you—not the end. I want to be the first to congratulate you for reaching this chapter because you now know more about LinkedIn than 95 percent of all LinkedIn members.

As I have mentioned many times throughout the book, most LinkedIn members never reach the milestone of seeing that magical message saying their profile is 100 percent complete. I hope you have, and if not, you need to commit yourself to that goal in the next day or so. You've seen the benefits of completing your profile, and it will make a world of difference to your business and career.

A lot of people still think of LinkedIn as just a website for finding a job. After reading this book, you now know that it's so much more. You've learned how to use LinkedIn to give you a huge competitive advantage over peers, co-workers, other businesses, job applicants, or consultants. It's time to put into practice what you have learned and blow away your competition.

Throughout the book, you've read about the power of LinkedIn and how you can use it to rise above your rivals. Let's recap a few of the highlights:

- Use LinkedIn as a business intelligence search engine to find the best employees, find a new job, connect with key decision-makers, monitor trends in your industry, keep an eye on your competitors, or increase your sales.
- Optimize your LinkedIn profile so you and your company can be easily found on LinkedIn and Google.
- Build your professional network with the right people, whether you decide to have a massive open network, build a small, niche network, or fall somewhere in between.
- Use LinkedIn tools so you can easily keep up with industry trends, connect with others, and automate many site functions.
- Use LinkedIn mobile apps so you can easily access the site from your phone or tablet to keep your profile up-to-date, read the latest industry news, connect with others, and find new prospects.
- Use LinkedIn's newsfeed to stay current by reading articles from other industry experts and then demonstrate your expertise by sharing and commenting on the content.
- Use LinkedIn Groups to build strong relationships with others, learn from other group members, and demonstrate your expertise.
- Establish a presence for your company on LinkedIn with a company page to spread the word about your products, employees, and culture; to recruit new employees; and to generate leads.
- Effectively use LinkedIn advertising to promote your brand, generate leads, recruit new employees, and promote events.
- Use premium services like Career, Business, Talent Solutions, or Sales Navigator to help you get the most out of LinkedIn.
- LinkedIn is constantly evolving, growing, and adding more great stuff, so stay tuned for developments as they occur.

Now that you qualify as an expert LinkedIn user, you have to apply that knowledge on a regular basis to maintain the competitive advantage you just gained. I could create a generic 30-day LinkedIn plan for you, but since everyone uses LinkedIn for different reasons, I recommend you design your own plan to fit your needs. Keep it very simple and ease into LinkedIn gradually. In no time you'll be logging in to LinkedIn every day.

Here are 20 suggestions to get you started:

1. Change the start page in your browser to LinkedIn.com so you automatically log in every time you open your browser.

2. Get in the habit of logging in to LinkedIn every day, and check out your newsfeed to read your industry news and articles and updates posted by your connections.

3. Check out the People You May Know widget on your LinkedIn homepage and connect with a few new people every week.

4. Recommend one person every week.

5. Ask for recommendations from your current co-workers or past co-workers and bosses.

6. Read some of the new questions and content posted in your newsfeed.

7. Join a Group and read some of the popular discussions.

8. Check out the profiles of people with the same job title as you and update your profile so it's more focused than theirs.

9. Follow some companies that are leaders in your industry.

10. Check out the Jobs section and see what new opportunities are out there—even if you aren't looking for a job.

11. As you become more comfortable with the way group discussions work, try posting some provocative questions. When you're even more comfortable, start answering other people's questions. Remember, don't self-promote! Just answer the questions in an unbiased way.

12. Help at least one person every day on LinkedIn by answering their question or by giving them a recommendation.

13. Add new multimedia content to your profile every week so it becomes more robust.

14. Learn one LinkedIn tool every week so you can become more efficient with LinkedIn.

15. Install the LinkedIn mobile apps on your phone or tablet.

16. Set a goal of connecting with at least one key 3rd-degree connection every week.

17. Practice using InMail by sending one to someone you know but aren't connected to. This will increase your chances of them opening it and replying, which helps your InMail score and lets you practice writing interesting InMails. Ask them for feedback to see if they would have opened the InMail if you were a stranger. Practice with them and review their InMail messages in return for helping you.

18. Upgrade to at least a Premium Business account after you become comfortable with the basic LinkedIn functions.

19. Do a Google search on your name and see if your LinkedIn profile comes up. If it does, does your profile headline in the search results let people know exactly what you do and how you can help them?

20. When you are comfortable with your LinkedIn profile, start promoting it by adding a link in your email signature, and add the LinkedIn badge to your blog and website.

Well, that was easy! Do one item each day for the next 20 days, and you'll be hooked on LinkedIn.

The key to success in business is consistency. If you consistently use LinkedIn every day to grow your professional network, help others, and demonstrate your expertise by answering questions, participating in group discussions, and displaying your blog posts, articles, and SlideShares in your profile, there is a good chance you will be considered a thought leader in your field. I've seen it happen again and again—when someone consistently posts fresh, relevant content and helps others, they are soon considered a leading expert in their field. What's stopping you from doing the same?

I've really enjoyed sharing my LinkedIn experience with you, and I hope you use the information wisely. If you use just a fraction of the tips in this book, I guarantee your career will never be the same.

Will you do me one more favor? When your career takes off because of what you learned in this book, please share your success story with me at ted@tedprodromou.com.

Here's to your LinkedIn success!

For additional updates and how-to videos, visit
https://tedpodromou.com/ultimateguideupdates.

Glossary

1st-Degree Connections: LinkedIn members whom you've agreed to connect with. Your 1st-degree connections are usually friends, co-workers, or colleagues. If you are a LinkedIn LION, your 1st-degree connections are anyone who sent you an invitation, since you want to connect with everyone. You can send messages to them directly without using InMail.

2nd-Degree Connections: A "friend of a friend," or the LinkedIn connections of your 1st-degree connections. You must request an Introduction from a 1st-degree connection if you want to connect with a 2nd-degree connection. You can only contact your 2nd-degree connections via an Introduction or InMail unless you are members of the same Group.

3rd-Degree Connections: The connections of your 2nd-degree connections, or the friends of your friends' friends. You must request an Introduction or use InMail to contact your 3rd-degree connections unless you are members of the same Group.

Activity Feed: Displays your network activity, such as joining/starting Groups, comments, profile changes, and application downloads. You can control which activities appear in your Activity Feed in your LinkedIn Settings.

Anonymous Viewers: You can choose to keep personal identification information private when looking at profiles. Recruiters often choose to stay anonymous to remain discreet.

Basic Account: The free LinkedIn account that most members use. The features of the basic account are limited but meet the needs of most LinkedIn members.

Company Page: A mini-website for your company on LinkedIn. You can post content, breaking company news, job openings, and product showcase pages.

Connection: LinkedIn members who have accepted an invitation to connect and become a 1st-degree connection.

Groups: LinkedIn Groups provide a place for professionals in the same industry or with similar interests to share content, find answers, post and view jobs, make business contacts, and establish themselves as industry experts. You can find Groups to join in the Groups Directory or view suggestions of Groups you may like. You can also create a new Group focused on a particular topic or industry.

Hashtags: You can follow popular topics by subscribing to related hashtags. To subscribe to hashtags, visit https://www.linkedin.com/feed/follow-hashtags/. When you post articles and status updates, include popular hashtags in your content so people who are following that topic will see it.

IDK Response: When you receive an invitation to connect, one of your options is to choose "I don't know this person" or IDK. If someone receives more than three IDK responses, their account may be suspended to prevent spamming. Always personalize your invitations with a greeting to let the person know why you want to connect with them and how you know them.

InMail: InMails are messages you can send directly to another LinkedIn member you're not connected to. Any member can purchase an InMail, or you can get them with a premium account.

Intermediary: The process whereby a 1st-degree connection must request an Introduction from a 2nd-degree connection to connect to a 3rd.

Invitations: Invitations are how you make connections on LinkedIn. When one LinkedIn member sends an invitation to another person who then accepts it, they become 1st-degree connections. If the person receiving the invitation isn't a LinkedIn member, she'll be prompted to join LinkedIn to accept the invitation. Each new connection can increase your access to thousands of professionals in your network.

LinkedIn Influencer: LinkedIn Influencer is a designation given to approximately 500 high-profile professionals who've been invited to publish on LinkedIn. They talk about broad topics of interest, such as leadership, management, hiring and firing, disruption, how to succeed, and more. The list of Influencers includes Sir Richard Branson, Bill Gates, Arianna Huffington, and Guy Kawasaki.

LinkedIn Salary: You can research your earning power in your industry and location using LinkedIn Salary. You can access Salary under the Jobs menu tab or by visiting https://www.linkedin.com/salary/.

LION: An acronym of "LinkedIn Open Networker," which is usually posted on people's profile as "Open Networker" or "LION." When you are a LION, you agree to connect with anyone, regardless of industry or connection, to increase your network size.

Network: Your LinkedIn professional network, which consists of a group of users who can contact you through connections up to three degrees away.

Newsfeed: The LinkedIn newsfeed is where you can customize news and content posted by LinkedIn Influencers, media outlets, and members.

Notifications: This is a menu item that shows you a snapshot of LinkedIn activity by you and your network. You are notified when people change jobs, have a birthday, and when people like, comment on, or share your posts. You can also see the Daily Rundown, which is a daily news summary.

Open Profile: A network premium members can join that allows any LinkedIn member to send them a free InMail, regardless of relationship.

Premium Business Account: A LinkedIn Premium account that offers more features for business users. Business accounts include five InMails per month, enhanced profile search results, expanded profiles, and Open Network, which allows you to message other Open Network members without being 1st-degree connections.

Premium Career Account: A LinkedIn Premium account for people looking for a job. You can choose Job Seeker Basic, Standard, or Plus to enhance your job search. Job Seeker accounts let you get introduced to the companies you want to work for. You can be contacted by anyone using Open Profile, and you can post a Job Seekers Badge on your LinkedIn profile.

Profile: Creating a LinkedIn profile is an excellent way to establish and own your professional identity online. LinkedIn profiles typically appear among the top search results when people search their names.

ProFinder: This is where you can find local service providers to hire for short-term projects.

Recommendations: A recommendation is a comment written by a LinkedIn member to endorse a colleague, business partner, student, or service provider. People interested in hiring or doing business with someone often consider recommendations when making their decisions.

Sales Navigator: LinkedIn's premium subscription tool for sales professionals who use LinkedIn to sell their products and services.

Skills: The Skills page is found under the More menu at the top of your homepage. LinkedIn Skills helps you discover the expertise that other professionals have and see how the demand for these skills is changing over time. The skills information shown is based on data LinkedIn members enter on their profiles.

SlideShare: LinkedIn's tool for sharing PowerPoint presentations, infographics, documents, and more. SlideShare used to be a separate website until LinkedIn purchased it in 2012 and integrated it into the site.

Status Updates: Your status updates are sent to your newsfeed and are visible to your connections. You can edit your status updates.

Talent Solutions: LinkedIn's collection of products to help you recruit the best employees. They include Recruiter, a tool to help you post and hire exceptional employees; Career Pages, which let people hear from current employees what it's like to work at your company; and Work With Us Ads, which let you target prospective employees with job listings.

Website Demographics: LinkedIn Website Demographics is a free reporting tool that provides advertisers with demographic information about the LinkedIn members visiting their website. After you add the LinkedIn Insight Tag to your website, you can use the site's demographic information to better understand your website visitors and improve your marketing.

What People Are Talking About Now: A sidebar widget on your LinkedIn homepage that shows you trending articles and news. This is a great resource you can use to share breaking industry news items to your network.

Who's Viewed Your Profile: When someone views your LinkedIn profile, you will be notified under the Notifications tab. This is valuable information that tells you if you are engaging the right audience on LinkedIn. Most of my profile views come from business development and sales professionals, which is my target audience.

Index